Cajun
Quick

**Other Books
by Jude W. Theriot, CCP**

New American Light Cuisine (1988)
La Cuisine Cajun (1986)
La Meilleure de la Louisiane (1980)

Cajun Quick

Jude W. Theriot

PELICAN PUBLISHING COMPANY
Gretna 1992

Library of Congress Cataloging-in-Publication Data

Theriot, Jude W.
    Cajun Quick / by Jude W. Theriot ; foreword by John Folse.
    Includes index.
    ISBN 0-88289-841-8
    1. Cookery, Cajun.   I. Title.
TX715.T382   1992
641.59763—dc20

                   92-20868
                      CIP

---

*The word "Pelican" and the depiction of a pelican are
trademarks of Pelican Publishing Company, Inc., and are
registered in the U.S. Patent and Trademark Office.*

Tabasco is a registered trademark of McIlhenny Company.

Manufactured in the United States of America

Published by Pelican Publishing Company, Inc.
1101 Monroe Street, Gretna, Louisiana 70053

To the three women in my life:

Debbie LeBlanc Theriot, my wife, my friend, my confidant, and my companion. She gives continued encouragement and effort to see my final product enhanced. She always insists on the highest standards, and is my toughest critic. The consequence of her involvement and evaluation is a finished outcome that is immeasurably improved. All my love!

Nicole Marie Theriot, my oldest daughter and a sensational person. She has provided me with the economic reasons for writing! (Have you raised a high-school student lately?) Nicole is a genuine and most amiable young lady who has her dad (notice I'm no longer "daddy") wrapped around her finger. She is the apple of my eye!

Christine Noelie Theriot, my youngest and baby daughter. She has already taught me that sleep is not really important! She is transforming our lives by helping us to remember just what is really meaningful and essential in this world. A new child can do many magnificent things for a daddy (I'm still a daddy to her) and a family. We are all so delighted and captivated by her presence.

With all my love for my three girls!

Contents

Foreword

South Louisiana holds two things close to its heart: its family and its food. For generations, nothing could be more true than the Cajun proverb, "In Louisiana, we live to eat, not eat to live." In no other region of the country do ingredients for the table receive the love—like a mother's love for her children—that they receive right here in Bayou Country.

The Acadians, or Cajuns as we are known today, were the French Catholics who left the coastal areas of France in the early seventeenth century in search of a new homeland. We settled in Acadia, a strip of land on the southeast corner of Quebec. Here, we were free to express our language and customs in the fertile regions of Port Royal and Grande Pre. In 1713, the Treaty of Utrecht granted possession of Acadia to the English, who changed the name to Nova Scotia. On August 11,1755, the Acadians were expelled from their homes and land in what has become known as "Le Grand Dérangement." After thirty years of exile, the Cajuns discovered a new land—the bayous of South Louisiana. Over two hundred years later, our customs and folklore remain intact, here in the "Cajun Triangle" of South Louisiana.

Up to and immediately following World War II, life in Cajun country was simple. Our *joie de vivre,* or "joy of living," was the order of the day in the swampland neighborhoods. The French Acadians had found a new homeland in the bayous of South Louisiana where devotion to family, food, religion, language, and customs could be freely expressed without fear of reprisal. Bayou Country was, for all practical purposes, cut off from the rest of the world.

This isolation made it imperative for the Cajun families to come together as a unit in order to socialize and to survive. Although we are hard-working by nature, our existence in this new environment allocated sufficient time for the preparation of good food—and the will to share it with good friends was inherent. Yes, time was cheap in those days, and the Cajuns made the most of it. It was quite ordinary for a venison roast to braise for hours in a black iron pot to the strains of a Cajun fiddle playing a melody on the front porch. As we approached the sixties, seventies, and eighties, life took on a a new focus and, as the words of a popular sixties song clearly stated, "The Times They [were] a Changing!"

Of course, we all realize the importance of change, whether it be in cultures or cuisine. There is a great evolutionary process taking place today in this far-removed South Louisiana landscape. Cajuns today have more access to the outside world, due not only to education and exposure, but also to increased mobility. Interstates now cross our swamplands as skyscrapers emerge from the bayous. Naturally, with the spotlight shining so brightly on our region, evolution of many sorts is inevitable.

The techniques of Cajun cuisine are also experiencing this evolutionary process. The time-honored traditions of hand-picked bayou ingredients and all-day simmmering in black iron pots are giving way to contemporary thinking. Innovative Louisiana chefs such as Paul Prudhomme, Leah Chase, and Alex Patout are as responsible as any for creating excitement over what the world has come to know as "Cajun cooking." Today, one would be hard pressed to find anyone, anywhere who has not tasted or even prepared a Cajun dish.

My good friend, Jude Theriot, has played a major role in preserving our wonderful flavors while addressing the issues of our modern-day Cajun kitchens. Jude, in a knowledgeable and interesting fashion, has created a timely work in *Cajun Quick* that recognizes the priorities of today's families everywhere. Although the desire for a good meal remains the highest priority, we are no longer willing nor able to devote the time necessary to create lavish culinary productions on a daily basis. We simply do not have the hours to spend in a kitchen preparing meals as our grandmothers did. Our world revolves at a faster pace and we must likewise adapt our culinary skills. The modern family, with all of its expertise in cooking and the desire to design interesting meals in minutes, will certainly find solace in this book.

We in Cajun Country will continue to demand great food made with regional ingredients. In these times, we have come to realize, however, that adjustments must be made in cooking techniques and time of preparation if we are to achieve these ends. We must never forget that a cuisine is a living thing that draws upon the very essence of the people who prepare it. Cajun cooking must continue to develop as it has over the past 250 years—with expert hands stirring and nurturing our unique recipes and techniques, passing them lovingly from mother to daughter, father to son, and friend to friend. I congratulate Jude for his book, giving all "us Cajuns" the wherewithall to create and share our magnificent feasts within the time restraints of the modern-day Bayou Country and the rest of the world.

CHEF JOHN D. FOLSE, CEC, AAC
National Chef of the Year, 1990-1991

Introduction

Here I am again, writing yet another book. From someone who always wanted to write just one good cookbook, this is number four!

What is my motivation for writing this book? I guess my main purpose is to present what I have learned in my ongoing development as a culinary professional. As time goes on, we all change, revise, rework, and re-create. This book contains all of these. In my travels around the country as a cooking school teacher, food consultant, speaker, and cooking demonstrator at various conventions, I have diligently tried to listen to my public.

First and foremost, you have told me loud and clear that you want more Cajun cooking! The notion that Cajun is a fad is DEAD. Cajun cooking has been around for too many years to just go away. It is the cooking of a modest people, who are close to the land and close to each other. It is not difficult to prepare, and the taste . . . well I'll just leave that judgement up to you. Now, I am not saying that it is the only style of cooking that is worthwhile—that wouldn't fit in with the Cajun way of thinking. However, I am going to say it is one of the most celebrated and distinctive styles of cooking in the world. Another reason it won't go away is the number of transplanted Cajuns around the country and, for that matter, around the world. No matter where a Cajun goes, his Cajun cuisine goes with him. It remains a part of a Cajun's being!

I have heard the petitions from across the country for more Cajun recipes. I have also studied the faces of my students as they experienced Cajun dishes for the first time. The gleam that is fixed on the face of the Cajun neophyte tells me that the story has a long way to go before the final chapter.

Secondly, I've heard from the people I've worked with that they want recipes that are easier to use and quick. Today's lifestyle mandates much of what we do and how we do it. Meals cannot take three or four hours to prepare anymore—nobody has that much time. The days of Mom at home, cooking all day and waiting for the family's arrival, are forever gone (and I'm sure many moms are elated by that). We need more quality recipes that can meet our families' needs and can be cooked in substantially less time. To that end, I have tried to produce recipes with traditional Cajun flavors that, for the most part, can be made in thirty minutes or less. Some of the recipes will take less time than that—they are down in the ten-minute range. A few recipes will take up to one hour, but that is a significant decrease from the old way of cooking similar dishes. There are recipes that are quite easy that really just have to be put in a pot or in the oven. The cook will have nothing to do but prepare to enjoy a good meal.

My goal is to get you from the stove to the table as quickly as possible without losing quality and taste. I have accomplished this in a number of ways. First, cooking at higher temperatures for less time improves a dish's flavors—the higher temperature seals in the natural juices of whatever you are cooking. Because the cooking time is shortened, the full taste of the ingredients remains captured in the dish. Secondly, I've developed a single seasoning mixture, **Cajun Seasoning Mix,** that works well on meats, poultry, seafood, vegetables, etc. This eliminates the need for multiple seasoning mixtures, thereby saving time in preparation. This seasoning mix helps to give a Cajun flair to almost anything on which it is used. Thirdly, cutting, pounding, slicing, or shaping the ingredients into thinner forms increases the surface area and decreases the time necessary in the pot. Finally, I have opened my cooking style to allow some already-prepared items like canned soups, canned or frozen vegetables, and items like a splendid new product in a jar called whole straw mushrooms. I've come to realize that it is okay to blend the old with the new, and that something that is packaged or frozen is not necessarily inferior or bad! A quality product can be made from other packaged quality products. I guess I have joined the twentieth century just in time for it to end!

I have realized that creating a meal oneself, even taking shortcuts, is a whole lot better than ordering out. When a family member takes the time (no matter how short or how long) to personally cook for the rest of the family, there is a bonding that takes place within the family that we, as a nation, can't really afford to do without. I chose the words "family member" carefully. Home cooking no longer is, nor should it be, Mom's chore (or perhaps "domain" is a better word). Every family member should be afforded the enjoyment of creating a dinner for the whole group. I see what it has done for my daughter Nicole. She is able to cook for her family now, and she has gained poise, self-confidence, and pride in a job well done. She is great at helping to test a recipe. Formerly, I had to depend only on my wife and myself for that, but now we've expanded the kitchen to include her as well. In fact, I'm trying to teach young Christine to cook, but my wife, Debbie, prefers that she learn to read and write first!

The third message I got from my travels is that people want to know dietary information for all recipes. They are not demanding that all be diet recipes by any means, but they want to know what is in what they fix. People used to want to know your zodiac sign; today, they want to know about your health and cholesterol level. I think that that is a sensible attitude to have. All the information about food content has made us aware that we are, in fact, what we eat. It is okay to eat high calorie recipes sometimes, as long as it is in moderation. It helps to know a recipe's contents to be able to pick and choose, depending on the week's and day's intake. All the recipes in this book include information on calorie, carbohydrate, fat, cholesterol, protein, fiber, and sodium content per individual serving.

Finally, the communiqué comes in loud and clear, that the public wants recipes that contain less fat than before. No fat at all is not the goal—just not the foods "swimming" in oils and fats that we used to see in almost all Cajun dishes. Actually, reducing the amount of fat has helped to speed the recipes up somewhat. The food comes in closer contact with the heat source and, therefore, cooks faster. I still use some deep frying, but when I do, I always use the lighter, unsaturated oils instead of the lards my grandmother used.

I hope you will find *Cajun Quick* as much fun to use as it was to develop. It is filled with a variety of distinctive recipes. I hope you enjoy my recipe names—they are a mixture of family names, friends' names, and ancestral names as well as names taken from the land of Louisiana itself. One of the novel experiences a cookbook author has is the naming of recipes. I take great delight in each recipe, so designating a name is the culmination of that satisfaction. Bon appetit!

Lagniappe

I have included a *lagniappe* with every recipe in this book. This is for the user's benefit. These sections are filled with many little hints and suggestions that will make cooking that particular recipe easier. It also contains general cooking tips and bits of enlightenment that I have gleaned from here and there. A lot of people tell me that they enjoy reading cookbooks as other people read novels. This is a special addition that will give the reader insights that should be beneficial to his or her cooking in general. I must admit, however, that I occasionally may just use the *lagniappe* section to talk to you.

Lagniappe is a Cajun French word that means "a little something extra" or "something for nothing." In the good old days, whenever a Cajun would shop at a store or stand, the proprietor would always throw something in with the purchase for good measure. It is somewhat similar to the "baker's dozen."

Well, the word has remained, but the custom, alas, is mostly gone. However, because I give you my *lagniappe* with each recipe, you get to experience firsthand just how it was. Additionally, you will always find a complete set of nutritional values per serving, along with occasional hints on freezing or refrigerating and bringing the food back to life for a "second showing." I also include ideas for related recipes.

I hope you take full advantage of the *lagniappe* sections while using the book. They will make the overall experience of *Cajun Quick* more rewarding, informative, and delicious!

NOTE: For all recipes, carbohydrate, fat, and protein values are given in grams; cholesterol and sodium values are given in milligrams. "Trace" indicates a negligible amount of that item. The values are for one serving or one tablespoon, unless otherwise indicated.

Cajun Quick

Appetizers

CRABMEAT DIP CALCASIEU

1 8-oz. pkg. cream cheese, softened
1/4 cup mayonnaise
1/4 cup green onions, chopped
2 tbsp. celery, finely chopped
1 tbsp. pimento, chopped
1/4 tsp. Tabasco sauce

1 tsp. Worcestershire sauce
1 tsp. salt
1/2 tsp. black pepper
1/4 tsp. fresh basil (or 1/8 tsp. dried)
1 tbsp. fresh lemon juice
1 lb. fresh crabmeat (lump or claw)

Mix together all the ingredients, except for the lemon juice and crabmeat, until well blended. Toss the crabmeat in the lemon juice; then gently fold it into the blended mixture. Serve as a dip with crackers, chips, or fresh vegetables. Serves 15 as a dip.

Lagniappe: What ease! What taste! When you start with fresh crabmeat, it really is hard to fail. You can make it in advance, but do not freeze. Be sure to keep it chilled until ready to serve.

This makes a wonderful stuffing for a ripe avocado half or a fresh red tomato. I also like to hollow out about 1/2 inch of a 1-inch-thick cucumber slice. I score the peel with a fork, leaving enough green for looks, then spoon a generous amount of the crabmeat dip into the 1/2-inch hole. I dust the top with a little paprika or drop a few flakes of fresh chives or finely minced parsley on top to give it a nice splash of green. It's pretty enough to take a picture of, but it is better to eat! Let your mind run with this dip—it is a great chilled crabmeat stuffing for just about anything.

Calories—99; Carb—2.2; Fat—7.2; Chol—48; Pro—6.5; Fib—Trace; Sod—232

CRAB DIP GUEYDAN

1/2 stick unsalted butter
6 green onions, chopped
3 cloves garlic, minced
1 celery stalk, minced
1/2 medium red bell
  pepper, chopped
1 tsp. fresh basil, minced
  (or 1/4 tsp. dried)
2 tbsp. all-purpose flour
2/3 cup milk
1/4 cup dry white wine
1/2 cup ripe California
  olives, pitted and
  chopped
5 mushrooms, chopped

1 cup Swiss cheese, grated
1/2 cup monterey jack
  cheese, grated or
  chopped
1/2 tsp. Tabasco sauce
1 tbsp. fresh lemon juice
1 tbsp. Worcestershire
  sauce
1 tsp. Cajun Seasoning Mix
  (see index)
1/4 cup fresh parsley,
  minced
1 lb. crabmeat (claw, lump,
  snow, or king crabmeat)

Heat a heavy, medium-sized skillet over medium heat. When it is hot, add the butter. When the butter begins to smoke, add the green onions, garlic, celery, red bell pepper, and basil. Sauté until the vegetables are limp—about 5 minutes. Add the flour and cook, stirring constantly, for 3 minutes.

Remove from heat and blend in the milk and white wine. Return skillet to heat, add the olives and mushrooms; then cook for 2 minutes. Add the rest of the ingredients, except for the crabmeat. Cook, stirring often, until the cheese is melted and blended into the sauce. Add the crabmeat, folding it in gently, and cook for 2 minutes to warm the crabmeat. Serve hot with corn chips or crackers. Serves 15 as a dip.

Lagniappe: Crabmeat is so versatile. It can be used in a sauce, under a sauce, as a stuffing, or it can stand alone. However, be advised that it is also very delicate. This dip can be made in advance and refrigerated. When you reheat it, put it on low and stir often until it is hot. It can be frozen, but the crabmeat tends to break up. You still get the great taste, but you lose the texture.

Calories—144; Carb—4.6; Fat—9.7; Chol—52; Fib—.5; Sod—180

ACADIAN SHRIMP DIP

1 lb. boiled shrimp, peeled and chopped	1/2 cup mayonnaise
1/2 cup green onions, minced	1 tsp. Cajun Seasoning Mix (see index)
2 cloves garlic, finely minced	1/2 tsp. Tabasco sauce
1 8-oz. pkg. cream cheese, softened	1 tbsp. Worcestershire sauce
	1 tsp. fresh lemon juice

In a medium-sized mixing bowl, blend all ingredients with an electric mixer at medium speed until well mixed. Chill for at least 15 minutes. Serve cold. Makes about 5 cups of dip.

Lagniappe: Quick, easy and good! You can prepare this dip up to 24 hours in advance and keep it chilled in the refrigerator. It actually tastes better if you make it the day before you serve it. I prefer to serve it with nice crackers rather than chips, but it's great either way. You can also enjoy it with fresh vegetables. It's a great quick party dip to bring at the last minute.

You can substitute 1 pound of crawfish for the shrimp to make **Acadian Crawfish Dip.** Just use the crawfish tails right from the plastic bag, they are already processed, so you don't need to cook them. **Acadian Crawfish Dip** is actually easier, because you don't have to boil them!

Calories—23; Carb—.7; Fat—1.5; Chol—12; Pro—1.3; Fib—Trace; Sod—35.4

SMOKED OYSTER DIP

1 pkg. Knorr's vegetable
  soup mix
1 cup sour cream
1 cup mayonnaise
1/4 cup Pickapeppa sauce
1 tsp. Tabasco sauce
1 tbsp. Worcestershire
  sauce

1 tbsp. green onion tops,
  minced
1 8-oz. pkg. cream cheese,
  softened
1 3 3/4-oz. can smoked
  oysters, chopped

In a medium-sized mixing bowl, mix together the soup mix, sour cream, mayonnaise, Pickapeppa sauce, Tabasco sauce, and Worcestershire sauce until blended. Add the green onions and cream cheese; then blend with an electric mixer or food processor until the dip is thoroughly blended and smooth. Fold in the oysters, and either pour into the serving bowl or refrigerate until you are ready to serve. The dip is much better if it chills for a few hours in the refrigerator. Serves 10.

Lagniappe: While trying to create a dip for a friend who really likes smoked oysters, I just started playing around with this recipe. It was a hit, so here it is. You can prepare this dip up to 24 hours in advance, and you can actually store it for 2 or 3 days in the refrigerator. However, be careful to put out only as much dip as you think you will need. If it stands unrefrigerated for a few hours, don't try to save it. Do not freeze this dip!

Calories—234; Carb—9; Fat—20; Chol—59; Pro—3.7; Fib—Trace; Sod—397

PINEAPPLE-WALNUT SPREAD

1 8-oz. pkg. cream cheese,
  softened
1/4 cup mayonnaise
1 cup crushed pineapple
2/3 cup chopped walnuts

1/2 cup finely chopped
  celery
1/4 cup diced red bell
  pepper
1/8 tsp. Tabasco sauce

In a mixing bowl, beat the cream cheese and mayonnaise with an electric mixer until smooth. Add the remaining ingredients, then mix with the mixer until completely blended. Cover and refrigerate until ready to serve. Makes about 3 cups of spread.

Lagniappe: This is great party food or everyday sandwich food. Just spread on bread to make a sandwich, or serve as an appetizer on crackers. I also like to surround a bowl of the spread with fresh cut raw vegetables for dipping. It's a true delight.

Calories—29; Carb—1.6; Fat—2.5; Chol—5; Pro—.6; Fib—Trace; Sod—25

STUFFED TOMATOES MICHELLE

12 cherry tomatoes
salt
black pepper
2 green onions, finely
  chopped
4 slices cooked bacon,
  crumbled

1 small clove garlic,
  minced
1 tbsp. chopped dill pickle
1/3 cup chopped lettuce
1/4 tsp. Tabasco sauce
2 tbsp. mayonnaise

Slice about 1/3 inch off of the top of each tomato. Use a small spoon or melon scoop to remove the seeds and pulp. Sprinkle lightly with salt and black pepper and set them on a plate, cut side down.

In a small mixing bowl, combine the remaining ingredients, mixing until well blended. Put equal amounts of the stuffing into each tomato; then chill until you are ready to serve. Serves 4.

Lagniappe: This is a quick and tasty appetizer, or it may serve as a nice garnish or vegetable. Preparation time is minimal, you can prepare them in advance, and you can store them in the refrigerator for up to 12 hours.

To lower the calorie count, use light mayonnaise. If you are in a hurry, you can substitute prepared bacon bits—they really do quite well.

Calories—201; Carb—5.6; Fat—18.8; Chol—22; Pro—3.0; Fib—.4; Sod—701

OLIVE SPREAD

1 8-oz. pkg. cream cheese, softened
1/4 cup mayonnaise
1/4 cup finely grated Swiss cheese
1/4 teaspoon Tabasco sauce
2/3 cup pimento-stuffed olives, chopped

1/2 cup ripe California olives, pitted and chopped
1/3 cup slivered almonds, toasted
1 tbsp. minced onion

Combine the cream cheese, mayonnaise, Swiss cheese and Tabasco sauce in a mixing bowl and beat with an electric mixer until smooth. Add the remaining ingredients, and mix together well. Cover and refrigerate until you are ready to serve. Spread on bread, crackers, or raw vegetables. Yields 3 cups.

Lagniappe: See **Pineapple-Walnut Spread** recipe for alternate uses for this spread. I prefer it spread on ribs of cut celery. I could eat the entire recipe this way. It also makes a nice hors d'oeuvre.

Calories—37; Carb—.8; Fat—3.0; Chol—5.5; Pro—.7; Fib—.1; Sod—143

ROQUEFORT DIP FOR VEGETABLES

2 cloves garlic, cut in
  quarters
2 tbsp. onion, chopped
1 tbsp. fresh basil, chopped
1 tbsp. fresh parsley,
  chopped
1 8-oz. pkg. cream cheese
1/4 cup mayonnaise

3 tbsp. milk
1 tbsp. white
  Worcestershire sauce
1/4 tsp. Tabasco sauce
1/4 tsp. salt
1/4 tsp. dry mustard
1/4 cup Roquefort cheese,
  crumbled

Put the garlic, onion, basil, and parsley into a food processor and blend at high speed until finely minced. Add the cream cheese, mayonnaise, and milk to the ingredients in the processor and mix at high speed for 2 minutes until smooth. Add the remaining ingredients, except for the cheese, and process again for about 1 minute. Pour the mixture into a mixing bowl and fold in the cheese. Cover the bowl and refrigerate it until you are ready to serve. This recipe is much better if allowed to stand for approximately 8 hours. However, you can serve it after 20 minutes—you just won't get the full power of the blend. Serve with plenty of fresh, raw vegetables. Serves 10 to 15.

Lagniappe: This dip can be prepared up to 4 days in advance and refrigerated. The more it sits, the more pronounced the flavor of the Roquefort cheese becomes. I also use this same recipe to make **Roquefort Salad Dressing.** Just add 1/4 cup more mayonnaise and 1/4 cup more milk, and you've created a wonderful salad dressing.

Calories—119; Carb—3.1; Fat—11; Chol—29.6; Pro—2.6; Fib—Trace; Sod—178

MUSHROOM MARINATE

2 lb. fresh small
mushrooms, brushed
clean
1/2 cup olive oil
1/4 cup almond oil (or
peanut oil)
1 1/2 cups white wine
vinegar
3 tbsp. balsamic vinegar
3 cloves garlic, minced
1 medium onion, chopped

1 medium red bell pepper,
diced
1 tbsp. black pepper
1/2 tsp. Tabasco sauce
1/4 cup Worcestershire
sauce
4 whole cloves
4 whole allspice
1/2 tsp. mustard seeds
1/2 tsp. celery seeds
1/4 cup sugar

Combine all ingredients in a large mixing bowl and mix together until blended. Pour into a large container that has a tight lid, cover, and refrigerate for at least 24 hours. Serve either as an appetizer or as a salad topping. Serves 12.

Lagniappe: Mushrooms are such fun to eat. You can make this dish up to a week in advance and still get excellent results. However, be sure to keep the container refrigerated.

As an appetizer, just serve in a large bowl with toothpicks. To make **Marinated Mushroom Salad,** start with a nice bed of shredded iceberg lettuce, and place about 1/2 to 3/4 cup of the marinrated mushrooms on top. Spoon about 1 tablespoon of the marinate over the salad and garnish with a little freshly chopped parsley. What a great salad! I recommend finding out what day the fresh mushrooms come in to your supermarket. Go that day, and pick out your mushrooms. You'll have your choice of the prettiest, and you can store them in your refrigerator so they will last longer and have fewer discolorations.

Calories—170; Carb—7.8; Fat—13.5; Chol—0; Pro—2.4; Fib—.8; Sod—63

MUSHROOM TOASTIES

25 rounds French bread,
   toasted and lightly
   buttered
1 lb. fresh mushrooms,
   finely minced
2 cloves garlic, finely
   minced
1/2 cup finely minced green
   onions
1/4 cup minced ripe
   California black olives

3 tbsp. unsalted butter
1/2 tsp. Tabasco sauce
1/2 tsp. salt
1/4 tsp. black pepper
1/4 cup grated parmesan
   cheese
1/4 cup grated romano
   cheese
sweet paprika

Preheat the oven to 375 degrees. Arrange the toast rounds on a cookie sheet. In a mixing bowl, combine the minced mushrooms, garlic, green onions, and California olives, and mix. Melt the butter in a medium-sized skillet over medium to high heat. When the butter begins to sizzle, add the mixed vegetables and sauté for 5 minutes. Add the remaining ingredients, except for the paprika. Continue to cook for about a minute; then remove from the heat and spread evenly on the toasted French bread rounds. Dust the tops with paprika and bake at 375 degrees for 2 to 3 minutes. Remove and serve hot as an appetizer or party food. Makes 25 rounds.

Lagniappe: To make the toasted French bread rounds, cut the french bread into 1/2 inch slices. Use a biscuit cutter to cut circles or you can leave the slices in their natural shape. Brush a small amount of butter on each round, toast in the oven for 3 to 5 minutes, then set the bread aside until you are ready to use it. You can make the bread rounds in advance and even freeze them if you like. Just be sure they are thawed before you use them in the recipe.

The spread can be made up to 48 hours in advance and refrigerated until you are ready to use it. If you refrigerate it, it will be easier to spread if you heat it either on the stove or in a microwave; then follow through with the recipe. This is an unusual but quite tasty recipe. You have to try it to really find out how good it is!

Calories—173; Carb—16.1; Fat—9.8; Chol—18.4; Pro—6.4; Fib—.7; Sod—449

STUFFED MUSHROOMS DAN JOSEPH

2 lb. large mushrooms
3 tbsp. olive oil
1/4 tsp. Tabasco sauce
1/2 teaspoon salt

1 recipe Stuffed Crabs,
    unbaked mixture only
    (see index)

Preheat the oven to 350 degrees. Clean the mushrooms with a pastry brush or a damp cloth. Remove the stems, and slightly widen the center of each cap with a melon scoop or spoon. (Do not throw away the stems and bits of mushrooms. Save for use in another recipe either by freezing or refrigerating.) In a small bowl, combine the oil, Tabasco sauce, and salt. Using a pastry brush, lightly coat the mushrooms with the oil mixture. Bake on a cookie sheet or a shallow baking pan at 350 degrees for 7 minutes. Remove from the oven, allow to cool, then stuff each cap with a generous amount of the crab stuffing. Raise the oven temperature to 400 degrees and bake for 12 minutes until the stuffing is golden brown. Serve hot. Serves 10.

Lagniappe: These mushrooms can be completely stuffed, baked, and either refrigerated or frozen for later use. They are a wonderful party food, a great appetizer, or the perfect thing to liven up almost any plate.

I like to make a batch and freeze them individually. I place them on a cookie sheet in the freezer for 24 hours; then remove them, put them into a quality freezer bag or a container with a tight lid, and put them back in the freezer. If someone pops in, I can serve a great little snack by defrosting and heating the caps in the microwave, or puting them directly into the oven at 300 degrees for 12 to 15 minutes.

Calories—239; Carb—19.2; Fat—12.7; Chol—91; Pro—14; Fib—1.1; Sod—548

STUFFED MUSHROOMS ALGIERS

24 large mushrooms
2 tbsp. olive oil
2 tbsp. unsalted butter
1 cup minced green onion
3 cloves garlic, minced
1/4 cup minced celery
1/4 cup diced bell pepper
1 tbsp. minced fresh basil
  (or 1 tsp. dried)
1 tsp. minced fresh
  rosemary (or 1/4 tsp.
  dried)

1 tsp. salt
1/2 tsp. black pepper
1/2 tsp. onion powder
1/4 tsp. Tabasco sauce
1/2 cup Italian bread
  crumbs
1/4 cup romano cheese
1/4 cup parmesan cheese
1/4 cup fresh parsley,
  minced
vegetable oil

Preheat the oven to 425 degrees. Clean the mushrooms by wiping them with a damp towel or brushing them with a pastry brush. Separate the stems and caps, and set the caps aside for later use. Finely chop the stems, and place them in a bowl. Heat a large skillet over medium heat. Add the olive oil and continue to heat until it begins to smoke. Add the butter and swirl it around until it melts—it will brown slightly. Sauté the finely chopped mushroom stems, onions, garlic, celery, and bell pepper for 4 minutes. Add the basil, rosemary, salt, pepper, and onion powder; then sauté for 3 more minutes. Mix in the Tabasco sauce, then the bread crumbs, cheeses, and fresh parsley. When thoroughly mixed, remove from the heat, and stuff each mushroom cap with about 1 tablespoon of the mix. Place stuffed caps on a lightly greased baking pan. Bake at 425 degrees for about 15 minutes. Serve hot. Serves 6.

Lagniappe: Aside from making an excellent appetizer, stuffed mushrooms complement almost any plate. They look especially nice with steaks and broiled fish. You can prepare these mushrooms completely in advance, except for the baking, and refrigerate or freeze them. Just remove them from the refrigerator and bake at 425 degrees for 15 minutes (or 17 minutes if frozen).

I use this recipe to make **Crab Stuffed Mushrooms Algiers** by simply adding 1 pound of crabmeat (usually clawmeat—the price is better than lump and it doesn't have as many shells) along with the

Tabasco sauce; then sauté for 3 additional minutes. Make **Oyster Stuffed Mushrooms Algiers**, by adding 1 pint of fresh, chopped oysters with the basil and rosemary, and sauté for 5 minutes, instead of the 3 the recipe above calls for. No matter how you make these stuffed mushrooms, they are GREAT!

Calories—165; Carb—10.9; Fat—12.8; Chol—19; Pro—6; Fib—1.1; Sod—539

CRAB MERINGUES

3 egg whites	1 1/2 cup fresh crabmeat
1/2 tsp. cream of tartar	(special or claw)
1/3 tsp. Tabasco sauce	1 cup mayonnaise
3/4 tsp. salt	20 toasted bread rounds
1/4 tsp. black pepper	paprika

Set the oven to broil. In a mixing bowl, combine the egg whites, cream of tartar, and Tabasco sauce; then whip the egg whites until they are stiff. Fold in the next four ingredients taking care not to deflate the egg whites. Spoon generous amounts of the mixture equally on top of each bread round, and dust with paprika. Place on a cookie sheet about 8 inches under the heat source, and broil for about 4 to 5 minutes until golden brown. Serve hot, straight from the oven. Serves 6.

Lagniappe: Other than the bread rounds, there's no advance preparation with this dish. If you like, use a biscuit cutter or cookie cutter to shape the slices of bread. Place the bread rounds on a cookie sheet, and bake at about 180 degrees until lightly toasted and somewhat dry. If you have a gas oven, put them in the oven with just the pilot light on, and leave them for up to 5 or 6 hours. They'll come out great. Don't worry about what to do with the leftovers—there won't be any!

Calories—239; Carb—10.4; Fat—30; Chol—68; Pro—6.4; Fib—Trace; Sod—600

CRAB AUNT YOLANDE

2 tbsp. olive oil
2 tbsp. butter
1 small onion, chopped
1 small red bell pepper, diced
1/4 cup minced celery
2 cloves garlic, minced
6 large mushrooms, thinly sliced
1 10 3/4-oz. can condensed cream of onion soup
1 3-oz. pkg. cream cheese, chopped into cubes
1/2 tsp. Tabasco sauce
1/2 tsp. salt
1/2 tsp. dried basil
1/2 tsp. black pepper
1/2 tsp. onion powder
1 lb. crabmeat (lump or claw)
2 tbsp. minced fresh parsley
1/2 cup seasoned bread crumbs
crackers or toasted bread rounds

Heat a large, heavy skillet over medium heat. When it is hot, add the olive oil and heat until it begins to smoke. Add the butter, swirl it around until it melts, then add the onion, red bell pepper, celery, and garlic. Sauté for 4 minutes. Add the mushrooms and sauté another 2 minutes. Stir in the soup, cream cheese, Tabasco sauce, and dried seasonings until heated throughout. Fold in the crabmeat, parsley, and bread crumbs. Remove from heat and spread on crackers or toasted bread rounds.

Lagniappe: You can make this quick and easy appetizer in advance and refrigerate it; but do not freeze it. To serve after refrigeration, heat in the microwave uncovered, stirring every minute, until warm. You can also just heat it in a skillet over low heat until it is heated thoroughly. This dish is also wonderful cold. You can use it as a cold spread straight from the refrigerator.

Notice that I recommend either lump or claw meat. The claw meat is excellent and, like the lump meat, has very few pieces of shell. However, the claw meat is about half the price. You can use snow crab, king crab, or dungeness crab; in fact, any crabmeat will do. I have even used the imitation stuff when crabmeat was not available.

Calories—146; Carb—7.9; Fat—8.8; Chol—54; Pro—8.5; Fib—.3; Sod—341

CAJUN FRIED CRAB BALLS PIERRE

1 small loaf French bread
1/2 cup milk
1/4 cup mayonnaise
2 large brown eggs, slightly
  beaten
1/2 cup finely chopped
  green onions
2 cloves garlic, minced
2 tbsp. minced red bell
  pepper
1 tbsp. finely chopped
  celery

1 1/2 tsp. Cajun Seasoning
  Mix (see index)
1/3 tsp. Tabasco sauce
1 tbsp. Worcestershire
  sauce
2 tbsp. dry white wine
1 lb. fresh crabmeat (lump,
  special, or claw meat)
flour
peanut oil

Chop or tear the bread into small pieces and place in a large mixing bowl. Pour the milk over the bread and mash the bread with your hands. Add the remaining ingredients, except for the flour and oil, to the bread mixture and blend together well. Roll the doughlike mixture into small, bite-sized meatballs and place on a tray. Cover with plastic and let them chill overnight in the refrigerator. (Note: you may omit this step, but the flavors will not blend together as well.) When you are ready to serve, roll each ball lightly in flour and either deep fry or pan fry in hot peanut oil until golden brown, about 4 minutes. Serve hot. Serves 6.

Lagniappe: Talk about heavenly eating. Although crabmeat is relatively expensive, one pound goes a very long way—as you can see with this recipe. This appetizer also makes a nice addition to a seafood platter, or may serve as a main dish. Five or six **Cajun Crab Balls Pierre,** a baked potato, and a nice green salad or cole slaw can make an excellent, quick and easy meal.

You can keep these crab balls for up to 3 days, as long as you keep them covered and refrigerated (below 40 degrees). Do not flour the balls before you refrigerate them—it makes them taste like they are coated with paper-mache. You can freeze them as well. Lay them unfloured on a tray in the freezer, let them freeze overnight, then put them into a large plastic bag and return them to the freezer. Drop them (flour is not necessary if they are frozen) into hot oil and cook for about

5 minutes instead of 4. Also, remember not to save the leftover oil. When you cook with peanut oil, it is only effective and beneficial one time.

Calories—467; Carb—40; Fat—24; Chol—173; Pro—23; Fib—.5; Sod—606

OYSTERS LANNETTE

2 slices bacon
3 tbsp. butter
1/4 cup flour
1 small onion, finely
  chopped
1/2 cup minced green onion
2 cloves garlic, minced
1/4 cup minced celery
1 small yellow or orange
  bell pepper, diced
2/3 cup evaporated milk
1/8 cup cognac
1/2 cup grated Swiss
  cheese

3/4 cup grated American
  cheese
1 cup chopped boiled
  shrimp, peeled and
  deveined
1 cup chopped spicy hot
  sausage, cooked
24 large raw oysters
1/4 cup fresh parsley,
  minced
3/4 cup seasoned bread
  crumbs

Preheat the oven to 425 degrees. In a medium-sized saucepan, fry the bacon until crispy. Remove the bacon, drain it on a paper towel, crumble it, and set it aside for later use. Add the butter to the saucepan, and when it is melted, add the flour. Stir the flour constantly for 2 minutes over medium heat. Add the onion, green onion, garlic, and celery; then cook for 3 more minutes. Stir in the milk and cognac until well blended. Add the cheeses, chopped shrimp, and sausage and cook for about one minute, until the cheeses start to melt. Add the oysters, and cook until they become puffy and white.

Remove the saucepan from the heat, carefully take the oysters out of the mixture, and place three oysters in each of eight 3-inch ramekins. Add the parsley to the sauce, and stir through. Spoon generous amounts of the sauce over the oysters and cover with bread crumbs. Bake in the preheated 425 degree oven for about 10 minutes. Serve at once. Serves 8.

Lagniappe: This is the supreme oyster dish. It looks good, tastes even better, and the sauce—well, you have to taste it to believe it! Be sure to serve with plenty of hot French bread because you'll want to soak up every drop of sauce.

You can make this dish in advance and refrigerate it before baking. You can refrigerate it for up to 3 days—just be sure it is well chilled and covered. All you have to do is heat the oven to 425 degrees and bake for 12 minutes. The extra 2 minutes is needed to raise the temperature of the oysters and sauce back to where they should be. Do not freeze this dish. Freezing causes it to break apart too much and loose much of the flavor.

This dish is listed as an appetizer, but you can use a larger serving dish, like a 6-inch baking shell or an au gratin dish, to make it an entree. Enjoy!

Calories—335; Carb—14.5; Fat—21.4; Chol—215; Pro—18.6; Fib—.5; Sod—785

OYSTERS DON LOUIS

6 slices bacon
12 large oysters (with half shells)
1 tsp. Cajun Seasoning Mix (see index)
rock salt
1 tbsp. Worcestershire sauce
1 tbsp. fresh lemon juice
1 tsp. Tabasco sauce

2 cloves garlic, minced
1 tsp. minced fresh rosemary (or 1/4 tsp. dried)
2 tbsp. chopped ripe California olives
6 slices hot pepper cheese, 1/4-inch thick, quartered
2 tbsp. minced green onion tops

Set the oven to broil. Fry the bacon in a medium-sized skillet over medium heat, until it is brown and crisp. Drain it on paper towels and set aside for later use. Dry each oyster with paper towels to get rid of excess water. Season each oyster with the **Cajun Seasoning Mix,** and place one oyster in each of the clean half shells. Pour enough rock salt into two large, sturdy tin pie pans to fill them to the rim and place six oyster shells on each bed of salt.

In a medium mixing bowl, combine the next six ingredients. Spoon equal amounts of this mixture over each of the twelve oysters. Crumble the bacon and sprinkle it evenly over the 12 oysters. Top each oyster with two of the quarters of hot pepper cheese. Place the oysters under the broiler, about 8 inches from the heat source, until the cheese is melted. Serve at once. Serves 2.

Lagniappe: You can double this recipe or triple, etc. just by increasing the amounts proportionately. This makes a pretty oyster dish that is so easy to prepare. To save time, you can fry the bacon, fill your pie pans with rock salt and stack them, mix together the lemon-olive mixture, and quarter the cheese in advance. The rest will be quick and simple.

I sometimes like to put chopped shrimp on with the crumbled bacon to give a different taste. Use about 2/3 cup of chopped boiled shrimp that has been peeled and deveined and simply put it on with the bacon. Cover it all with the cheese (the melting of the cheese holds it all together, so be sure to place the two quarters of cheese to cover the whole oyster). I call this dish with shrimp **Baked Oysters Eugene.** Both Eugene and Don Louis are my great uncles, my grandfather Theriot's brothers.

Calories—942; Carb—12; Fat—81; Chol—450; Pro—31; Fib—.8; Sod— 2318

OYSTER FRITTERS POUPONNE

1 1/2 cup flour
1 1/2 tsp. baking powder
1/2 tsp. baking soda
1 tsp. salt
1/2 tsp. cayenne pepper
1/2 tsp. black pepper
1/4 tsp. white pepper
1/2 tsp. garlic powder
1/4 tsp. dry sweet basil
3 large eggs, beaten
1/2 cup milk

1 qt. oysters (in water)
1 medium onion, minced
1/4 cup finely chopped red
    bell pepper
2 tbsp. minced celery
1 clove garlic, minced
1/2 cup minced fresh
    parsley
1/2 tsp. Tabasco sauce
peanut oil

   Preheat the oil to 375 degrees in a large pot or deep fryer. In a large mixing bowl, combine the first nine ingredients using a wire whisk. Blend in the eggs, milk, and enough of the oyster liquid to make a thick batter. Add the onion, bell pepper, celery, garlic, and parsley. Blend thoroughly. Chop the oysters into large pieces, and fold them and the Tabasco sauce into the batter. Spoon the batter by tablespoon into the hot peanut oil. Fry until golden brown. Serve hot. Serves 4 to 6.

Lagniappe: This is a great way to serve oysters to people who won't eat them raw. Serve the fritters with **Jude's Special Seafood Sauce** or **Tartar Sauce.**

   You can substitute a pound of crabmeat to make **Crab Fritters Pouponne** or you can use 1 1/2 pounds of shrimp to make **Shrimp Fritters Pouponne.** (The shrimp will need to be boiled, peeled, deveined, and chopped before being added to the batter.) All in all, this is an easy dish, a great party food, or a wonderful seafood entree.
   You can make this batter in advance and refrigerate it for up to 8 hours before frying. Just stir it well, then spoon it into the hot oil. Remember to use peanut oil because it can withstand the high temperatures, and it imparts a slightly nutty taste to the fritters that will keep them guessing. Do not freeze this dish.

Calories—530; Carb—45.7; Fat—26; Chol—609; Pro—28; Fib—.5; Sod—802

OYSTERS MANUEL

1/2 cup chili sauce
1/2 cup catsup
1/2 tsp. Tabasco sauce
3 cloves garlic, minced
1 tbsp. minced shallots
1 tbsp. minced fresh basil
  (or 1 tsp. dried)
1 tsp. salt

12 large oysters (with half
  shells)
6 slices bacon, halved
12 toothpicks
5 lb. rock salt
2 tbsp minced fresh parsley
4 lemon wedges

Preheat the oven to 400 degrees. In a mixing bowl, combine the chili sauce, catsup, Tabasco sauce, garlic, shallots, basil, and salt and set aside. Pat each oyster dry with a white paper towel. Wrap each oyster with 1/2 slice of bacon and secure it with a toothpick. Place each oyster in its half shell. Fill two sturdy tin pie pans with rock salt, spoon equal amounts of the chili sauce mixture over each oyster, and place six oyster shells on each bed of rock salt.

Bake at 400 degrees for about 15 minutes. When done, the top of the bacon should be crisp. Remove pans from the oven, sprinkle the oysters with the fresh parsley, and garnish with lemon wedges. Place the pie pans on cool plates and serve hot. Serves 2.

Lagniappe: You can double or triple this recipe with ease. Just keep the proportions constant. This is about as close to raw oysters as you can get. Serving oysters on the half shell in an old pie pan is a tradition in Louisiana. The rock salt really adds to the dish: it prevents the shells from moving, it keeps the oysters hot longer, it gives a little crust of salt around the edges, and it looks pretty.

To clean oyster shells, scrub them well, boil them in hot water for about 20 minutes, then just wash them in the dishwasher—it does a great job. Ask your seafood supplier to keep some nice large shells for you, and you'll have a wonderful serving dish for oysters. Remember that the shells must be clean! The reason restaurants have stopped using real shells is the time it takes to clean them properly.

Calories—710; Carb—39; Fat—52; Chol—360; Pro—23; Fib—.1; Sod—3438

SHRIMP ANNA BRIN

2 lb. large shrimp
1 tsp. Cajun Seasoning Mix
   (see index)
1 stick unsalted butter
1 tbsp. minced shallots
3 cloves garlic, minced
1 tsp. grated fresh ginger
2 cups dark brown sugar
2 cups light brown sugar

1/4 cup honey
1 tsp. Tabasco sauce
2/3 cup distilled white
   vinegar
2/3 cup port wine
1 large onion, sliced
1 large red bell pepper, cut
   into strips

Peel and devein the shrimp, leaving the last section of the tail on the shrimp. Season the shrimp with **Cajun Seasoning Mix** and set aside. Heat a large, heavy skillet over medium-high heat, then add the butter. When the butter begins to smoke, add the shallots, garlic, and ginger. Cook for 30 seconds, then add the shrimp. Sauté for 2 1/2 minutes, remove the shrimp with a slotted spoon, and place them on a warm platter.

Reduce the heat to medium, then add the sugars, honey, and Tabasco sauce, stirring constantly for 3 minutes. Remove from heat, and carefully stir in the vinegar (it may splatter or cause a rush of steam). Return to the heat, add the port wine and the onions, and cook until the mixture thickens and the amount of liquid is reduced by about 1/3. Add the cooked shrimp and the red bell pepper. Reduce to a simmer, and allow the shrimp to cook for about 2 minutes, stirring occasionally. Serve right away. Serves 8.

Lagniappe: I had difficulty deciding where to put this recipe. I chose to put it in the appetizer section because it could start any meal off with a bang. Sweet shrimp, cooked the Cajun way, are like none you have ever tasted before. Serve them in individual dishes with plenty of sauce. Leaving the tail on creates a beautiful effect. If you use this as an entree, you can serve it over rice.

Don't make this dish in advance. Although it won't hurt the sauce at all, the shrimp continue to cook, and become overcooked, if not eaten right away. What you can do is prepare the sauce in advance; then later add shrimp that have been sautéed in butter. The sauce alone can be refrigerated nicely for up to one week. In fact, it can be frozen for later use.

If you like scallops, you can make **Scallops Anna Brin,** by substituting 1 2/3 pounds of scallops for the shrimp. Be prepared for a unique and tasty treat!

Calories—607; Carb—129; Fat—13.4; Chol—205; Pro—22.2; Fib—.3; Sod—258

SHRIMP MARIE LOUISE

1/3 cup olive oil
4 cloves garlic, minced
1 tbsp. minced shallots
1/3 cup minced fresh parsley
1/2 tsp. black pepper
1 tsp. chopped fresh oregano (or 1/4 tsp. dried)

1/2 tsp. chopped fresh rosemary (or 1/8 tsp. dried)
1 1/2 lb. jumbo shrimp, peeled and deveined
1/2 lb. fresh mushrooms, sliced
1 tbsp. fresh lemon juice
lemon wedges

Heat a heavy skillet (use one that has a cover) over medium heat. When hot, add the olive oil, and heat until it begins to smoke. Sauté the garlic, shallots, parsley, pepper, oregano, and rosemary for 2 minutes. Add the shrimp and mushrooms; then cover the skillet for 4 minutes, shaking the pan often. Remove the cover, add the lemon juice, and stir. Serve immediately with lemon wedges as a garnish. Serves 4 as an appetizer.

Lagniappe: Because I think this dish is a spectacular appetizer, I put it in this section. Although my wife prefers it as a meal, I am writing the book—so you see where it is. (Boy, will I pay for this one!) Seriously, it is great as an appetizer or an entree—the choice is yours.

There is no need to make this in advance, it barely takes any time to cook. Serve it with plenty of hot fresh bread, and you won't even have to do the dishes—the bread will be used to wipe the plates clean.

Calories—343; Carb—7.8; Fat—19; Chol—257; Pro—34.5; Fib—.5; Sod—830

SHRIMP DANIEL

1/4 cup vegetable oil
2 tbsp. creole mustard
1 tbsp. red wine vinegar
1/2 cup minced green
  onions
2 tbsp. minced celery
2 cloves garlic, minced
1 tsp. horseradish
1 tsp. Tabasco sauce

1 tsp. minced fresh basil
  (or 1/4 tsp. dried)
1 tbsp. minced fresh
  parsley
1/2 tsp. salt
1/2 tsp. black pepper
1 recipe Spicy Boiled
  Shrimp (see index)
1/2 head iceberg lettuce

In a mixing bowl, combine the oil, mustard, and vinegar. Whip with a wire whisk or electric mixer until well blended. Fold in the remaining ingredients, except for the shrimp and lettuce. Prepare **Spicy Boiled Shrimp** according to the recipe. Peel and devein the shrimp, and mix them in with the sauce mixture. Cover and refrigerate for a few hours.

When you are ready to serve, make a nice bed of lettuce on your salad plates and spoon the shrimp equally onto the lettuce. Serve chilled. Serves 4.

Lagniappe: This entire dish may be prepared up to 24 hours in advance and stored in the refrigerator, tightly covered. Do not freeze this sauce. You can make the sauce alone up to 3 days in advance; if you add the shrimp, four to six hours before serving.

As an entree, serve the dish with plenty of hot French bread and either ice cold beer or a light, dry white wine.

Calories—465; Carb—11.3; Fat—17.3; Chol—515; Pro—66.3; Fib—.8; Sod—2130

SHRIMP REMOULADE

1 cup mayonnaise
1/4 cup creole mustard
1 tbsp. horseradish
1 tsp. Tabasco sauce
1 tsp. Worcestershire sauce
3 cloves garlic, finely
  minced
2 tbsp. sweet paprika
2 tbsp. red wine vinegar
1/2 tsp. onion powder

1/2 cup chopped fresh
  parsley
1 cup chopped green
  onions
2 tbsp. chopped celery
1 recipe Spicy Boiled
  Shrimp (see index)
1/2 head lettuce
lemon wedges

In a large mixing bowl, combine the mayonnaise, mustard, horse-radish, Tabasco sauce, Worcestershire sauce, garlic, paprika, vinegar, and onion powder. Whip with a wire whisk or electric mixer until well blended. Fold in the parsley, green onions, and celery.

Prepare the shrimp according to the **Spicy Boiled Shrimp** recipe and peel them (devein if you like, but it is not necessary). Fold the shrimp into the sauce, cover, and refrigerate until you are ready to serve. Although you may serve right away, chilling for a few hours blends the spices.

When you are ready to serve, cut the lettuce into strips and arrange it as a bed on the serving plates. Spoon generous amounts of the shrimp mixture over the lettuce, and garnish with a wedge or two of lemon. Serve chilled. Serves 4.

Lagniappe: This is a quick, and quite good remoulade. It can be served as a salad or as an appetizer—either way it is delicious. You can prepare this dish up to 24 hours in advance, and store it tightly covered in the refrigerator. However, do not cut the lettuce until you are ready to serve so it will be crisp. Bon appetit!

Calories—594; Carb—28; Fat—56.8; Chol—531; Pro—67; Fib—1.2; Sod—2444

CHEDDAR KRISPS

2 cups grated sharp
  cheddar cheese
2 sticks unsalted butter,
  softened
2 cups self-rising flour
2 cups Rice Krispies cereal
1 tbsp. Worcestershire
  sauce

1/2 tsp. Tabasco sauce
1/4 tsp. onion powder
1/4 tsp. sweet basil
1/4 cup finely minced green
  onions

Preheat the oven to 325 degrees. Combine all ingredients in a large mixing bowl. Mix until well blended. Form small, 1-inch balls, like meatballs, and place on a lightly greased cookie sheet. Press them down—just a little—with your thumb. Bake for 18 to 20 minutes; then remove from the cookie sheet and allow to cool. Serve warm or cool. Makes about 8 dozen.

Lagniappe: This is a great appetizer to make and eat. It freezes well, and stores unfrozen in a tight container for several days.
    You can make **Swiss Krisps** by substituting 2 cups of Swiss cheese for the cheddar. This is a great after-school snack for kids. If you substitute margarine for the butter, I would suggest that you add 2 teaspoons of powdered Butter Buds to give you the real butter taste without the cholesterol.

Calories—39; Carb—2.6; Fat—2.8; Chol—8.0; Pro—.9; Fib—Trace; Sod—53

SPICY ROASTED PECANS

1 1/2 cups pecan halves
2 tsp. canola oil
1 tbsp. sugar
1 tsp. salt

1/2 tsp. onion powder
1/4 tsp. garlic powder
1/2 tsp. cayenne pepper
1/4 tsp. dried ground basil

Preheat the oven to 450 degrees. Put the pecan halves in a mixing bowl and pour the oil over them. Toss to mix; then stir in the remaining ingredients. Pour the pecans onto a large cookie sheet and bake until they are nicely browned, about 7 minutes. Allow them to cool; then put them into a container with a lid for use as needed. Makes 1 1/2 cups of spicy roasted pecans.

Lagniappe: This is a great party dish. It is also great as a snack. I like to add whole pecans to green salads to add that special crunch and piquant flavor. Make them and develop your own use for them—who knows, you might just want to eat them like popcorn. Be careful, these are habit forming.

Calories—45; Carb—1.2; Fat—3.6; Chol—0; Pro—.3; Fib—.2; Sod—96

HOLLY'S SNAPPY APPETIZER

3/4 cup chopped ham
1/4 cup chopped pepperoni
1/2 cup mayonnaise
1/2 cup finely chopped
   hazel nuts
1/4 cup chopped pimento-
   stuffed green olives
1/4 cup chopped black
   olives

1/8 cup capers
1/4 tsp. Tabasco sauce
1/4 tsp. fresh basil (or 1/8
   tsp. dried)
20 French bread rounds,
   toasted
paprika

In a large mixing bowl, fold together the first nine ingredients and mix well. Spoon a generous amount on each bread round, dust lightly with paprika, and serve. Makes 20 rounds.

Lagniappe: This can easily be made in advance and refrigerated until ready to use. I use a biscuit cutter to shape the bread rounds. French bread is best, but if you don't have French bread, any bread will do— even whole wheat or rye. To toast them, put them in a 180-degree oven until they are nice and dry. You can lightly butter the bread, or even use seasoned butter, before putting it in the oven.

This is a great hors d'oeuvre to serve while waiting for all your guests to arrive. It is also simple enough that your children can make it for you.

Calories—115; Carb—7; Fat—7; Chol—8.6; Pro—3.1; Fib—.4; Sod— 397

PECAN BALLS

4 oz. cream cheese,
  softened
1/4 cup grated sharp
  cheddar cheese
1/4 cup grated Swiss
  cheese
1 tbsp. finely chopped
  green onions

2 tbsp. chopped black
  olives
1 tsp. chopped pimento
1/4 tsp. Tabasco sauce
1/4 tsp. fresh lemon juice
1/3 cup roasted pecans,
  chopped

In a mixing bowl or a food processor, blend together all ingredients, except the pecans. Form the mixture into balls. Pour the chopped pecans onto a plate, and roll the balls over the pecans with enough pressure to make the pecans stick to the cheese mixture. Place pecan-covered balls on a plate, cover with plastic wrap, and chill for 30 minutes to an hour. Serves 4.

Lagniappe: This appetizer can be served on crackers or alone. It can also be rolled into one big ball and served with crackers around it for a nice party dish.

It will store for up to one week in the refrigerator, so it can be made well in advance. If you have a larger crowd, you can make it in increased quantity without disturbing the outcome. Experiment with other cheeses and vary some of the other ingredients to make other nice cheese balls.

Calories—226; Carb—3.1; Fat—21.3; Chol—45; Pro—15.4; Fib— .5; Sod—227

Gumbos and Soups

QUICK SEAFOOD GUMBO

1 cup peanut oil
1 cup flour
2 large onions, chopped
2 ribs celery, chopped
3 cloves garlic, minced
1 medium bell pepper,
  chopped
1 10-oz. can stewed
  tomatoes
3 qt. fish stock
2 1/2 tsp. Cajun Seasoning
  Mix (see index)
1/2 tsp. Tabasco sauce

1 tbsp. Worcestershire
  sauce
2 bay leaves
2 lb. shrimp, peeled and
  deveined
1 lb. crabmeat
1 pint oysters
1 cup finely chopped green
  onions
1/2 cup finely chopped
  fresh parsley
cooked white rice
filé powder

Be sure that all the prep work (chopping, peeling, mincing, etc.) is done ahead of time. Have all the ingredients lined up and ready for use. Heat a large, heavy stock pot or gumbo pot (at least 3 gallon size) over high heat. When it is hot, add the peanut oil. When the oil begins to smoke, add the flour, stirring constantly with a wire whisk for about 3 minutes. Take great care not to splash the hot mixture. This will make a roux that should be a dark, rich brown color.

Stirring constantly, add the onions, celery, garlic, and bell pepper. Reduce the heat to medium, and sauté the vegetables in this dark mixture for 3 more minutes. Stir in the stewed tomatoes and cook for 2 more minutes. Add the seafood and cook for 12 minutes over medium heat. Finally, add the green onions and parsley and cook for 5 more minutes. Serve in large soup bowls over cooked white rice. Spoon filé powder on top of each serving, according to taste. Serve hot. Serves 8.

Lagniappe: Yes, you can make speedy gumbo—but you will have to take care not to burn yourself with the hot roux. You can make gumbo in advance and either refrigerate or freeze it. The dish will taste better if it is made a day early, and chilled in the refrigerator. To reheat, just pour back into the pot, place it over low heat, and serve it when it's hot.

For a different flavor, two pounds of crawfish (or one pound of crawfish and one pound of shrimp) can be substituted for the two pounds of shrimp in the recipe. You can use this recipe to make **Shrimp Gumbo** by replacing all of the seafood with 3 1/2 pounds of peeled and deveined shrimp. To make **Oyster Gumbo,** use 1 1/2 quarts of oysters as the only seafood; to make **Crawfish Gumbo,** use 3 pounds of peeled and deveined crawfish tails. Also, if you don't have any fish stock, you may substitute chicken stock, chicken broth, or even warm water.

Gumbo is a Cajun staple, and must be tasted before it is judged. Many people from outside Louisiana tend to judge it by it's looks (it is not very pretty), but the smell and taste are what makes it so wonderful. It is an old Louisiana dish that was created by the Creoles of New Orleans in an attempt to imitate Bouillabaisse. Because they didn't have access to the necessary ingredients, they made substitutions. Later, the Cajuns made other changes. Today, we have almost as many kinds of gumbo as we have people in Louisiana. It has become a personalized dish—everyone makes his own gumbo.

The word *gumbo* comes from an African word meaning "okra." Not all gumbos contain okra, but they all carry the original name. Almost every true gumbo starts with a dark brown roux and is topped with filé powder—the ground up leaves of the sassafras tree. Filé powder gives gumbo a unique flavor. For those not familiar with filé, I would recommend adding a little at a time to the individual serving. Filé powder added to the pot has a tendency to thicken the gumbo and add a somewhat bitter taste (which I happen to find pleasing—but you may not).

This is "The Gumbo Gospel according to St. Jude."

Calories—468; Carb—23.4; Fat—28.4; Chol—272; Pro—29; Fib—.8; Sod—512

SEAFOOD COUBILLION

1 24-oz. can whole
  tomatoes
1 lb. fresh fish filets
1/2 cup peanut oil
1/2 cup all-purpose flour
1 large onion, chopped
2/3 cup chopped celery
3 cloves garlic, minced
1/2 cup chopped fresh
  parsley
3 cups chicken stock,
  chicken broth or fish
  stock
1 1/2 cup dry white wine

1/2 large fresh lemon
2 tbsp. Worcestershire
  sauce
1/2 tsp. Tabasco sauce
2 bay leaves
2 tsp. Cajun Seasoning Mix
  (see index)
1 1/3 lb. fresh shrimp,
  peeled and deveined
1 pint fresh oysters
1/2 cup chopped green
  onions
cooked white rice
  (optional)

Chop tomatoes and place them in a bowl with their juice and the liquid from the can. Set aside. Cut the fish filets into bite-sized pieces and set aside. Be sure that all other ingredients are respectively chopped, minced, peeled, deveined, and ready to use.

Heat a large (2 1/2 gallon) stock pot or saucepan over high heat. When it is hot, add the peanut oil. When the oil begins to smoke, stir in the flour. Stirring constantly with a wire whisk, cook for 2 minutes (be careful, if this roux mixture splashes on you, it will burn severely). When it is a light brown color, add the onions, celery, garlic, and parsley. Reduce the heat to medium, and sauté for 4 minutes, stirring constantly. Slowly add the stock, tomatoes with their liquid, and the wine. Squeeze the lemon juice into the mixture and stir well. Add the Worcestershire sauce, Tabasco sauce, bay leaves, and **Cajun Seasoning Mix.**

Bring the mixture to a boil; then reduce to a simmer for 7 minutes. Add the seafood, simmer over low to medium heat for 5 more minutes, then add the green onions. Simmer for one more minute, and serve piping hot in bowls with rice on the side. Serves 6 to 8.

Lagniappe: This dish, that was originally made with scraps of unused pieces of seafood, has become a Cajun favorite over the years. The name *Coubillion* may not make sense to you because it really should be Court Bouillon—but it has taken on a slang name over the years.

Seafood Coubillion is a rich stock soup that can be eaten as a soup or as the main meal. You can prepare this dish completely in advance, and refrigerate or freeze it. If frozen, just thaw in the refrigerator, heat over low-medium heat and serve. As with all dishes that have a roux—a cooked mixture of flour and oil—it actually improves with refrigeration. I like to make it the day before serving, because it is always better if the flavors have a chance to blend together.

Be sure to have all the ingredients lined up before you start to make the roux. This is a fast-moving dish, and the roux will darken too much if you are not able to move on immediately.

Calories—886; Carb—20; Fat—72.4; Chol—286; Pro—28; Fib—.6; Sod—437

SPEEDY SHRIMP BISQUE

1 1/2 lb. fresh shrimp, peeled and deveined
1 10 3/4-oz. can condensed cream of mushroom soup
1 10 3/4-oz. can condensed cream of celery soup
1 cup water
1/2 cup milk, warmed
1/2 cup finely chopped onion
1/2 medium red bell pepper, finely chopped
1 clove garlic, minced
1/2 tsp. salt
1/2 tsp. Tabasco sauce
1/4 tsp. black pepper
1/4 cup minced green onion tops
1/4 cup minced parsley

Combine all the ingredients, except the last two, in a large saucepan over medium heat. Stir over heat for 12 minutes. Add the green onions and parsley and cook for 3 more minutes. Serve hot. Serves 6.

Lagniappe: This may not be as good as regular bisque; but considering the time difference, it is a close second. This recipe could only be easier if you bought it in a can. This is a recipe that you do not want to share. Tell them it's an old family secret, because once they see how simple it is, they won't think you are such a good cook!

Do not freeze this dish. You can make it completely, and refrigerate it for up to 24 hours before serving—that will give you time enough to hide the soup cans.

Calories—219; Carb—15; Fat—7; Chol—182; Pro—25; Fib—.2; Sod—1121

SHRIMP SOUP ROSALIE

1/2 cup flour
1/4 cup unsalted butter
1 1/4 qt. milk, warmed
1 cup chicken broth
1 lb. small shrimp, peeled
**   and deveined**
1 tsp. salt

1/2 tsp. Tabasco sauce
1/4 tsp. white pepper
1 tsp. minced fresh basil
**   (or 1/2 tsp. dried)**
1/2 cup sherry wine
1 tbsp. white
**   Worcestershire sauce**

In a large soup pot, sauté the flour in the butter over medium heat for 5 minutes. Stir in the milk, broth, and shrimp; then blend the flour into the liquid. Cook over low to medium heat for 5 minutes; then add the remaining ingredients. Cook for 5 more minutes and serve hot. Serves 6.

Lagniappe: Do not freeze this soup—it breaks apart and will look terrible. You can completely prepare it, then refrigerate it for up to 2 days. Just cover it and store it in the refrigerator. To reheat, warm over low heat until hot. Do not boil this soup.

This recipe can be used to make **Crawfish Soup Rosalie** or **Crab Soup Rosalie** by substituting 1 pound of crawfish or lump crabmeat for the shrimp. The rest of the recipe remains the same. This soup is wonderful with French bread and a green salad. It makes a tasty light lunch or evening meal.

Calories—331; Carb—20; Fat—16; Chol—164; Pro—23; Fib—Trace; Sod—747

BLACK-EYED PEA SOUP

2 ham hocks
2 cups dried black-eyed
  peas
2 quarts water
2 cups dry vermouth
1 cup chopped smoked
  ham
1 small onion, chopped
1 small sweet red bell
  pepper, diced
2 cloves garlic, minced
1 stalk celery, chopped
1/4 cup minced parsley

2 tsp. minced fresh basil
  (or 1/2 tsp. dried)
1 tsp. salt
1/2 tsp. black pepper
1/4 tsp. white pepper
1/2 tsp. Tabasco sauce
2 whole bay leaves
3 carrots, sliced
2 10 3/4-oz. cans
  condensed cream of
  potato soup
1/2 cup finely chopped
  green onions

Combine the ham hocks, dried beans, water, and vermouth in a large stock pot; then bring to a boil over high heat. Let the mixture boil for 6 minutes uncovered. Add the remaining ingredients, except for the potato soup and green onions. When the soup begins to boil again, reduce the heat to medium. Cook for 10 minutes at a low, rolling boil; then remove the ham hocks and stir in the condensed potato soup. Continue to cook over medium heat for 5 more minutes; then add the green onions. Stir in well and cook for 2 more minutes. Serve hot. Serves 6.

Lagniappe: This is a very hearty soup. It is also a great way to use dried peas or beans. Feel free to substitute navy beans or pinto beans for the black-eyed peas to make **Navy Bean Soup** or **Pinto Power Soup.** The list is endless, and only your imagination limits the choices. These soups can be made in advance and refrigerated for later use. Just place over medium heat until it is heated through.

Calories—326; Carb—26; Fat—13; Chol—41; Pro—18.4; Fib—1.5; Sod—1250

CAJUN BLACK BEAN SOUP

1 lb. dry black beans
1 lb. andouille sausage
1/4 lb. ham
1 cup dry red wine
water
1/4 cup olive oil
1/4 cup peanut oil
2 large onions, chopped
1 large green bell pepper,
  chopped
1 large red bell pepper,
  chopped

4 cloves garlic, minced
1 cup finely chopped celery
1/4 cup minced carrots
1 tsp. salt
1/2 tsp. Tabasco sauce
1/2 tsp. black pepper
1/2 tsp. sweet basil
1 tbsp. Worcestershire
  sauce
2 tbsp. red wine vinegar

Wash the black beans well. Cut the andouille into 1/2-inch slices and chop the ham into bite-sized pieces. Combine the beans, sausage, ham, and wine in a large pot (use one that has a lid). Add enough water to the pot to cover the ingredients, and place the pot over high heat. Bring to a hard boil for 5 minutes; then reduce to a rolling simmer.

Place a large skillet over medium-high heat. When it is hot, add the olive oil and peanut oil. When the oil starts to smoke, add the chopped vegetables, and sauté for about 5 to 7 minutes, or until they are limp. Add the sautéed vegetables and the remaining ingredients to the bean pot, cover, and cook for 30 to 45 minutes, until the beans are tender. When the beans are ready, remove about 2 cups of them, mash them with a fork, then return them to the soup pot. Serve hot. Serves 6.

Lagniappe: This is a great flavorful soup that can serve as a main course. It can be prepared up to 3 days in advance and refrigerated until you are ready to use (advance preparation actually improves the flavor). This soup can also be frozen after it is completely cooked. To reheat, just thaw in the refrigerator, heat over medium heat until it comes to a low boil, then serve.

I like to add chopped pieces of chicken to this soup to create an even heartier meal. I simply had to experiment with these little black beans—they were the only beans in the supermarket that I had never used before. So here you have them!

Calories—574; Carb—19.3; Fat—44.8; Chol—70; Pro—21.8; Fib—1.2; Sod—1517

CREAM OF CELERY SOUP

2 cups diced celery	**1/4 cup unsalted butter**
2 1/4 cups water	**1/4 cup finely chopped**
1/2 tsp. chopped fresh basil	**onions**
(or 1/8 tsp. dried)	**1/4 tsp. minced garlic**
1 tsp. salt	**1/4 cup all-purpose flour**
1/4 tsp. Tabasco sauce	**2 cups half-and-half cream**

In a saucepan over medium heat, combine the celery, water, basil, salt, and Tabasco sauce; then bring to a boil. Reduce the heat to a simmer, cover, and cook for about 10 minutes.

While the celery mixture cooks, melt the butter in a 2 1/2-quart saucepan over medium heat. When it begins to smoke, add the onions and garlic and sauté for 2 minutes. Add the flour and cook for 3 minutes, stirring constantly.

Remove from heat and use a wire whisk to blend the half-and-half cream into the roux (flour mixture). Return to the low heat, stirring constantly, until the sauce begins to thicken. Add the cooked celery mixture and cook over low heat until the soup is thick enough to coat a spoon. Serve hot. Serves 4.

Lagniappe: You can use this soup as a base or any time your recipe calls for cream of celery soup. Remember that this soup is not condensed, so you would have to modify any recipe that calls for canned soup. You can make it in advance and freeze or refrigerate it for later use. This recipe makes about seven cups of soup.

Calories—253; Carb—13; Fat—20; Chol—21; Pro—4.7; Fib—.4; Sod—671

CREAM OF ONION SOUP

3 tbsp. unsalted butter
3 medium onions, chopped
1/2 cup minced celery
1/4 cup unsalted butter
1/4 cup all-purpose flour
1 cup milk

1 cup half-and-half cream
1 cup beef broth
1/4 tsp. Tabasco sauce
1 tsp. salt
1/4 tsp. white pepper

In a heavy skillet over medium heat, melt the 3 tablespoons of butter. When it begins to smoke, add the onions and celery and sauté for 8 minutes, until the onions begin to brown nicely.

While the onions and celery cook, melt the 1/4 cup of butter in a heavy, 2 1/2-quart saucepan over medium heat. When it is melted, add the flour and stir constantly for 4 minutes. Remove from the heat, stir in the milk and half-and-half cream, then return to the heat. Cook, stirring often, until the sauce thickens.

When the onions have cooked, add the beef broth to the skillet and let it simmer for 1 minute. Pour the contents of the skillet into the saucepan, stir in well, and season with Tabasco sauce, salt and pepper. Let the soup thicken over medium heat for about 2 minutes, taking care not to allow it to boil. Serve hot. Serves 4.

Lagniappe: If you don't like onions floating in your onion soup, then run the onions through a food processor or blender until they are completely pureed. This works quite well to make a smooth soup. Personally, I like the taste, texture, and bite of real pieces of onions in my onion soup, so I do not run it through a blender—but the choice is really yours.

You can make this soup in advance and refrigerate it. You can freeze it, but I don't recommend it because onions loose quite a bit of their flavor when they are frozen. It is at it's pinnacle just after preparation.

It is necessary to brown the onions because browning helps to sweeten the onion in the soup. As the starch (gluten) leaves the onion under heat, it begins to turn to sugars. Sugars and heat combine to create a sweet caramel. Therefore, to get the flavor of onion that I want in this dish, you must be sure to brown the onions.

Calories—366; Carb—17.6; Fat—30.4; Chol—68; Pro—7.4; Fib—.6; Sod—851

CREAM OF BROCCOLI SOUP I

1/4 cup unsalted butter
1 medium onion, chopped
1 stalk celery, chopped
1 small bell pepper, diced
2 cloves garlic, minced
1/2 lb. smoked ham, diced
1 10 3/4-oz. can condensed
  cream of chicken soup

2 1/2 cups fresh broccoli
  florets
1 1/4 cup milk, warm
1/2 tsp. Tabasco sauce
1/2 tsp. salt
1/2 tsp. dried basil
2 tbsp. minced fresh
  parsley

In a large saucepan over medium-high heat, heat the butter until it begins to sizzle; then sauté the onion, celery, bell pepper, and garlic for 5 minutes. Add the ham and sauté for 2 more minutes. Add the remaining ingredients, except for the parsley, reduce the heat to low-medium, and simmer for 12 minutes. Add the fresh parsley and simmer for 1 more minute. Serve hot. Serves 4.

Lagniappe: Quick can still be so good! This is a real treat—but don't tell anyone that you used canned soup—everyone will think you are a real whiz in the kitchen.

You can vary the types of creamed soup you make by just substituting your favorite vegetable. To make **Cream of Summer Squash Soup,** just replace the broccoli with 2 1/2 cups of yellow squash cut into 1/2-inch circles—the rest of the recipe remains the same. I also like to make **Cream of Asparagus Soup** by substituting 2 1/2 cups of fresh asparagus pieces (a little over a pound of asparagus), for the broccoli. **Cream of Carrot Soup** can be made by using the same recipe with 2 1/2 cups of sliced fresh carrots. The number of choices is phenomenal. Have a blast!

Calories—423; Carb—14; Fat—29; Chol—74; Pro—13.5; Fib—2; Sod—1498

CREAM OF FRESH BROCCOLI SOUP II

1 bunch broccoli (about
  1 1/4 lb.)
3 cups chicken stock or
  chicken broth
1/4 cup butter
2/3 cup chopped onion
1/4 cup minced celery
1 tbsp. diced bell pepper
2 tbsp. chopped fresh
  parsley

3 tbsp. all-purpose flour
3 large egg yolks, beaten
1 cup heavy cream
1 cup milk
1 tsp. salt
1/2 tsp. Tabasco sauce
1/2 tsp. white pepper
1/4 tsp. black pepper

Wash the broccoli, trim off any bad spots, and cut it into small pieces. Put the broccoli into a heavy saucepan (about 3-quart) with enough water to cover it. Bring to a boil over medium heat for exactly 2 minutes. Add the chicken stock, bring the liquid back to boiling, then reduce to a simmer. Let the broccoli simmer for 5 minutes; then remove from the heat and allow to cool.

In a skillet over medium heat, melt the butter until it begins to smoke. Add the onion, celery, bell pepper, and parsley. Sauté for 3 minutes; then add the flour and cook for 3 minutes. Combine the roux (flour-oil mixture) with the cooling broccoli, and mix together well. Pour the mixture into a blender or food processor and blend until the broccoli is finely chopped. Return to the pot and bring to a simmer.

As the soup begins to thicken, combine the beaten eggs, heavy cream, and milk in a separate bowl. Add enough of the hot soup to the cream mixture to make it quite hot; then pour it into the soup pot. Continue to simmer and blend in the remaining ingredients. Be sure not to allow this soup to boil after the cream mixture has been added. Serve hot. Serves 6.

Lagniappe: Here we have another magnificent cream soup. This one is not heavy, but it is bona fide and quite pleasurable. You can do a lot with this recipe. You can substitute 1 1/4 pounds of the vegetable of your choice and make this cream soup the way you want it. I like to use asparagus, tender young carrots, or fresh leeks.

This soup can be made in advance and stored in the refrigerator for up to 4 days. I don't like to freeze this soup, the egg-cream mixture really doesn't respond well to extreme temperatures. Bon appetit!

Calories—333; Carb—10; Fat—29; Chol—221; Pro—10; Fib—.8; Sod—798

CREAMY CORN SOUP

5 ears fresh corn
3 tbsp. unsalted butter
3 1/3 tbsp. flour
1 qt. milk
2 tbsp. minced celery

2 tbsp. minced onion
1 tsp. salt
1/4 tsp. Tabasco sauce
1 tsp. black pepper

Shuck, wash, and remove silk from the corn. Cut the corn off the cob into a mixing bowl to get as much of the "corn milk" as possible. Mashing it with a spoon and stirring constantly, cook the corn in a medium-sized saucepan or skillet over medium heat for 4 minutes. Remove from the heat and set aside for later use.

In a 2 1/2-quart saucepan, melt the butter over medium heat. Add the flour, stirring continuously, for 3 minutes. Add the celery and onions and cook for 1 minute. Remove from the heat to add the milk, salt, Tabasco sauce, and black pepper. Blend in well and return to heat. When the mixture begins to thicken, add the corn, scraping the bottom of the pot to be sure you get all of the liquid too. Cook for 4 more minutes over low to medium heat. Serve warm. Serves 6.

Lagniappe: This is a great soup and a great base for other soups. Add 1/2 pound of fresh lump crabmeat to this soup for a scrumptious **Corn and Crab Soup,** or add a pint of fresh oysters to make **Oyster and Corn Soup.** There are many other possibilities—try them and see.

You can make this soup in advance and refrigerate or freeze it. It is quick and easy, and the flavor is magnificent.

Calories—302; Carb—38; Fat—13; Chol—38.5; Pro—7; Fib—.6; Sod—485

CREAM OF MUSHROOM SOUP

1 lb. mushrooms
1 tbsp. fresh lemon juice
2 cups beef stock or beef
  broth
1/4 tsp. Tabasco sauce
1 tsp. salt
1/4 cup unsalted butter
1/2 cups finely chopped
  onions

2 tbsp. minced celery
1/8 tsp. minced garlic
1/4 cup all-purpose flour
3 cups milk
1 cup half-and-half cream
2 tbsp. minced fresh
  parsley

Wash (yes, wash) and trim the mushrooms of all bad spots. Chop the mushrooms and put them in a 2-quart saucepan with the lemon juice, beef stock, Tabasco sauce, and salt. Bring to a boil over medium heat; then cover and reduce to simmer for 15 minutes.

While the mushrooms are simmering, melt the butter over medium heat in a 3-quart stock pot or saucepan. When the butter begins to smoke, add the onions, celery, and garlic and sauté for 3 minutes. Add the flour and stir constantly as it cooks for 3 minutes. Remove from the heat, blend in the milk and cream, then return to the heat. Allow the sauce to thicken.

When the mushrooms are cooked, add the mushroom mixture to the white sauce and blend in well. Allow the soup to simmer for about 2 minutes to blend flavors, garnish with fresh parsley, and serve. Serves 4 to 6.

Lagniappe: This is another splendid soup or a spectacular base for sauces or gravies. You can use this soup in other recipes instead of condensed canned soup, but you will have to compensate for this by taking about 1/2 cup of liquid out of the dish, and adding an extra 1/2 cup of the soup. One can of condensed soup is about 1 1/4 cups. Therefore, you would use between 1 3/4 and 2 cups of this soup in its place, and decrease the liquid in the recipe by about 1/2 cup.

This soup can be made in advance and refrigerated or frozen for later use. Thaw it in the refrigerator, and heat over low heat until warm.

Calories—251; Carb—16; Fat—17; Chol—40; Pro—8; Fib—.7; Sod—731

CREAM OF WALNUT SOUP

1 lb. walnuts
2 cups water
1 cup cooked white long-
grain rice
2 tbsp. sugar
1 tsp. salt

2 tbsp. minced chives
1 tsp. grated orange rind
2 cups half-and-half cream
1 qt. milk
1/4 tsp. Tabasco sauce
1/2 tsp. white pepper

In a medium-sized saucepan over medium heat, add the the walnuts and water, and bring to a boil. Reduce the heat to simmer for 6 minutes. Reserving the liquid, place the walnuts in a food processor or blender and process until they become a paste. Add the cooked rice, sugar, and salt; and process for 2 minutes more.

Heat the reserved walnut-water until the liquid is reduced to about 1/4 cup. Add the reduced liquid, the chives, and orange rind to the mixture in the processor. Blend at full power for 1 minute. Add the half-and-half and mix until well blended. Pour the mixture and the milk into a 3-quart saucepan or stock pot. Add the Tabasco sauce and pepper and allow the soup to simmer for about .5 minutes. Serve hot. Serves 6.

Lagniappe: You cannot imagine the multiple flavors of this soup. It is intense, yet delicate. This is a soup to be reckoned with—and also a great base for other soups, sauces, or gravies. Try experimenting with this one.

This soup can be made in advance and either refrigerated or frozen. If you freeze it, thaw it in the refrigerator until you are ready to serve, then heat on low until hot.

Calories—744; Carb—32; Fat—63; Chol—25; Pro—14; Fib—1.6; Sod—229

FRESH TOMATO-BASIL SOUP

2 tbsp. canola oil
1/2 cup chopped green
   onions
1 tbsp. minced celery
1/3 cup diced carrots
2 cloves garlic, minced
2 large tomatoes, skinned
   and diced
3 tbsp. chopped fresh basil

1 cup chicken stock or
   chicken broth
1 tsp. Cajun Seasoning Mix
   (see index)
1 cup half-and-half cream
1/2 cup milk
2 tbsp. minced fresh
   parsley

Heat the oil in a large, heavy saucepan over medium heat. When the oil smokes, add the onions, celery, carrots, and garlic; then sauté for 4 minutes. Add the tomatoes and basil and sauté for 3 minutes. Add the chicken stock and **Cajun Seasoning Mix** and bring the liquid to a boil. Cover and let the soup cook for 10 minutes. Remove from the heat and cool.

Puree the liquid in a blender or food processor. Combine the pureed liquid, the half-and-half and the milk in the saucepan. Return it to the heat until hot. Do not boil this soup because it will separate. Garnish each bowl of soup with minced parsley. Serve hot. Serves 4.

Lagniappe: This is a nice summer soup. I love to use fresh tomatoes and herbs while they are in season. Basil is easy to grow anywhere in the country. I keep it outside in the summer so it will flower and seed. I choose one nice plant at the end of the summer and cut it back to about 1 foot high—which is almost only one stalk. When it begins to send out new sprouts, I dig it up (with the dirt around it) and pot it to bring indoors for the winter. It does nicely in a window that gets the sun from the south or east. Be sure to time the arrival of winter right—I get caught by an early winter every now and then.

As far as the soup is concerned, it can be made in advance and refrigerated for up to 3 days. Just heat over a low fire when you are ready to serve. This makes a nice side soup, or even a light luncheon soup. Don't let the cream scare you, there is enough tomato in this soup to keep it light and fresh!

Calories—211; Carb—9; Fat—15; Chol—7; Pro—9; Fib—1; Sod—373

SUMMER SQUASH SOUP

2 lb. fresh yellow summer
  squash
1 tsp. salt
2 whole allspice
3 tbsp. sugar
1 tsp. fresh lemon juice
3 tbsp. butter

3 tbsp. flour
3 cups milk
1 cup half-and-half cream
1 recipe Whipped Cream
  (see index)
fresh zest curls lemon

Clean the squash, cut out any bad pieces, and trim the tips of both ends of the squash. Place in a large pot, cover with water, and add 1/2 teaspoon of the salt and the allspice. Boil the squash over high heat for 5 minutes. Remove from the heat and allow the squash to sit in the liquid for 3 minutes. Remove the squash from the liquid and place it in a food processor or blender. Add the sugar, the remaining 1/2 teaspoon of the salt, and lemon juice. Process for 2 minutes until the mixture is very smooth.

In a 3-quart saucepan over medium heat, melt the butter. Add the flour and cook, stirring constantly, for 4 minutes (this is making a roux). Remove the pan from the heat to blend in the milk and half-and-half cream. The sauce should thicken somewhat when you return it to the heat. Add the blended squash and reduce the heat to low. Cook over low heat while you are making the whipped topping. Serve warm, topped with a large dab of whipped cream and zest curls of lemon. Serves 4 to 6.

Lagniappe: This soup takes advantage of a white sauce made from a roux. Very often, people do not realize that a roux is just a light mixture of flour and some oil (in this case, butter). In Louisiana, when we refer to roux, we mean a dark brown roux. A roux is made by cooking flour in oil for at least three minutes. It is used to jell sauces, soups, or any hot liquids. It also helps to disperse the essence of the flavor throughout the complete dish. Each grain of flour absorbs flavor and deposits it back on your taste buds. This means that you get a blended flavorful taste in every bite.

You can make this soup in advance and refrigerate or freeze it for later use. Don't dress it with the whipped cream until you are ready to serve. If you freeze it, defrost it in the refrigerator until it is completely thawed. Heat at low temperature until warm, then dress with the whipped cream and serve.

Calories—405; Carb—28; Fat—45; Chol—147; Pro—8.6; Fib—.8; Sod—222

CHILLED AVOCADO SOUP

1 qt. chicken stock or chicken broth	3 large avocados, peeled and pitted
1/2 cup chopped onion	1/2 lemon
1/4 cup chopped celery	3/4 tsp. salt
2 tbsp. minced parsley	1/2 tsp. black pepper
1 tbsp. chopped fresh basil (or 1 tsp. dried)	1/4 tsp. Tabasco sauce
1/4 cup chopped green onions	1/2 cup heavy cream
	2 strips bacon, cooked and crumbled

Bring the first six ingredients to a boil in a large saucepan over high heat; then reduce heat to medium and cook for 7 minutes. Remove from heat, allow the liquid to cool for a few minutes, then pour it into a blender and blend until the vegetables are mixed into the liquid.

Slice the avocado into thin slices, then squeeze the lemon over it. Add the avocado, salt, pepper, and Tabasco sauce to the blender and blend until the mixture is smooth and creamy. Cover and chill. When you are ready to serve, stir in the heavy cream, pour into bowls, and sprinkle with crumbled bacon. Serve cold. Serves 4.

Lagniappe: This is an easy soup to serve, because it is served straight from the refrigerator. It can be stored for up to 48 hours if you keep it tightly covered (plastic wrap works best) and well chilled. Do not freeze this soup. I like to serve this soup in the summer. Although it has heavy cream in it, it is still a light soup.

Calories—425; Carb—26.1; Fat—33.2; Chol—23; Pro—11.5; Fib—5.4; Sod—885

POTATO SOUP MILLER

2 medium baking potatoes, peeled	3 tbsp. unsalted butter
1 cup turnip, sliced	3 tbsp. all-purpose flour
1/2 cup chopped celery	2 cups milk
1/2 cup chopped onion	1/4 cup Tabasco sauce
1/4 cup chopped carrots	1/4 cup white pepper
1 1/2 cups boiling water	1 teaspoon salt
1 1/2 cups beef stock or beef broth	

Peel, slice, and chop the first five ingredients as indicated above. Wash and drain them, then place in a large mixing bowl and cover with boiling water. Let the vegetables stand for about 10 minutes, tossing them once or twice. Put the vegetables into a large stock pot with the beef stock and bring to a boil. Reduce heat and simmer for 15 minutes.

While the vegetables are simmering, melt the butter in a heavy, 2 1/2-quart saucepan over medium heat. Add the flour and cook for 4 minutes, stirring constantly. Remove from the heat, blend in the milk and remaining ingredients, then return to the heat until the sauce thickens nicely.

When the vegetables are tender from simmering, carefully pour them and their liquid into a food processor or blender. (Be sure the use all the liquid because this vegetable stock enhances the taste of the soup.) Process at high speed until completely liquified. Add this puree to the sauce mixture and stir in well. Serves 6.

Lagniappe: This is another soup that can either stand alone or add to a wonderful entree. This soup added to gravies, enhances their composition and flavor. It makes a nice base to use in recipes instead of canned potato soup. Please note that canned soups, for the most part, are condensed. You can't just substitute equal amounts. You can make this soup in advance and refrigerate it.

Calories—156; Carb—15.3; Fat—10; Chol—27.5; Pro—4.3; Fib—.6; Sod—643

SWEET POTATO SOUP

1 tbsp. flour
2 qt. ice cold water
2 1/2 lb. fresh sweet
  potatoes
boiling water
1/2 tsp. salt

1 tsp. fresh shredded ginger
2 cups milk
2 cups half-and-half cream
1/4 cup sugar
1 tbsp. brandy
2 tsp. chopped fresh mint

Mix together the flour and ice water in a large bowl. Peel the sweet potatos, cut them in half, then drop them immediately into the ice water. Let them stand in the ice water for 5 minutes. Remove them from the cold water and put them into a large saucepan or stockpot. Cover with boiling water, and add the salt and fresh ginger. Boil until the potatoes are very tender. Remove the potatoes, reserving 1 cup of the hot liquid. Put the potatoes into a food processor or blender (if you use a blender, add some of the reserved hot liquid to get the blender to work), and process until the potatoes are whipped and light, about 1 1/2 minutes.

Pour the whipped potatoes into a 3-quart saucepan or stock pot and blend in the 1 cup of reserved hot potato water and remaining ingredients, except for the mint. Cook over low heat until the soup comes together and is heated throughout. Do not bring to a boil, just let it simmer. Serve hot topped with mint. Serves 6.

Lagniappe: This is a novel and most pleasing soup. If you can't get good sweet potatoes, you can substitute yams. If you are wondering about purpose of the flour in the ice water, it is there to react with the starch in the potato to prevent the potato from turning dark. This gives your soup that marvelous orange-yellow color.

If you don't have a blender or food processor, you can mash the potatoes with a fork or slotted spoon—they just won't be quite as light and wispy as those done in the food processor. This soup can be made in advance, but the color starts to change over time. Flavor is not harmed by refrigeration.

Calories—329; Carb—49; Fat—12.5; Chol—14; Pro—7; Fib—1; Sod—278

Salads and
Salad Dressings

SHRIMP SALAD

1 1/3 lb. boiled shrimp,
  peeled and deveined
2 large hard-boiled eggs,
  chopped
2/3 cup mayonnaise
1/2 cup chopped celery
1/3 cup chopped sweet
  pickles
1/3 cup minced green
  onions
1/4 cup minced parsley
1/4 cup diced sweet red
  bell pepper

1/4 cup shredded carrots
2 tsp. prepared yellow
  mustard
1/2 tsp. Tabasco sauce
1 tsp. Worcestershire sauce
2/3 tsp. Cajun Seasoning
  Mix (see index)
1/2 head iceberg lettuce
1 head red tip lettuce
  lettuce
paprika

Chop the peeled and deveined boiled shrimp into bite-sized pieces. In a large mixing bowl, combine all but the last three ingredients until well blended. Taste the mixture, and adjust seasoning if necessary. Chill until ready to serve.

Chop the half head of iceberg lettuce into very thin slices, so it appears to have been shredded. Arrange one or two nice leaves red tip lettuce on each salad plate. Pile some of the shredded lettuce on the leaves, and spoon a generous amount of the shrimp salad over the lettuce. Sprinkle with paprika and serve. Serves 4.

Lagniappe: This is an excellent salad for almost any occasion. You can make it in advance and refrigerate for up to 48 hours, until you are ready to serve. Don't chop the lettuce until you are ready to serve and be sure to keep the shrimp well-refrigerated.

You can also use this salad to make **Shrimp Stuffed Avocados.** Just hollow out the center of a half avocado, and stuff it generously with the shrimp mixture. I like to use the red tip lettuce as a base for the avocado—and often even the shredded iceberg lettuce. The red tip lettuce can be replaced—in either recipe—by any other fancy-leaf lettuce. Either way, this makes a great salad, appetizer, or entree.

Calories—424; Carb—26.5; Fat—15.6; Chol—379; Pro—37.5; Fib—2; Sod—773

CREAMY SHRIMP DAIGLE

1 cup sour cream
1/4 cup mayonnaise
1/2 large lemon, juiced
2 tbsp. white wine vinegar
1 tsp. fresh tarragon (or 1/4
   tsp. dried)
1/2 cup chopped green
   onions
2 tbsp. minced parsley
1 tsp. Tabasco sauce

1 tsp. black pepper
1/2 tsp. salt
1 tsp. sugar
1 recipe Spicy Boiled
   Shrimp, peeled (see
   index)
1/2 head iceberg lettuce
paprika
lemon wedges

In a large mixing bowl, combine all the ingredients, except the shrimp, lettuce, paprika and lemon wedges. Fold in the peeled **Spicy Boiled Shrimp.** Cut the lettuce into strips and arrange it as a bed on each of 6 salad plates. Spoon equal amounts of the mixture on top of the lettuce. Sprinkle with paprika, and garnish with a lemon wedge. Serve chilled. Serves 6.

Lagniappe: You can make the shrimp mixture in advance and refrigerate for up to 24 hours. If you do make it in advance, don't cut the lettuce until you are ready to serve. This makes a nice salad or appetizer.

Calories—148; Carb—7.6; Fat—5.0; Chol—93; Pro—17.4; Fib—.5; Sod—784

CRABMEAT STUFFED AVOCADO

3/4 cup mayonnaise
2 tsp. olive oil
1 tsp. Creole mustard
1 clove garlic, minced
2 tbsp. diced sweet red bell
  pepper
2 large eggs, hard-boiled
  and chopped
1 stalk celery, diced
1/4 cup minced green
  onions

2 tbsp. minced fresh
  parsley
1/2 tsp. salt
1 tsp. black pepper
1/2 tsp. Tabasco sauce
1 lb. fresh lump crabmeat
3 large avocados, peeled
  and pitted
1 large lemon, juice only
paprika
lemon wedges

In a large mixing bowl, blend together the mayonnaise, olive oil, mustard, and garlic. Fold in the next eight ingredients. When the mixture is completely blended, gently fold in the crabmeat, taking care not to break up the nice big lumps.

Squeeze the juice of the lemon over the avocado halves to help prevent discoloration. Place a heaping amount of the crabmeat mixture in each avocado half. Dust with paprika and garnish with a lemon wedge. Serve chilled. Serves 6 as an entree salad.

Lagniappe: This is a summer salad special. It is light, yet quite filling. It looks great and tastes outstanding. It really is difficult to mess up lump crabmeat. Don't use the special white crabmeat for this dish—there are too many shells. There is nothing so disturbing as to find a piece of shell in every bite of salad. If lump is not available, the claw meat is okay. It is also low on shells. It tastes just as good, but it just doesn't have the nice color of the fresh lump crabmeat.

You can use this recipe to make **Crabmeat Stuffed Tomatoes** by substituting three tomatoes for the avocados and eliminating the lemon juice. I like to hollow out some of the tomato center to make a basket of sorts for the crabmeat salad. This dish is quite pretty, tasty, and colorful with the red of the tomato, the white of the crabmeat, and the yellow of the lemon.

Calories—423; Carb—22.4; Fat—30.6; Chol—158; Pro—18.7; Fib—2.7; Sod—504

RED BEAN SALAD

1 15-oz. can red beans,
  drained
1/2 cup diced yellow bell
  pepper
1/2 cup minced celery
1 small onion, sliced into
  thin rings
1/2 cup chopped sweet
  pickles
1/2 cup diced American
  cheese
1/2 cup diced white
  American cheese
1/4 cup chopped green
  onions
1/4 cup shredded carrots
2 large eggs, hard-boiled
  and chopped
3/4 cup mayonnaise
1 tsp. prepared yellow
  mustard
1 tsp. Worcestershire sauce
1/4 tsp. Tabasco sauce
1/2 tsp. salt
1/2 head iceberg lettuce,
  shredded

Combine all ingredients, except the lettuce, in a large mixing bowl. Mix until well blended. On salad plates, make beds of shredded lettuce, and spoon generous amounts of the red bean mixture onto the lettuce. Serve chilled. Serves 6.

Lagniappe: This salad can be made in advance, and refrigerated for up to 8 hours if you toss it every once and a while. Because it wilts quickly, don't shred the lettuce until just before you plan to serve. This is a nice alternative to plain green salad with all the benefits. It's quick and easy, and has a very generous serving size.

You can make **Black-eyed Pea Salad** or **White Bean Salad** by substituting a can of black-eyed peas or large white beans for the red beans.

Calories—330; Carb—29; Fat—18.4; Chol—117; Pro—9.8; Fib—22.3; Sod—1162

BEAN SALAD ACADIE

1 15 to 16-oz. can green
  beans
1 15 to 16-oz. can kidney
  beans
1 15 to 16-oz. can wax
  beans
1 15 to 16-oz. can lima
  beans
1 cup canola oil
1/4 cup extra virgin olive
  oil
1/2 cup red wine vinegar

1/4 cup sugar
1 tsp. Tabasco sauce
1 tsp. salt
1 tsp. minced fresh basil
  (or 1/4 tsp. dried)
1/4 cup minced onions
2 cloves garlic, minced
1/4 cup chopped ripe
  California olives
1 medium sweet orange
  bell pepper, cut into
  strips

Drain the liquid from the cans of beans, and set the beans aside. In a large mixing bowl, blend together the oils, vinegar, sugar, Tabasco sauce, salt, basil, onions, and garlic until the mixture is smooth. Fold in the olives, bell pepper, and drained beans; cover and refrigerate until you are ready to serve. Serve chilled. Serves 6 as a salad or vegetable.

Lagniappe: This recipe is basically dump, dump, and serve. This is a great bean salad to bring to a party or buffet. You spend minutes preparing it, but it tastes like you slaved for hours. It can be made 48 hours in advance and stored in the refrigerator. Feel free to vary or substitute different beans according to your individual preference — just try to keep 4 cans of beans in the salad.

Calories—678; Carb—42; Fat—50; Chol—0; Pro—11; Fib—7; Sod—1041

BROCCOLI SALAD JACQUES

3/4 cup canola oil
3/4 cup red wine vinegar
1 tsp. balsamic vinegar
1/2 tsp. salt
1/2 tsp. Tabasco sauce
1 tbsp. sugar
1 medium red bell pepper,
cut into strips

1 medium onion, chopped
1/4 cup chopped ripe
California black olives
2 bunches broccoli
1 head iceberg lettuce

In a large mixing bowl, combine the oil, vinegars, salt, Tabasco sauce, and sugar and let it stand for 5 minutes. Add the bell pepper, onions, and olives and toss. Cut the broccoli into bite-sized florets and add it to the vinegar mixture. Toss well. Cover tightly with plastic wrap, and let the salad stand for 4 to 8 hours in the refrigerator.

When you are ready to serve, cut the lettuce into thin slices and arrange it to form a bed on your salad plates. Spoon generous amounts of the broccoli mixture over the lettuce. Serve chilled. Serves 6.

Lagniappe: This is a colorful and somewhat different salad. It is easy to make and can be made up to 48 hours before serving. The longer the broccoli marinates in the vinegars, the more tangy it becomes.

You can make **Cauliflower Salad Jacques** by substituting 1 large head of cauliflower for the 2 bunches of broccoli. Either way, it is quite a treat!

Calories—315; Carb—11.5; Fat—28.6; Chol—0; Pro—23; Fib—11.3; Sod—669

SALAD LUC

1 bunch broccoli
1 head cauliflower
3 tender young carrots
1 gallon water
1 tbsp. salt
10 whole black
   peppercorns
3 tbsp. olive oil

3 cloves garlic, minced
1 tbsp. minced fresh basil
1 cup mayonnaise
1/2 cup sour cream
1/4 cup Creole mustard
1/2 tsp. Tabasco sauce
1 tsp. Worcestershire sauce

Wash and drain the broccoli, cauliflower, and carrots. Cut the broccoli and cauliflower into florets and slice the carrots at an angle. Heat the gallon of water in a large pot (at least 3-gallon size) over high heat. When the water is boiling, add the carrots and cook for 3 minutes. Add the cauliflower and cook, at full boil, for 2 minutes; then add the broccoli florets and cook for 2 more minutes. Remove from the heat, let the vegetables stand in the water for 5 minutes, then drain.

Heat a small skillet over medium heat. Add the olive oil, let it heat, then sauté the garlic and basil for 3 minutes. Remove from the heat and set aside to cool.

In a large bowl, mix together the remaining ingredients until well blended. Add the cooled olive oil and mix in well. Toss the broccoli, cauliflower, and carrots lightly with the dressing mix. Either serve at once or chill before serving. Serves 6.

Lagniappe: This is a wonderful mixed salad with great color and outstanding flavor. You can make it up to 2 days in advance and store in the refrigerator until you are ready to serve. Just toss lightly before serving. However, I must warn you that, if someone discovers this salad in the refrigerator, it may disappear before serving time.

Calories—227; Carb—22.6; Fat—20.5; Chol—10.7; Pro—5; Fib—3.6; Sod—1537

SUMMER MIXED GREEN SALAD

1 head red tipped lettuce
1 head romaine lettuce
1 lb. fresh young spinach
1 small sweet red bell
   pepper, cut into strips
1 small purple onion, thinly
   sliced

1 small carrot, thinly sliced
1/4 cup toasted pecan
   halves
1/2 recipe Honey Dressing
   (see index)

Wash each head of lettuce and drain on paper towels. Wash the spinach, and chop it into small pieces. Tear the lettuce into bite-sized pieces and combine them with the chopped spinach, bell pepper, onion, carrot, and pecans in a large salad bowl. Toss together well. Prepare the dressing as the recipe indicates, and pour it over the salad. Toss until the everything is well coated with dressing. Serve on salad plates. Serves 6.

Lagniappe: You can use this green salad with other dressings, but it is just perfect with the **Honey Dressing.** The only advance preparation I recommend is washing the greens and cutting the pepper and onions. Don't tear the greens or chop the spinach until you are ready to serve.

Calories—128; Carb—14; Fat—8; Chol—0; Pro—4.3; Fib—2.3; Sod—38.6

CHILLED CUCUMBER SALAD

3 medium cucumbers
1 tsp. salt
1 tsp. black pepper
1/2 tsp. Tabasco sauce

1 tbsp. minced onion
1/2 cup distilled white
   vinegar
1/4 cup red wine vinegar

Skin the cucumbers and cut them into 1/4-inch slices. In a large mixing bowl, combine the cucumbers and the rest of the ingredients. Mix well. Let the mixture chill for at least 10 minutes in the refrigerator before serving. Serve cold. Serves 6.

Lagniappe: This salad makes a great snack during the summer. I like to make it about 24 hours in advance and store it in the refrigerator. Be sure to keep it covered and chilled. The cucumbers remain crisp and taste like a homemade pickle. I assume it will be good for a few days, but I can't say for sure because they are always gone the first day. I really don't know what happens to them!

Calories—47; Carb—6.3; Fat—.3; Chol—0; Pro—.9; Fib—.9; Sod—384

QUICK CAN CAN FRUIT SALAD

1 16-oz. can pear halves
1 8-oz. can crushed
   pineapple
1 3 1/2-oz. pkg. orange
   jello

1 cup seedless grapes, cut
   in half
1 banana, sliced
1/2 cup chopped pecans
1 9-oz. carton Cool Whip

Cut the pear halves into bite-sized pieces. Pour the juices from both cans of fruit into a small saucepan, and add the jello. Heat over low heat until the jello melts. Remove from the heat and stir in the pineapple, pear pieces, grapes, and banana. Pour into a mixing bowl and add the pecans and Cool Whip. Mix well. Chill 1 to 2 hours until the jello sets. Serve as a fruit salad. Serves 4.

Lagniappe: This is a mixture of my favorite fruits. I create recipes for my taste. If you have different tastes, substitute! You can change any or all of the fruit, and the flavor of the jello. I promise it won't hurt my feelings! This recipe is a jumping-off point. I always recommend to people to make the recipe as it is the first time. Then, make notes in the margins (that's why they are there) on the changes you would like to make. When you look at the recipe later, you'll know what you recommended doing to change it into your own recipe.

Calories—303; Carb—57; Fat—8.8; Chol—0; Pro—3.5; Fib—3; Sod—65

CAJUN NEW POTATO SALAD

2 lb. small new potatoes
1 tbsp. salt
3/4 cup mayonnaise
1/8 cup peanut oil
3 tbsp. red wine vinegar
1/2 tsp. Tabasco sauce
1/2 cup chopped green
  onions

1/4 cup chopped celery
1 tbsp. minced bell pepper
1/4 cup chopped sweet
  pickles
1/2 cup sliced black olives
1/2 cup diced ham (or
  crumbled bacon)

Place the potatoes in a large saucepan and fill with cold water to about 2 inches over the potatoes. Add the salt, and bring to a boil over high heat. Boil for about 15 minutes, or until the potatoes are soft when by pierced with a fork. Drain potatoes and set aside.

In a large bowl, use a wire whisk to whip together the mayonnaise, peanut oil, vinegar, and Tabasco sauce. Add the remaining ingredients and mix in well. Add the potatoes (they will still be warm), and blend in. Serve at once. Serves 6.

Lagniappe: This is a great potato salad that can be a side dish or an entree. It is quick and easy. I don't like to make it ahead of time because it is so good hot. Be sure to save any leftovers. It isn't bad cold. Feel free to use any type of meat in the place of the ham or bacon. You can also just leave the meat out entirely.

Calories—382; Carb—41; Fat—14.8; Chol—19; Pro—7.2; Fib—1.1; Sod—1131

GRAND PRE SALAD DRESSING

1 cup red wine vinegar
2 cloves garlic, crushed
1 tsp. diced shallots
2 tbsp. diced sweet red bell
  pepper
2 tbsp. minced fresh
  parsley

1 tsp. minced fresh basil
2 tbsp. capers
1/2 tsp. black pepper
1 tsp. salt
1/2 tsp. paprika
1/4 cup olive oil

In a clean 1-quart mayonnaise jar that still has the lid, combine all the ingredients. Cover with the lid (if it leaks, use a piece of plastic wrap between the jar and the lid), and shake for 1 minute. Let the dressing stand for at least 15 minutes before serving. Keep it cold in the refrigerator until you are ready to serve. Makes about 1 1/2 cups.

Lagniappe: This is a dressing I threw together once when company was coming for dinner and I realized that I had no dressing for the salad. It turned out quite well, so I offer it to you—as I did to my company! Although I recommend a mayonnaise jar in the recipe, it would certainly be okay to use one of those nice dressing jars—it will even look fancier!

I just write these recipes as I make them, folks. This dressing will store for several days in the refrigerator. Feel free to replace the basil with any other fresh herb that you like. I just really like the taste of fresh basil, and I always have more than enough growing around here.

Calories—43; Carb—1.1; Fat—4.5; Chol—0; Pro—.1; Fib—Trace; Sod—193

GREEN ONION DRESSING

1 bunch green onions
1 cup mayonnaise
1/2 cup sour cream
1/4 cup white wine vinegar
1/2 fresh lemon, juice only
2 cloves garlic, minced
1/2 cup minced fresh
  parsley
2 tbsp. minced fresh basil

1 tbsp. minced fresh chives
1 tsp. salt
1/2 tsp. black pepper
1/4 tsp. Tabasco sauce
1/4 tsp. celery seeds
1/2 tsp. onion powder
1/4 tsp. minced fresh
  tarragon (or 1/8 tsp.
  dried)

Finely chop the green onions, tops and bottoms. Measure one cup of the onions, and combine them with the rest of the ingredients in a food processor or blender. Process at full power for 2 minutes. Pour into a salad dressing bottle that has a lid, cover tightly, and refrigerate until you are ready to serve. Makes just under 1 quart of salad dressing.

Lagniappe: You can make this salad dressing up to 4 days in advance and refrigerate it. If you plan to use it right away, be sure to allow it to chill in the refrigerator for at least 20 minutes. Flavors will blend more thoroughly if the dressing is allowed to stand for at least 24 hours. Use this dressing on your favorite green salad.

Calories—19; Carb—1.4; Fat—1.5; Chol—2; Pro—.1; Fib—Trace; Sod—64

BUTTERMILK DRESSING

2 cups buttermilk
2 cups mayonnaise
1 tsp. minced fresh basil
1 clove garlic, minced
2 tbsp. diced pimento
1/4 tsp. Tabasco sauce
1/4 tsp. white pepper

1 1/2 tsp. salt
1/2 tsp. black pepper
1/2 tsp. onion powder
1/2 tsp. garlic powder
1/8 tsp. nutmeg
1/8 tsp. hot dry mustard

In a large mixing bowl or blender, mix all the ingredients together until well blended. Pour into a salad dressing container and cover tightly. Store in the refrigerator until you are ready to use. Makes about one quart.

Lagniappe: Easy! Easy! Easy! Pour and mix. That's about as easy as they get, folks. You can make this dressing and serve it right away, or you can store it for up to 1 week. It is a great way to top any green salad. It also makes a great dip for raw vegetables. If you are watching calories, you can use light mayonnaise to significantly reduce the calories.

Calories—32; Carb—2.2; Fat—2.5; Chol—2; Pro—.3; Fib—Trace; Sod—61

CAJUN FRENCH DRESSING

1 cup red wine vinegar
1 small onion, chopped
2 cloves garlic, minced
1/3 cup sugar
1/2 cup chili sauce
1 tsp. paprika

1/2 tsp. Tabasco sauce
1 tbsp. Worcestershire
  sauce
1/2 tsp. white pepper
1/2 cup olive oil
1/2 cup vegetable oil

Pour the red wine vinegar into a blender or food processor with the onion and garlic. Blend or process at high speed for 2 minutes. Add the remaining ingredients, except for the oils, and blend at high speed for 2 more minutes. While blending, slowly drizzle in the olive oil and the vegetable oil. Continue processing until all of the oil is blended. Pour into a serving bottle and refrigerate until you are ready to serve. Makes about 4 cups of salad dressing.

Lagniappe: After you try making and serving homemade salad dressings, you will stop using the store-bought kinds. There is so much more depth to homemade dressing, and it really tastes better. This dressing will be good for a few weeks if kept covered and cold in the refrigerator.

If you don't have a blender or food processor, you'll have to chop the vegetables ultra-fine, and use a wire whisk to blend the ingredients and whip in the oil by hand. It can be done, but I bet after a few times, you'll want to buy a blender or processor.

Calories—43; Carb—.9; Fat—4; Chol—0; Pro—.1; Fib—Trace; Sod—31

HONEY DRESSING

3 tbsp. honey
1/2 cup white wine vinegar
3 tbsp. olive oil
1/4 tsp. dried sweet basil

1/4 tsp. dry mustard
1/4 tsp. Tabasco sauce
3 tbsp. toasted sesame
seeds

In a medium-sized mixing bowl, combine all the ingredients and whip with a wire whisk until the dressing is well blended. Pour into a jar, and chill until you are ready to use. Makes about 1 cup.

Lagniappe: This is an excellent dressing for any green salad. It is quick and easy, and has a unique taste. The sesame seeds really bring out the taste of the honey. This dressing will keep for at least a week in the refrigerator if tightly covered.

To toast sesame seeds, just pour them into a hot skillet and shake them around for a minute or so. You can also pour them onto a plate, put them in the microwave for 1 minute, stir, then heat for another minute at full power.

Calories—106; Carb—8.3; Fat—8.5; Chol—0; Pro—.6; Fib—Trace; Sod—2

Breads

FRESH PLUM BREAD

2 cups all-purpose flour
3/4 cup sugar
1/2 cup light brown sugar,
  firmly packed
1/4 tsp. salt
1 tsp. baking powder
1/2 tsp. baking soda

1 1/2 cups chopped fresh
  plums
1 large brown egg, slightly
  beaten
2 tbsp. unsalted butter,
  melted
2/3 cup chopped pecans

Preheat the oven to 350 degrees. In a large mixing bowl, combine the flour, sugar, brown sugar, salt, baking powder, and baking soda. In another large mixing bowl, combine the chopped plums, egg, and butter and mix together well. Add the pecans to the plum mixture, then slowly blend the flour mixture into the plum mixture until well mixed. Pour into a lightly greased and floured 9 by 5-inch loaf pan. Bake at 350 degrees for about 45 minutes, or until a toothpick inserted into the center of the bread comes out clean. Let the bread cool, then remove from the pan. Serve warm or at room temperature. Makes one loaf.

Lagniappe: This is good breakfast bread that goes exceptionally well with coffee. You can use it as you would any other bread. This mixture also makes superb muffins—just bake for about 15 to 20 minutes in a muffin pan.

You can freeze this bread for later use. It is a moist and very delicate bread, so it will probably crumble if cut when it is still hot. You can heat it up in the oven or microwave—by the slice or by the loaf.

Calories—215; Carb—40.3; Fat—5.3; Chol—31; Pro—3; Fib—.3; Sod—108

PEACH OATMEAL BREAD

1 1/2 cups all-purpose flour
1 tsp. baking soda
1 1/4 tsp. baking powder
1/2 tsp. salt
1 tsp. nutmeg
1/2 tsp. cinnamon
1/4 tsp. orange peel spice
3/4 cup light brown sugar,
  packed

2 large brown eggs, lightly
  beaten
1/3 cup unsalted butter,
  melted
2 cups chopped fresh
  peaches, pitted and
  peeled
1 cup chopped pecans
1 1/2 cups oats

Preheat the oven to 350 degrees. In a large mixing bowl, combine the flour, baking soda, baking powder, salt, nutmeg, cinnamon, and orange peel spice. In a separate bowl, blend together the brown sugar, eggs, and butter until creamy. Add the dry mixture slowly into the wet mixture, stirring until it is smooth, then fold in the peaches and pecans.

Using an electric mixer (or a large spoon with a strong arm), mix in the oats. Pour into a greased and lightly floured 9x5x3-inch loaf pan, and bake at 350 degrees for about 1 hour or until a toothpick stuck into the center of the bread comes out clean. Remove the bread from the oven, allow it to cool for a few minutes, then serve. Serve warm or cool. Makes one loaf of bread.

Lagniappe: Peaches are very easy to use and they bake very well. They blend nicely with the oats to produce a bread that you will enjoy immensely. I like to use this as a coffee bread or a breakfast loaf, but it can be used as you would any bread. You can use the same recipe to make nice muffins. In fact, it only takes about 15 to 20 minutes to cook the muffins—so if you are in a hurry, try the muffins instead.

You can make the bread in advance and let it sit on the counter, somewhat covered until you are ready to serve. You can also freeze it for later use. To serve, just let the bread thaw, covered on the counter (another rule broken!), until you are ready to serve. If you like it hot, I suggest heating by the slice for 30 seconds in the microwave (I do use the microwave occasionally).

Calories—202; Carb—28.6; Fat—8.5; Chol—53; Pro—3.3; Fib— .6; Sod—159

FIG PRESERVE BREAD

1/2 cup unsalted butter
1 cup sugar
2 large brown eggs, slightly
 beaten
2 tsp. vanilla
1 1/2 cups fig preserves

2 cups all-purpose flour
1/2 tsp. baking soda
1 tsp. baking powder
1/2 tsp. salt
1/4 tsp. ground ginger
1 cup chopped pecans

Preheat the oven to 350 degrees. In a mixing bowl, cream the butter with an electric mixer. Add the sugar and continue to cream. Mix in the eggs and vanilla, then the fig preserves. In a separate bowl, combine the remaining ingredients. Blend this flour mixture, a little at a time, into the creamed mixture, until all the flour mixture is absorbed. Pour into a lightly greased and floured 9x5x3-inch loaf pan and bake at 350 degrees for 45 minutes to 1 hour. A toothpick stuck into the middle of the bread should come out clean when it is done. Allow the bread to cool for a few minutes, then cut and serve. Makes one loaf of bread and serves about 6.

Lagniappe: With all those homemade fig preserves around, this recipe is a must. It makes a very moist bread that can be served at breakfast, with tea, or with any meal. I like it with a glass of milk. It's also nice with a dab of whipped cream.

Although the cooking time tends to remove this recipe from the quick range, it is still an easy bread to make. Just whip it up, pour it out, and bake. While the bread is baking, you are doing nothing but wishing it would hurry!

Calories—693; Carb—119; Fat—24; Chol—90; Pro—6; Fib—7; Sod—320

PEANUTTIER NANNA LOAF

1 3/4 cups all-purpose flour
2 1/2 tsp. baking powder
1/2 tsp. baking soda
1/2 tsp. salt
1/4 tsp. lemon peel spice
1/8 tsp. ground ginger
1/3 cup light brown sugar, packed
1/2 cup sugar

3/4 cup crunchy peanut butter
1/3 cup vegetable shortening
2 large brown eggs, lightly beaten
2 medium ripe bananas, mashed
1 tsp. fresh lemon juice

Preheat the oven to 350 degrees. In a large bowl, blend together the flour, baking powder, baking soda, salt, lemon peel spice, and ground ginger. In a separate mixing bowl, cream together the brown sugar, sugar, peanut butter, shortening, and eggs with an electric mixer until smooth and fluffy.

Mix together the mashed bananas and the fresh lemon juice. Beat the banana mixture into the creamed mixture about 1/4 at a time. Beat in the flour mixture gradually—just until the flour is blended in. Pour the batter into a 9x5x3-inch greased and floured loaf pan, and bake for about 1 hour, or until a toothpick inserted into the center of the loaf comes out clean. Makes one loaf, serves about 6.

Lagniappe: Use this as a breakfast bread, a snack bread, or coffee bread. You can make it in advance and cover it until you are ready to serve. Of course, the fresher it is, the better. This bread freezes well. To serve, leave covered on the kitchen counter until it is defrosted, then serve. If you want it warm, use the microwave. I like to serve it with butter or margarine, but the bread is moist enough to eat alone—it's up to you.

Calories—470; Carb—61.8; Fat—17.1; Chol—102; Pro—10.3; Fib—1; Sod—511

SWISS CORNBREAD

1 1/2 cups buttermilk
2 large brown eggs, slightly
   beaten
1 medium onion, finely
   chopped
1/4 cup diced red bell
   pepper
3 tbsp. unsalted butter
1 1/4 cup grated Swiss
   cheese
1 cup yellow cornmeal

1/2 cup white cornmeal
   (fresh ground or stone
   ground)
1 1/4 tsp. baking powder
3/4 tsp. baking soda
1 tsp. salt
1/2 tsp. black pepper
2 tbsp. fresh parsley,
   minced
1/4 tsp. Tabasco sauce
butter

Preheat the oven to 400 degrees. Combine and thoroughly mix the first five ingredients in a large mixing bowl. Fold in the Swiss cheese. In another mixing bowl, combine the yellow and white cornmeal, baking powder, baking soda, salt, and black pepper. Use a wire whisk to blend together. Slowly mix the cornmeal mixture into the Swiss cheese mixture. Blend in the Tabasco sauce and parsley. Lightly butter 10x10-inch baking pan, and pour the batter into the pan. Bake at 400 degrees for about 30 minutes. Serve hot with plenty of butter.

Lagniappe: Cheese and cornbread go well together. Seasoned cornbreads are widely used in Cajun country. There are hundreds of variations that you could develop, and all of them would have merit. You can make this bread in advance, and it will keep at room temperature for a few days. Like any other bread, it is best eaten when fresh. I also like to use seasoned cornbreads in stuffings. It adds zest to the finished product.

Calories—187; Carb—21.3; Fat—6; Chol—86; Pro—9.5; Fib—.8; Sod—453

CORN PONE

1 cup white cornmeal
1 cup yellow cornmeal
1 tbsp. all-purpose flour
1/2 tsp. baking powder
2 tbsp. sugar

1/2 tsp. salt
1 1/4 cup plus 2 tbsp.
  water
2 tbsp. unsalted butter

Preheat the oven to 450 degrees. In a large mixing bowl, combine the corn meals, flour, and baking powder. In a small, heavy saucepan, add the sugar, salt, and water. Bring to a hard boil over high heat. When the water is boiling, pour it over the cornmeal and stir. Cover and let it stand for about 10 minutes. Remove the cover and shape the mixture with your hands into 4 by 1-inch cakes. Place on a lightly greased baking tray, and bake for about 20 minutes at 450 degrees. Makes about one dozen cakes.

Lagniappe: This is an old and very simple recipe. Serve it as a light supper with jelly, syrup, preserves, butter, and a tall glass of milk. Or you can just serve it plain as your bread at mealtime. It is obviously a great breakfast food. I like them warm—straight from the oven—but they can be eaten at room temperature as well. You can make them in advance and store them as you would any bread.

Calories—107; Carb—19; Fat—2.6; Chol—5.5; Pro—2; Fib—.7; Sod—117

PEPPERONI BISCUITS

2 cups Bisquick mix
3/4 cup diced pepperoni
1/4 cup sliced ripe
  California pitted olives
2 tbsp. minced onions

1/4 tsp. Tabasco sauce
1/4 cup grated mozzarella
  cheese
2/3 cup milk

Preheat the oven to 450 degrees. In a large mixing bowl, combine all ingredients, mixing until the Bisquick mix is thoroughly moistened. Place the dough on a lightly floured work surface. Knead with your hands about 6 times; then roll the dough to about 2/3-inch thickness. Cut the dough into circles with a biscuit cutter; then place it on a lightly greased baking sheet. Bake at 450 degrees until the biscuits are a golden brown, about 9 minutes. Makes about 1 dozen biscuits.

Lagniappe: This can be a biscuit or a meal. You can serve them alone or as you would any other biscuit or bread. I like to eat these with a little butter and a tall glass of milk. It is better than a sandwich.

You can make the biscuits in advance, and store them in the refrigerator until you are ready to use them. Just reheat them in a 350-degree oven for about 3 minutes. I have to admit that they are much better straight from the oven. Buy your pepperoni in bulk, it is considerably cheaper than getting it in those small packages.

Calories—246; Carb—14.4; Fat—17.3; Chol—26; Pro—8.4; Fib—.3; Sod—860

DROP BISCUITS

1 1/4 cups all-purpose flour	**2 tbsp. unsalted butter,**
1 3/4 tsp. baking powder	**cold**
1/2 tsp. baking soda	**1/2 tsp. freshly grated**
1/2 tsp. salt	**orange rind**
1/4 tsp. nutmeg	**3/4 cup heavy cream**

Preheat the oven to 425 degrees. In a large mixing bowl, sift together the flour, baking powder, baking soda, and nutmeg. Chop the butter into small pieces, and cut it into the flour mixture until the flour becomes mealy. Add the orange rind and the cream, and mix together until the mixture forms a stiff batter. Drop the batter by spoonful onto a greased baking sheet. Bake at 425 degrees until the biscuits are a light brown, about 15 minutes. Serve hot. Makes about 20 biscuits.

Lagniappe: This is a quick and easy biscuit that tastes like you really worked at it. The hint of orange will have your diners guessing. I like to serve these biscuits with plenty of fig preserves, ça c'est bon!

Calories—73; Carb—5.7; Fat—5.8; Chol—17.6; Pro—.9; Fib—Trace; Sod—79

BASIL BUNS

1 tube refrigerated crescent
  dinner rolls
1 tbsp. Dijon mustard
1 tbsp. minced fresh basil
  (or 1 tsp. dried)
2 tbsp. finely minced onion

1/3 lb. hot breakfast
  sausage
2 tsp. unsalted butter,
  melted
paprika

Preheat the oven to 375 degrees. Open the package of rolls and separate each of the triangles of dough. Spread the mustard lightly and evenly on one side of each triangle. Sprinkle with the basil and onion. Break the ground sausage into small pieces, spread it out evenly on the rolls, then roll the crescent rolls according to package directions. Lightly brush with melted butter, dust lightly with paprika, and bake for 10 minutes at 375 degrees. Serves 4 to 6.

Lagniappe: This is an example of taking a prepared item and making it into an original creation. There are countless possibilities with prepared roll mixes. Try this one, then start creating your own. Send me your ideas, who knows, they might appear in my next book!

You can make these in advance and refrigerate them, covered, until you are ready to bake. Serve as you would any dinner roll or use as an appetizer.

Calories—314; Carb—18.2; Fat—4.3; Chol—45; Pro—10.5; Fib—.1; Sod—568

APPLE WALNUT MUFFINS

1 3/4 cups all-purpose flour
1/4 cup sugar
2 1/2 tsp. baking powder
1/2 tsp. baking soda
1/2 tsp. salt
1/2 tsp. nutmeg
1 large brown egg, slightly
  beaten

3/4 cup milk
1 tbsp. honey
1/3 cup unsalted butter,
  melted
1 cup diced apples
1/2 cup chopped walnuts

Preheat the oven to 400 degrees. In a large bowl, combine the flour, sugar, baking powder, baking soda, salt, and nutmeg. In another large mixing bowl, cream the egg, milk, honey, and butter with an electric mixer until smooth. Slowly beat in the flour, adding about 1/4 of the flour mixture at a time. Do not overbeat. Fold in the apple pieces and the walnuts evenly. Grease and lightly flour muffin tins, or use 1 dozen paper muffin cups. Fill the muffin tins about 3/4 full. Bake for about 17 minutes, or until a toothpick stuck into the center of the muffin comes out clean. Serve hot with plenty of butter or margarine. Makes 12 muffins.

Lagniappe: These are great for breakfast, snacks, or as a dinner roll. This is a quick and easy muffin that has a distinctive blend of flavors. You can make them in advance and store them, covered tightly, for 3 to 5 days. You can also freeze them for later use. Let them thaw on the counter until defrosted, and warm them in the microwave if desired.

Use this recipe to make **Pecan Date Muffins** by substituting 3/4 cup of chopped dates for the cup of apples, and 2/3 cup of chopped pecans for the walnuts in the above recipe. I think you'll find both recipes to be spectacular.

Calories—166; Carb—21; Fat—8; Chol—40; Pro—3; Fib—.4; Sod—216

ORANGE DATE NUT MUFFINS

1 cup dates
2 cups all-purpose flour
2 1/2 tsp. baking powder
3/4 tsp. baking soda
1/4 tsp. salt
1/8 tsp. orange peel spice
1/2 cup milk
1/4 cup fresh orange juice

1 tbsp. grated fresh orange peel
1/4 cup butter
1/2 cup sugar
1 large brown egg, slightly beaten
2/3 cup chopped pecans

Preheat the oven to 450 degrees. Wash the dates in cold water, chop them into small pieces, then set them aside for later use. In a large mixing bowl, combine the flour, baking powder, baking soda, salt, and orange peel spice. Mix together the milk, orange juice, and fresh orange peel in another bowl.

In a large bowl, cream the butter and sugar until fluffy, then add the egg and beat about 1 minute. Add the milk mixture, flour mixture, dates, and pecans alternately to the creamed mixture, using about 1/4 of each mixture at a time, until all is used. Pour into lightly greased muffin tins, filling each cup about 3/4 full. Bake at 450 degrees for 18 to 20 minutes. A toothpick stuck into the middle of the muffin should come out clean. Serve hot with plenty of butter. Makes about 12 muffins.

Lagniappe: I worked on this recipe for some time. I ate a muffin similar to this on my travels, and I made a note of the combination. However, I couldn't remember where or when I ate the muffin. Well, once I started, I couldn't rest until I was satisfied with the recipe. Here it is, an Orange Date Nut Muffin like the one I had somewhere, sometime.

Many people ask me where I get my recipes. Well, I am always thinking about recipes. If I go somewhere, and like something, I write down what it is, and why I like it. Then I jot down how I think it was made. Some time later, when I'm in the mood (or whenever I find my notes), I'll give it a try in the kitchen. The rest is history! Another way I create recipes is just by finding raw vegetables, fish, meat, or poultry that look inviting. I buy what looks new, fresh and tempting; I bring it home and experiment. If I like the resulting dish, it becomes a new recipe! So much for my secrets. Now eat your muffins, they are getting cold!

Calories—206; Carb—33.5; Fat—7; Chol—34; Pro—2.8; Fib—1.6; Sod—166

PAIN PERDU
(Lost Bread)

3 extra large eggs	**1/4 cup milk**
1/4 cup sugar	**6 slices stale bread**
1/2 tsp. vanilla extract	**2 tbsp. peanut oil**
1/2 tsp. cinnamon	**powdered sugar (optional)**
1/2 tsp. nutmeg	**syrup (optional)**

Heat a large, heavy skillet over medium-low heat. In a large bowl, beat the eggs until frothy. Add the remaining ingredients, and beat until the sugar is dissolved. Place the bread, one slice at a time, into the mixture, coating both sides of the bread. Carefully transfer coated bread to the hot skillet, and fry about one minute on each side until the bread is lightly browned. Serve hot with powdered sugar or syrup. Serves 3.

Lagniappe: This is a Cajun breakfast staple! It is great breakfast food that is fast and easy. My wife gave me this recipe. She got it from her grandmother, Marie Segura LeBlanc. It is simple Cajun food at its best. Serve it alone, or as the bread with breakfast.

Calories—332; Carb—41; Fat—17.1; Chol—276; Pro—10.8; Fib—Trace; Sod—325

BLUEBERRY PANCAKES

2 cups Bisquick mix
2 1/2 tsp. sugar
1/4 tsp. nutmeg
1/4 tsp. orange peel spice
2 tsp. vanilla extract

2 large brown eggs, beaten
1 cup milk
3 tbsp. canola oil
1 cup fresh blueberries

In a large mixing bowl, sift together the Bisquick, sugar, nutmeg, and orange peel spice. Beat in the vanilla, eggs, and milk with a wire whisk until smooth. Heat a large skillet over low-medium heat, add the canola oil and let it get hot. Pour about 1/3 cup of pancake batter into the skillet for each cake—you should be able to get two or three cakes at a time in the pan, depending on the size. Drop a handful of berries in the batter just after pouring it into the skillet.

Cook the cake until it is set enough to flip. Turn each cake carefully to avoid splattering the oil in the pan. When each cake is nicely browned, remove them from the skillet, and serve with plenty of butter or margarine and your favorite syrup. Makes about 10 nice pancakes.

Lagniappe: This is the traditional Sunday breakfast in the Theriot household—for Debbie and me, that is. Nicole likes her pancakes plain, so I leave the blueberries out of hers. That is why I really like this recipe—you add the berries (as few, or in my case, as many as you like) to the batter after it is in the pan.

To make **Rasberry Pancakes,** substitute 1 cup of raspberries for the blueberries, and follow the recipe. I also like to make **Blackberry Pancakes** when fresh blackberries are in season. All you need do is use 1 cup of blackberries instead of the blueberries.

Calories—176; Carb—19; Fat—9.4; Chol—3.1; Pro—.4; Sod—295

CREPES

3 large brown eggs, beaten
1 cup milk
1/8 tsp. Tabasco sauce
2 tbsp. unsalted butter,
  melted
1 cup all-purpose flour
1 tbsp. sugar

1/4 tsp. nutmeg
1/4 tsp. baking powder
1/4 tsp. baking soda
1/8 tsp. lemon peel spice
  (or fresh grated lemon
  peel)
1/4 tsp. salt

Mix the eggs, milk, Tabasco sauce, and butter together. Combine the remaining ingredients; then add them to the egg mixture. Beat with a wire whisk until smooth. Cover and let the batter stand for at least 15 minutes. Heat a medium-sized non-stick skillet over low to medium heat until it is hot. Pour about 1/4 cup of batter into the skillet and swirl it around to cover the entire bottom evenly. Cook until the crepe is lightly browned, about 30 to 45 seconds; then flip it over and lightly brown the other side. Slide the crepe onto a sheet of waxed paper. Repeat the process until all crepes are cooked. Makes about 12 crepes.

Lagniappe: Crepes can be made well in advance and frozen or refrigerated until you are ready to use them. To freeze, layer the crepes, in groups of 4, between sheets of waxed paper. Place them in a ziplock bag and store flat in the freezer to keep them from tearing. To use frozen crepes, let them thaw completely at room temperature, then separate them as you need them. Crepes can be stored in the refrigerator for about 4 days. I find that it is easier to make a large batch of crepes at one time, then freeze what I don't need. If you have time, leave the crepe batter covered and refrigerated for about 2 hours before use — you will get nicer crepes.

Calories—91; Carb—9.4; Fat—4.3; Chol—85; Pro—3.4; Fib—Trace; Sod—112

Seafood

CRAB CREPES GUEYDAN

1 recipe Crepes (see index)
1 recipe Crab Dip Gueydan
 (see index)
1 recipe Hollandaise Sauce
 (see index)

2 tbsp. minced fresh
 parsley
lemon wedges

Preheat the oven to 325 degrees. Open the 12 crepes into full circles. Spoon 3 generous tablespoons of **Crab Dip Gueydan** in the center of each crepe; then roll it into a tube with the crabmeat filling in the center. Place two rolled crepes into each serving dish, and bake at 325 degrees for 10 minutes. Remove and cover with a generous amount of **Hollandaise Sauce.** Garnish with the fresh parsley and lemon wedges. Serve at once. Serves 6.

Lagniappe: To make a nice appetizer, you can double the number of crepes and only put 1 1/2 tablespoons of dip in each. These crepes can be made, filled, and frozen or refrigerated until you are ready to serve. Do not bake them or put the sauce on until you are ready to serve. To serve from the freezer, just thaw in the refrigerator, bake as above, then proceed according to the recipe.

You can be a little creative with this dish by adding a few steamed broccoli florets or nice cooked sweet peas to each crepe. This will bring the house down!

Calories—748; Carb—32; Fat—53.3; Chol—548; Pro—35.2; Fib—1.3; Sod—831

LUMP CRABMEAT MICHELLE

1 stick unsalted butter
1/2 cup chopped green
  onions
1/4 cup diced sweet red
  bell peppers
2 tbsp. diced green bell
  pepper
2 tbsp. finely chopped
  celery
1 clove garlic, minced
1 lb. fresh lump crabmeat

1 1/4 tsp. Cajun Seasoning
  Mix (see index)
1 7-oz. jar whole straw
  mushrooms, drained
2 tbsp. minced fresh
  parsley
1/2 tsp. minced fresh basil
  (or 1/8 tsp. dried)
3 tbsp. fresh lemon juice
1/4 tsp. Tabasco sauce
1/2 cup sauterne wine

Heat a large, heavy skillet over medium heat. Melt the butter and let it begin to smoke. Sauté the green onions, red and green bell peppers, celery, and garlic for 3 minutes, stirring often. Add the crabmeat, **Cajun Seasoning Mix,** straw mushrooms, parsley, basil, lemon juice, and Tabasco sauce and simmer for 10 minutes. Shake the pan often to prevent sticking and to blend the ingredients. Do not stir because stirring breaks up the lumps of crabmeat. Add the wine and blend in well. Let the dish simmer for 2 more minutes; then serve hot. Serves 4.

Lagniappe: This is a very flavorful dish. The wine seems to bring the crabmeat to life. Do not prepare this dish in advance or refrigerate it. It must be eaten fresh. I like to serve plenty of hot bread with this dish to soak up the liquid. It is light and tasty. I recommend serving this recipe in individual dishes because there is a lot of liquid. You want to serve the crabmeat in its liquid to intensify its flavor.

Calories—369; Carb—8; Fat—26; Chol—154; Pro—22.4; Fib—.5; Sod—240

CRAB CASSEROLE PORT ROYAL

3 tbsp. unsalted butter
1 cup julienne carrots,
 1 1/2-inches long
1 cup chopped fresh
 asparagus, 1-inch pieces
1 cup chopped celery, 1/2-
 inch slices
1 small onion, diced
1 10 3/4-oz. can condensed
 cream of celery soup
1 cup dry white wine
1 1/3 cups milk
1 lb. lump crabmeat
1 lb. tortellini, dried or
 frozen

1 tbsp. minced fresh basil
 (or 1 tsp. dried)
1/2 tsp. salt
1/2 tsp. black pepper
1/2 tsp. Tabasco sauce
1/4 tsp. dry mustard
1/4 cup minced fresh
 parsley
1 cup grated Swiss cheese
1/4 cup slivered toasted
 almonds
paprika

Preheat the oven to 350 degrees. In a large skillet over medium heat, melt the butter and let it sizzle. Add the carrots, asparagus, celery, and onion and sauté for 7 minutes. Mix in the remaining ingredients, except for the cheese, almonds, and paprika; then remove from the heat. Fold in 1/2 of the Swiss cheese, then pour the mixture into a lightly greased 3-quart casserole dish. Top with the remaining cheese, then the almonds, and dust with paprika. Bake at 350 degrees for 45 minutes. Remove from the oven, let the dish stand for 5 minutes, then serve warm. Serves 6.

Lagniappe: This is an easy, yet distinctive casserole. While the cooking time is over 30 minutes, that is the bulk of the total preparation time.

You can use this recipe to make **Shrimp Casserole Port Royal, Crawfish Casserole Port Royal,** or **Catfish Casserole Port Royal** by respectively substituting 1 1/3 pounds of peeled and deveined, raw shrimp; 1 pound of fresh, peeled crawfish tails; or 1 1/2 pounds of catfish, cut into bite-sized pieces for the crabmeat.

This casserole can be made completely and baked in advance and frozen or refrigerated. Keep the casserole tightly covered when it is in the refrigerator or freezer. To reheat, just thaw in the refrigerator and bake, uncovered at 350 degrees, for about 12 minutes until it is heated through.

Calories—396; Carb—18.3; Fat—22; Chol—123; Pro—28; Fib—.8; Sod—925

CRABMEAT NOELIE

1 stick unsalted butter
3/4 cup chopped onion
1/2 cup chopped green
**   onions**
1 clove garlic, minced
2 tbsp. minced celery
1 lb. lump crabmeat (or
**   king crabmeat)**
1 tsp. Cajun Seasoning Mix
**   (see index)**

1/4 tsp. Tabasco sauce
1 tsp. Worcestershire sauce
1/4 cup sherry wine
4 slices bread, toasted and
**   cut into points**
1 tbsp. fresh parsley
1 tsp. paprika
lemon wedges

Heat a heavy, medium-sized saucepan over medium heat. Melt the butter until it begins to smoke, then sauté the onion, green onion, garlic, and celery for 5 minutes. Add the crabmeat and **Cajun Seasoning Mix,** and sauté for 1 minute, blending the crabmeat into the mixture. Add the Tabasco sauce, Worcestershire sauce, and sherry; reduce the heat to low; and simmer for 3 minutes, shaking the pan often to prevent sticking. Spoon over the toast points, sprinkle with paprika, and garnish with the parsley and lemon wedges. Serves 4.

Lagniappe: Other ways to serve this are in a nest of potatoes or on a bed of noodles cooked al dente. This recipe allows you to enjoy the taste of the crabmeat. Don't do anything in advance and serve it as you finish cooking. In fact, I recommend cutting the recipe in half if you are only serving two. It does not reheat well—the crabmeat begins to fall apart.

Calories—412; Carb—17; Fat—27; Chol—154; Pro—24; Fib—.5; Sod—359

STUFFED CRABS

1 lb. crab claw meat
1/2 cup minced onion
1/2 cup minced celery
1 clove garlic, minced
1/4 cup diced red bell
   pepper
1 tsp. minced fresh basil
2 tbsp. minced fresh
   parsley
2 tbsp. minced green onion
   tops
1 1/2 cups French bread,
   chopped into small
   pieces

1 cup cracker crumbs
1 tsp. salt
1/2 tsp. black pepper
1/4 tsp. white pepper
1/2 tsp. dry hot mustard
1 tsp. onion powder
1/4 tsp. Tabasco sauce
1 tbsp. Worcestershire
   sauce
1 tsp. soy sauce
1 jumbo egg, beaten
1/2 cup milk
1/2 stick unsalted butter,
   melted

Preheat the oven to 375 degrees. Put the crabmeat into a large bowl and remove any shells. Mix in all the ingredients, except for the last six. In a small bowl, combine the last six ingredients, then pour them into the mixing bowl with the crab mixture. Stir until the mixture is very moist. Stuff the mixture into cleaned crab shells, ceramic shells, or casserole dishes. Bake at 375 degrees for 18 minutes. The top should be a golden brown and the stuffing should be completely hot. Serve hot. Serves 6 to 8.

Lagniappe: This is a super mixture. I use it to make my **Stuffed Shrimp** (see index), and to stuff other fish. You'll find it to be very useful. The recipe can be made in advance, and either refrigerated or frozen. You can completely bake it and wrap individually for freezing or refrigerating. Keep frozen until you are ready to use. To reheat, place in the microwave under a piece of wax paper and cook, turning frequently until warm.

You will see this recipe in a number of other dishes in this book. Use it to create your own originals, then write and tell me all about it—it might appear in my fifth book!

Calories—292; Carb—28; Fat—11.4; Chol—135; Pro—19; Fib—.7; Sod—760

STUFFED EGGPLANT CROWLEY

2 large purple eggplant
1 gallon water
2 tsp. salt
1 recipe Stuffed Crab,
   unbaked mixture only
   (see index)

paprika
2 tbsp. minced fresh
   parsley

Wash the two eggplants well and cut off the stems. Boil the gallon of water in a 3-gallon stock pot. Add the salt; then boil both whole eggplants for 4 minutes over high heat. Remove eggplants and let them cool enough to handle. Cut each eggplant in half lengthwise, and scoop the pulp out of the center, leaving about 1/4 inch around the skin. Place the pulp in the boiling water for 2 minutes; then remove it from the heat. Let the pulp sit in the hot water for 7 minutes.

Preheat the oven to 425 degrees. Remove the eggplant pulp from the water and drain in a colander. When completely drained, mix the cooked eggplant pulp with the crab stuffing. Put about 1/4 of the stuffing mix into each eggplant half, sprinkle with paprika, and place on lightly greased baking dishes or cookie sheets. Bake for 15 minutes at 425 degrees. Remove, garnish with fresh parsley, and serve. Serves 4.

Lagniappe: What can I say? This is easy, quick, pretty, and tasty. This is superb. Eggplant and crabmeat were made for each other—and brought together by the Cajuns. You can make this dish in advance and freeze or refrigerate it until you are ready to serve. To serve, thaw in the refrigerator, and bake at 350 degrees for 12 to 15 minutes until completely hot. It is hard to top this!

Calories—503; Carb—50; Fat—20.5; Chol—202; Pro—30.1; Fib—2.8; Sod—1720

CRAWFISH ANDREE BRUN

1 stick unsalted butter
1 medium onion, finely
  chopped
2 ribs celery, finely
  chopped
2 cloves garlic, minced
1/2 cup diced bell pepper
2 tbsp. all-purpose flour
1 13-oz. can evaporated
  milk
1/4 tsp. Tabasco sauce
3/4 tsp. Cajun Seasoning
  Mix (see index)
1 tsp. minced fresh basil
  (or 1/4 tsp dried)

1/2 tsp. minced fresh sage
  (or 1/8 tsp. dried)
1/4 tsp. ground nutmeg
1/8 tsp. ground ginger
2 cups cornflakes, toasted
  lightly
1 lb. fresh crawfish tails,
  peeled and deveined
1/4 cup minced fresh
  parsley
1 cup cracker crumbs
1 tbsp. unsalted butter
fresh lemon wedges

Preheat the oven to 400 degrees. Heat a large, heavy skillet over medium heat. Melt the butter until it begins to smoke; then add the onions, celery, garlic, and bell pepper. Sauté for 3 minutes, stirring constantly. Add the flour and cook, stirring often, for 3 more minutes. Blend in the evaporated milk with a wire whisk until the sauce is smooth. Blend in the Tabasco sauce, **Cajun Seasoning Mix,** basil, sage, nutmeg, and ginger.

In a bowl, combine the cornflakes, crawfish, and parsley. Fold the mixture in with the contents of the skillet until thoroughly mixed. Pour into a large casserole dish or individual au gratin dishes. Cover with the cracker crumbs and dot with small pieces of the butter. Bake at 400 degrees for 15 to 20 minutes. Serve hot garnished with lemon wedges. Serves 4.

Lagniappe: This dish can be made in advance and refrigerated for later use. It can be frozen, but the crawfish get a little tough and don't look as good. The taste is still great, but you lose eye appeal. To serve, just heat at 350 degrees for about 10 minutes until heated through.

You can use this recipe to make **Lump Crabmeat Andree Brun** by substituting 1 pound of lump crabmeat for the crawfish. You can also make **Baked Shrimp Andree Brun** by replacing the crawfish with 1 1/3 pounds of fresh shrimp (peeled and deveined), and adding the shrimp after the milk to the flour roux, instead of later with the cornflakes and parsley, allowing it to cook for 2 minutes before continuing with the recipe.

To toast the cornflakes, spread the flakes out on a cookie sheet, and bake at 350 degrees for 7 minutes. This gives a unique flavor to the flakes and enhances the dish.

Calories—571; Carb—61; Fat—38; Chol—165; Pro—33; Fib—.9; Sod—572

QUICK FRIED CRAWFISH TAILS

peanut oil (for frying)
1 lb. fresh crawfish tails,
peeled and deveined
2 tsp. Cajun Seasoning Mix
(see index)

2/3 cup all-purpose flour
2 tbsp. cornstarch
3 tbsp. seasoned bread
crumbs

Preheat the peanut oil to 375 degrees in a deep fryer or a large saucepan. Season the crawfish tails with 1 teaspoon of the **Cajun Seasoning Mix.** Put the other teaspoon of **Cajun Seasoning Mix** in a paper or plastic bag with the flour, cornstarch, and bread crumbs; then shake it to mix the ingredients. Place the crawfish in the bag, and shake to coat them with the mixture. Drop the crawfish into the hot oil, and cook about 5 minutes until they are golden brown and begin to float to the surface. Drain on paper towels and serve at once. Serves 4.

Lagniappe: You've probably heard about Cajun Popcorn—now you have it. It is nothing more than fried crawfish tails. This is about the easiest recipe for fried crawfish you will find, and the taste is sumptuous. Serve them immediately after frying, they lose their quality quickly. If you can help it, don't refrigerate after cooking and definitely do not freeze!

Calories—278; Carb—24; Fat—9; Chol—61; Pro—24.4; Fib—.2; Sod—249

BAKED CRAWFISH CASSEROLE CRYSTAL

2 lb. fresh crawfish tails,
  peeled and deveined
2 1/2 cups diced French
  bread
1/2 cup dry vermouth
1/4 cup unsalted butter
1 cup chopped green
  onions
1/4 cup diced green bell
  pepper
1/4 cup diced red bell
  pepper

1/4 cup minced celery
2 tbsp. minced carrots
2 cloves garlic, minced
4 hard-boiled eggs,
  chopped
1 cup evaporated milk
1/2 tsp. Tabasco sauce
1 tsp. Worcestershire sauce
1 1/2 tsp. Cajun Seasoning
  Mix (see index)
1/2 cup finely chopped
  fresh parsley

Preheat the oven to 375 degrees. Chop one pound of the crawfish, leaving the other pound whole. In a large mixing bowl, pour the vermouth over the French bread and set it aside for later use. Heat a large, heavy skillet over medium heat; then melt the butter. When it begins to smoke, sauté the green onions, green and red bell pepper, celery, carrots, and garlic for about 3 minutes until the vegetables are very limp. Add the crawfish, sauté for 1 minute, then add the wine-soaked French bread and cook, stirring constantly, for 2 minutes. Remove from the heat and mix in the remaining ingredients. Lightly butter a 3-quart casserole dish, and pour the crawfish mixture into the dish. Bake at 375 degrees for 30 minutes. Serve hot. Serves 6.

Lagniappe: This dish may be prepared in advance and either refrigerated or frozen. To bring it back to life, thaw it in the refrigerator and bake at 350 degrees until hot. I also like to serve this recipe in individual casseroles or au gratin dishes. The frozen individual dishes make great Cajun T.V. dinners. I wrap them tightly in plastic wrap, label and date them, then freeze. These are perfect when you are looking for a single serving for lunch or dinner alone. (Debbie uses them for when I am gone — which is not very often, of course!)

You can use this recipe to make **Baked Scallop Casserole Crystal,** by using 2 pounds of fresh scallops instead of the crawfish. Sauté the scallops for 3 minutes instead of 1 minute when you add them to the skillet. Crawfish tails are, for the most part, already cooked when you buy them. Because they were boiled before they were peeled, they require less cooking time. You can also make **Baked Shrimp Casserole Crystal** by replacing the crawfish with 2 1/2 pounds of shrimp. Peel and devein the shrimp, and divide them into two equivalent stacks. Chop half of them, and leave the other half whole. Cook the shrimp for 3 minutes, just as you would scallops. Be sure to stir them around and shake the pan while cooking.

Calories—429; Carb—23; Fat—20; Chol—303; Pro—39; Fib—.9; Sod—471

SHRIMP MISS HOLLY

1 1/3 lb. fresh shrimp, peeled and deveined
1 10 3/4-oz. can cream of mushroom soup
1 10 3/4-oz. can cream of onion soup
1/4 cup dry white wine
1 tbsp. Worcestershire sauce
3/4 tsp. salt
1/2 tsp. Tabasco sauce
1/2 tsp. black pepper
1/2 cup minced green onions
2 cloves garlic, minced
2 tbsp. finely chopped red bell pepper
1/2 cup uncooked long grain white rice

Preheat the oven to 350 degrees. In a large mixing bowl, combine all of the ingredients and mix thoroughly. Pour the mixture into a lightly greased 2-quart casserole dish and bake for 1 hour at 350 degrees, or until the rice is cooked. Remove from the oven, cool for 3 minutes; then serve hot. Serves 4 to 6.

Lagniappe: This is almost too easy to be in a cookbook. It takes longer, from start to finish, than most of the recipes in this book, but I think you will agree that this is quick, easy—and so good!
   This dish may be frozen for later use. Just bake, wrap, and freeze. Defrost it in the refrigerator and reheat, covered, at 200 degrees for about 15 minutes. You can also reheat it in the microwave.

Calories—489; Carb—31; Fat—12.2; Chol—303; Pro—43.3; Fib—.3; Sod—2167

STUFFED SHRIMP THERIOT

1 1/2 pounds large shrimp, unpeeled
3 tbsp. Cajun Seasoning Mix (see index)
1 recipe Stuffed Crabs (see index), unbaked
2/3 cup all-purpose flour
2/3 cup seasoned bread crumbs
1/2 cup cornmeal
2 large brown eggs, slightly beaten
1/4 cup milk
1/4 tsp. Tabasco sauce
1/2 tsp. dried sweet basil
1 tbsp. Worcestershire sauce
peanut oil (for frying)

Peel the shrimp, leaving on the last segment of shell and the tail. Devein the shrimp, then butterfly them by cutting the shrimp along the backs, about three-fourths of the way through. Spread the shrimp open at the cut and season the shrimp with one teaspoon of the **Cajun Seasoning Mix.** Stuff the tail with two heaping tablespoons of crab stuffing. Mold it with your hands, pressing it into the shrimp, and folding a little of the shrimp around the stuffing. Put the stuffed shrimp on a tray or cookie sheet and refrigerate for an hour or two. Refrigeration helps seal the shrimp and crabmeat stuffing.

In a paper bag or mixing bowl, combine one teaspoon of the **Cajun Seasoning Mix** with the flour and mix until well blended. In a second bag or bowl, combine the bread crumbs, cornmeal, and one teaspoon of the **Cajun Seasoning Mix** and mix well. In a mixing bowl, beat the eggs, milk, Tabasco sauce, basil, and Worcestershire sauce until smooth. Place the shrimp, a few at a time, into the flour mixture, and gently shake. Remove and dip in the egg wash, then put the shrimp into the bread crumb mixture and coat. Either deep fry or pan fry with peanut oil until the shrimp are a nicely browned. Repeat the process until all the shrimp are cooked. Serves 6.

Lagniappe: Although this may appear to be a long recipe, it really is easy. I prefer to make the stuffed shrimp up to the refrigeration stage, then let them sit overnight in the refrigerator. I simply flour, egg wash, bread, and fry. It takes longer than thirty minutes from start to finish; but this recipe must be in this book because once you've made the crab stuffing, you are more than halfway there.

Stuffed shrimp can be served as an entree, as an appetizer, or as a party food. I like to serve it with plenty of tartar sauce. Bon appetit!

Calories—611; Carb—39.8; Fat—29.7; Chol—411; Pro—45.7; Fib—.7; Sod—1279

SHRIMP ETOUFFEE

1 stick unsalted butter
1 large onion, chopped
1/2 cup chopped celery
2 cloves garlic, minced
1 medium sweet red
   pepper, diced
3 tbsp. flour
1 1/2 cups chicken stock,
   chicken broth, or water
2 lb. large raw shrimp,
   peeled and deveined

1/2 tsp. Tabasco sauce
2 tsp. Cajun Seasoning Mix
   (see index)
1/2 cup minced fresh
   parsley
3/4 cup finely chopped
   green onions
cooked white long grain
   rice

Heat a heavy skillet over medium heat. Melt the butter until it begins to smoke, then sauté the onion, celery, garlic, and red pepper for 4 minutes, stirring often. Add the flour and cook, stirring constantly, for 4 minutes. Blend in the stock (or water) until the sauce thickens. Mix in the shrimp, Tabasco sauce and **Cajun Seasoning Mix.** Allow the shrimp to cook for about 5 minutes, stirring often. Add the parsley and green onions, and cook 1 more minute. Serve hot over white rice. Serves 4.

Lagniappe: This dish may be prepared in advance and refrigerated until you are ready to serve. If you refrigerate, do not add the parsley and green onions until you reheat it. To reheat, simmer over low heat for about 3 minutes, stirring often. Add the parsley and green onions, cook for 1 minute, then serve. You can also freeze this recipe prior to adding the parsley and green onions. Thaw in the refrigerator, then proceed as above.

Calories—536; Carb—16.9; Fat—30.5; Chol—413; Pro—34; Fib—.9; Sod—961

SHRIMP SAUTE EMELUSE

3 tbsp. olive oil
3 tbsp. unsalted butter
2 tbsp. minced shallots
3 cloves garlic, minced
3 tbsp. finely minced
  carrots
1 tbsp. chopped fresh
  rosemary leaves (or 1 tsp.
  dried)
2 lb. large shrimp, peeled
  and deveined

1 2/3 tsp. Cajun Seasoning
  Mix (see index)
1/2 tsp. Tabasco sauce
1 tsp. soy sauce
1/2 cup champagne
1 tbsp. fresh lemon juice
1/4 cup minced fresh
  parsley
lemon wedges

Heat a large skillet over medium-high heat. Add the olive oil. When it smokes, add the butter, swirling it around until it melts. When the butter starts to smoke, sauté the shallots, garlic, and carrots for 2 minutes. Stir in the rosemary, shrimp, and **Cajun Seasoning Mix.** Sauté for about 3 to 4 minutes until the shrimp are nicely browned on both sides. The shrimp should curl together and turn pink from the head to the tail. Add the Tabasco sauce, soy sauce, champagne, and fresh lemon juice. This will produce a bit of steam, so shake the pan lightly and stir. Mix in the parsley and serve garnished with lemon wedges. Serve hot. Serves 4.

Lagniappe: This is a quick dish that really must be eaten right after cooking to get the full benefit of the splendid flavors. Do not do anything in advance but peel the shrimp and chop the vegetables. This dish will be a hit at any meal or dinner party.

If you keep shrimp in your freezer, you can do this dish anytime. I encourage buying shrimp in frozen five-pound blocks from a seafood supplier. Don't be concerned that the shrimp is frozen, you will be buying a quality product. When you get "fresh" shrimp at the market, it usually has been frozen. To defrost some shrimp, just run a little cold water over one end of the block until you have the amount of shrimp that you need.

Remember that shrimp are sized for you. Shrimp labeled "21-25" have an average of 21 to 25 shrimp tails per pound. If you count out about 23 of these shrimp, you will have close to a pound. Shrimp frozen this way last a long time (up to 4 months) in your freezer. You'll never be short of shrimp again!

Calories—453; Carb—7.9; Fat—23.6; Chol—371; Pro—47.1; Fib—.3; Sod—675

FIRE SHRIMP

3 lb. jumbo shrimp with heads, unpeeled
1 tbsp. Cajun Seasoning Mix (see index)
2 sticks lightly salted butter (do not use unsalted)
1 tsp. black pepper
2 tsp. crushed red pepper
1 tsp. Tabasco sauce
2 tbsp. Worcestershire sauce
1 small onion, minced
4 cloves garlic, minced

Set the oven to broil. Wash and drain the shrimp. Season them with the **Cajun Seasoning Mix.** In a baking pan large enough to hold three pounds of shrimp, melt the butter. Lay the shrimp in the melted butter, cover with the remaining ingredients, and stir around until well mixed. Place about 8 inches under the broiler, and broil for 25 to 30 minutes.

Stir the pan every 5 minutes or so, to ensure that both sides of the shrimp get cooked. When the time is up, pour into a large bowl and serve hot. Serves 4.

Lagniappe: Serve with a green salad and plenty of fresh French bread. Be sure to have plenty to drink—this dish is very hot. You can serve this dish after the shrimp are cooled and easier to handle. Be sure to have paper towels to wipe your hands (and face). It is hot, it is quick, it is easy, and it is scrumptious!

You can do everything in advance. Melt the butter, put the shrimp in, cover with the ingredients, then refrigerate until you are ready to broil. I really like to do this, because the flavors get into the shrimp shells even more. If you are a bit squeamish about the shrimp heads, take them off—but do leave the shells on or you will ruin the dish.

Calories—817; Carb—8.6; Fat—55.2; Chol—652; Pro—70.3; Fib—.2; Sod—1045

SHRIMP NICOLE MARIE

2 tbsp. olive oil
2 tbsp. unsalted butter
2 tbsp. finely chopped
  shallots
3 cloves garlic, minced
1 fresh sweet banana
  pepper, cut into strips (or
  1/2 medium bell pepper)
1/2 sweet red bell pepper,
  cut into strips
1 tbsp. chopped fresh
  rosemary (or 1 tsp. dried)

1 1/3 lb. large shrimp,
  peeled and deveined
1 tsp. salt
1/2 tsp. black pepper
1/2 tsp. Tabasco sauce
1/4 cup dry white wine
1 tbsp. fresh lemon juice
1/2 tsp. soy sauce
1/4 cup minced fresh
  parsley
fresh lemon wedges

Heat a large skillet over medium-high heat, then add the olive oil. When the oil is heated, add the butter and swirl it around until it melts. When both oils are hot, sauté the shallots, garlic, banana pepper, and sweet red pepper for 2 minutes. Add the rosemary and shrimp and sauté for about 3 to 4 minutes until they are nicely browned on both sides. The shrimp should curl up and turn pink from head to tail.

Stir in the remaining ingredients, except for the parsley and lemon wedges. The liquids should create a bit of steam and the pot will deglaze. Reduce the heat to low, shake the pan a few times to prevent the shrimp from sticking, and simmer for 2 more minutes. Add the parsley and stir through. Serve at once, garnished with a wedge or two of fresh lemon. Serves 4.

Lagniappe: This is a fast-moving dish that must be served right after cooking. The only thing that you can do in advance is peel and devein the shrimp and chop the vegetables—except for the parsley. Remember that fresh parsley loses its taste quickly after it is cut. I recommend cutting fresh parsley by rolling it into a ball, and chopping it right before you add it to a dish. That puts the flavor into the dish rather than into the air. You can serve this dish over rice or egg noodles, it is quite nice. This simple dish will win you raves!

Calories—303; Carb—6.2; Fat—15.7; Chol—247; Pro—31.6; Fib—.3; Sod—847

SHRIMP SPAGHETTI

1/2 cup lemon juice
1/2 cup orange juice
1/2 cup dry vermouth
1/2 cup chicken stock or
  chicken broth
1/4 cup soy sauce
1/2 tsp. Tabasco sauce
1 tbsp. grated lemon peel
1 tbsp. grated orange peel
1 tbsp. sugar
1/4 cup olive oil1
1/2 lb. fresh shrimp, peeled
  and deveined
1 1/4 tsp. Cajun Seasoning
  Mix (see index)

1 small yellow bell pepper,
  cut into strips
1 small red bell pepper, cut
  into strips
2 cloves garlic, minced
1/2 cup diced carrots
1/4 cup diced celery
1/2 cup chopped green
  onions
1/4 cup minced fresh basil
3 tbsp. cornstarch
1 12-oz. pkg. spaghetti,
  cooked al dente
1/4 cup minced fresh
  parsley

In a mixing bowl, combine the lemon juice, orange juice, vermouth, chicken stock, soy sauce, Tabasco sauce, lemon peel, orange peel, and sugar. Mix together well, cover, and set aside for later use.

Heat a large, heavy skillet over medium-high heat. Add the olive oil and heat until it smokes, then sauté the shrimp for about 3 minutes until they are browned on both sides.

Season with the **Cajun Seasoning Mix,** then add the bell peppers, garlic, carrots, and celery. Sauté for 3 minutes. Add the green onions and fresh basil, then sauté for 1 more minute.

Stir the cornstarch into the liquid juice mixture until it is dissolved; then pour this liquid into the skillet. Stir for about 1 minute until the sauce begins to thicken. Continue to cook for 2 more minutes.

Put the cooked spaghetti in a very large mixing bowl, pour the shrimp mixture over it, add the parsley, and toss until the spaghetti is coated. Serve at once. Serves 4.

Lagniappe: This dish is a full meal with fresh hot bread and a nice green salad. It's a new twist on spaghetti. The tangy sauce, the fresh shrimp, and the pasta blend together to create a pretty dish that will draw "oohs" and "aahs!"

You can use this recipe to make **Crawfish Spaghetti** by substituting 1 1/2 to 2 pounds of crawfish for the shrimp. Sauté the crawfish for 1 minute instead of the 3 minutes required to cook the shrimp. The rest of the recipe remains the same.

Calories—405; Carb—83.8; Fat—21.4; Chol—343; Pro—49.7; Fib— 1.1; Sod—1851

SHRIMP JEANNETTE

1 1/2 lb. large shrimp, unpeeled
1 carrot
1 celery stalk
1 small red bell pepper
1/4 lb. snow peas
3 tbsp. olive oil
2 tbsp. unsalted butter
2/3 cup whole blanched almonds
1/2 cup chopped onion
1 tbsp. minced fresh ginger
2 cloves garlic, minced

1 7-oz. jar whole straw mushrooms, drained
1/2 cup dry white wine
2 tsp. Worcestershire sauce
1/3 tsp. Tabasco sauce
2 tbsp. soy sauce
1 tsp. Cajun Seasoning Mix (see index)
3 cups cooked white rice
1/2 cup chopped green onions
1/4 cup minced fresh parsley

Peel and devein the shrimp, leaving the last section of shell and the tail on the shrimp. Set aside. Cut the carrots and celery stalk at an angle into 1/8-inch slices. Cut the red bell pepper into strips 3 inches long, trim the ends of the snow peas, and set aside ready to use.

In a large skillet over medium heat, heat the almonds until they become toasted, about 3 minutes. Pour them into a glass or metal bowl to hold for later use. Wipe the skillet and return it to the heat. Heat the olive oil in the hot skillet until it starts to smoke; then swirl in the butter. Add the carrots, celery, onion, fresh ginger, and garlic; then sauté for 2 minutes.

Add the shrimp and cook for about 3 minutes until they are pink from head to tail. Add the bell pepper and snow peas, and sauté for 1 1/2 more minutes. Stir in the whole straw mushrooms, heat for about

1/2 minute; then blend in the white wine, Worcestershire sauce, Tabasco sauce, and soy sauce. Add the **Cajun Seasoning Mix** and cooked rice, and heat until the rice is warm and coated. Mix in the green onions, toasted almonds, and parsley. Serve hot, straight from the skillet. Serves 6.

Lagniappe: This dish is a meal by itself. It is swift and simple to make and will earn you rave reviews. This is one of those meals that you can make in front of your guests. They will be so impressed by the fact that you are cooking in front of them that they won't notice just how easy the dish is to make.

I recommend doing all of the prep work (toasting the almonds, cutting the vegetables, peeling and deveining the shrimp, and cooking the rice) in advance. This makes the actual cooking time just under ten minutes. It is a sort of Cajun stir fry. I think you may notice in this book that I enjoy serving one-dish meals. They are easy to cook, easy to serve, and easy to clean up. Just serve it with a nice green salad or fruit salad, and plenty of fresh hot bread.

Calories—463; Carb—39.7; Fat—20.2; Chol—185; Pro—30.8; Fib—2.3; Sod—622

OLD FASHIONED SHRIMP STEW

1/4 cup canola oil
1/4 cup all-purpose flour
1 medium onion, chopped
1/2 cup chopped celery
2 cloves garlic, minced
1 small bell pepper,
  chopped
2 1/2 lb. shrimp, peeled
  and deveined
1 large tomato, skinned
  and diced

2 cups chicken stock,
  chicken broth, or water
2 tsp. Cajun Seasoning Mix
  (see index)
1/4 cup chopped green
  onions
1/4 cup minced fresh
  parsley
cooked white rice

Heat a large saucepan over high heat. Add the oil and heat until it begins to smoke. Add the flour, stirring constantly and thoroughly with a wire whisk. This will make a dark brown roux. Cook for 2 minutes over high heat, then turn to medium heat and add the onion, celery, garlic, and bell pepper. Cook for 2 minutes; then add the shrimp. Allow the shrimp to cook for 3 minutes, stir in the diced tomato, and cook for 1 more minute. Add the stock and **Cajun Seasoning Mix** and cook for 15 minutes. Finally, stir in the green onions and parsley, heat for 2 more minutes, and serve hot over cooked white rice. Serves 6.

Lagniappe: Cooking a dark brown roux like this can be dangerous if you are not careful. You don't want to let it splash on you, because it will burn you like you've never been burned before. You must pay attention to the recipe, and be sure to have all your prep work done before you start. The roux will burn if you don't give it your full attention. Once you add the shrimp, the roux will cool down significantly, and you can begin to relax.

This is a stew that lends itself to seafood because seafood likes to cook quickly. You can use this recipe to make **Crawfish Stew** by substituting 2 pounds of crawfish for the shrimp. This stew actually tastes better if it is made in advance, and refrigerated or frozen. To reheat, just thaw in the refrigerator (never on the counter), and heat over a low fire until heated through.

Calories—260; Carb—10.5; Fat—13.4; Chol—290; Pro—41.6; Fib—.6; Sod—754

SHRIMP BOURG

1/4 cup unsalted butter
2 lb. shrimp, peeled and
  deveined
1 clove garlic, minced
1 tbsp. minced shallots
1/4 cup chopped celery
2 tbsp. minced carrots
1 small red bell pepper, cut
  into strips
1 small yellow bell pepper,
  cut into strips
2/3 cup extra dry vermouth
1/2 cup ripe California
  olives, pitted and halved
1 7-oz. jar whole straw
  mushrooms, drained
2 tsp. Cajun Seasoning Mix
  (see index)
1/4 tsp. Tabasco sauce
3 tbsp. lime juice
1/4 cup minced fresh
  parsley
cooked white rice or
  noodles

Heat a heavy skillet over medium-high heat, then add the butter. When the melted butter is beginning to brown, add the shrimp and sauté for about 3 minutes. They should begin to turn a nice pink color from head to tail. Add the garlic, shallots, celery, and carrots and sauté for 2 minutes. Add the bell peppers, sauté for 1 minute, then add the wine and allow it to absorb (deglaze) the pan drippings. Add the remaining ingredients and cook, stirring often, for 3 more minutes. Serve hot over cooked white rice or the noodles of your choice. Serves 4 to 6.

Lagniappe: This is a recipe that is just perfect for those little straw mushrooms. Their texture and taste are phenomenal. They are a relatively new product on the shelves, so look for them—I think you'll like them.

This dish is quite easy to prepare, and can be done just before serving. I don't recommend cooking in advance, but to save time, do all your prep work early. Enjoy!

Calories—412; Carb—10.8; Fat—18.4; Chol—363; Pro—48.4; Fib—1.4; Sod—668

SHRIMP PERRINE

2 tbsp. olive oil
2 cloves garlic, minced
1 1/3 lb. fresh shrimp,
  peeled and deveined
2 tbsp. tomato paste
1 tsp. Cajun Seasoning Mix
  (see index)
1/2 cup dry vermouth
1/2 cup hearty burgundy
  wine

1/2 tsp. Tabasco sauce
1 tsp. paprika
1/4 cup brandy
1 tsp. fresh thyme (or 1/4
  tsp. dried)
2 tbsp. fresh minced
  parsley

Heat a medium-sized skillet over medium-high heat. Add the olive oil, and when it smokes, sauté the garlic for 1 minute. Add the shrimp and brown on both sides for about 3 minutes. They should turn pink from head to tail. Blend in the tomato paste and **Cajun Seasoning Mix.** Stir in the wines, Tabasco sauce, and paprika; cover and cook for 6 minutes, shaking the pan often to prevent sticking. Uncover, add the brandy and thyme and cook for 2 more minutes. Stir in the parsley and serve hot. Serves 4.

Lagniappe: You have probably noticed that I always tell you to heat the pot before adding the oil. There is a simple reason for this. When you add cold oil to a hot pot, it prevents sticking and allows you to use much less oil, because it spreads out faster and more evenly in a hot pot. I also instruct you to let the oil begin to smoke prior to adding other ingredients. This indicates that the oil is at its highest temperature, which sears whatever you are cooking and seals in the juices and flavors.

This is a quick recipe; but don't be fooled, it is delicious. Cooking and preparation time are so minimal that I would not recommend trying to do anything but peeling and deveining the shrimp in advance.

Calories—275; Carb—5.7; Fat—9.6; Chol—231; Pro—31.8; Fib—.1; Sod—179

SPICY BOILED SHRIMP

1 gallon cold water
2 tbsp. salt
12 whole black
  peppercorns
5 whole bay leaves
1 large lemon, sliced
1 small onion, quartered
  (leave the skin on)
2 stalks celery, chopped
2 cloves garlic, crushed
10 whole cloves

1/2 tsp. dried thyme leaves
1/4 cup fresh chopped basil
  (or 1 tbsp. dried)
4 sprigs fresh parsley
2 tbsp. sugar
1 fresh or pickled whole
  cayenne pepper (or a
  jalapeno pepper)
3 lb. fresh shrimp tails,
  unpeeled

In a large stock pot over high heat, combine all the ingredients except for the shrimp, and bring to a hard rolling boil. Let the mixture boil for 2 minutes; then add the shrimp. Once the liquid begins to boil again, wait exactly 3 minutes; then turn the heat off. Let the shrimp stand in the liquid for 5 more minutes. Drain the shrimp and serve at once. Serves 4.

Lagniappe: Plain boiled shrimp are great with **Jude's Special Seafood Sauce** (see index). Cover your table with old newspapers and place the shrimp right in the middle of the table—Cajun style. Serve with a cold, crisp green salad, French bread, and the sauce.

If you wish to serve the shrimp chilled, drain the hot shrimp and immediately cover them with ice. Once the shrimp are cold, put them in an airtight container and refrigerate until you are ready to serve. Refrigerated, they will keep nicely for 24 hours. You can hold them longer, but they begin to lose their quality. Never keep them for more than 36 hours.

Calories—360; Carb—3.2; Fat—6; Chol—520; Pro—69; Fib—0; Sod—2158

SHRIMP CREOLE

1/2 cup canola oil
1 medium onion, chopped
1 medium bell pepper, chopped
1 cup chopped celery
2 cloves garlic, minced
1/2 cup minced green onions
1 14-oz. can stewed tomatoes
1 15-oz. can whole tomatoes, chopped
1 cup chicken broth
1 tsp. salt
1/2 tsp. Tabasco sauce
1 tsp. black pepper
1/4 tsp. white pepper
1 tsp. fresh basil (or 1/4 tsp. dried)
2 whole bay leaves
2 lb. large shrimp, peeled and deveined
2 tbsp. cornstarch
3 tbsp. water
cooked white rice
2 tbsp. fresh minced parsley

Heat a large, heavy saucepan over high heat. Add the oil, and when it starts to smoke, sauté the onions, bell pepper, celery, garlic, and green onions for 3 minutes. Drain the stewed tomatoes and chopped whole tomatoes, reserving their juice; then add them to the saucepan and sauté for 3 more minutes over high heat. Add the tomato juices, chicken broth, salt, Tabasco sauce, black and white pepper, basil, and bay leaves. Cook for 1 minute over high heat; then add the shrimp and reduce the heat to medium. Bring the liquid to a boil, and cook the shrimp until they turn pink from head to tail, about 3 minutes.

Blend together the cornstarch and water, and stir the mixture in with the hot shrimp. The sauce will begin to thicken at once. Stir well. Serve over cooked white rice and garnish with parsley. Serves 6.

Lagniappe: This is a magnificent shrimp creole. I wouldn't have believed how good it was if I had not tried it myself. Cooking at high temperatures seems to seal in the natural sweetness of the vegetables and shrimp. You can make this dish in advance and refrigerate or freeze it, or you might just want to freeze the leftovers for another day. To reheat, just thaw in the refrigerator and heat over a low fire until heated through. What a treat!

Calories—388; Carb—15.9; Fat—22; Chol—231; Pro—34.1; Fib—1.5; Sod—1069

SCALLOPS AND ANGEL HAIR PASTA

1 gallon water
2 tsp. salt
2 cups chardonnay (or dry white wine)
1 tbsp. finely chopped shallots
1 clove garlic, minced
1 tbsp. chopped fresh basil
1 1/3 lb. scallops
3 tbsp. Dijon mustard
3 tbsp. unsalted butter, chilled
1/2 tsp. Tabasco sauce
1 tsp. salt
1/2 tsp. black pepper
1 10-oz. pkg. angel hair pasta
1 1/2 tbsp. olive oil
1 tbsp. minced fresh parsley

Add the salt to the gallon of water, and start it to boil over a medium-high heat. In a large, heavy skillet over medium heat, combine the wine, shallots, garlic, and basil. Bring to a boil; then reduce to a low simmer. Add the scallops and cook for about 2 to 3 minutes until they turn white. Remove the scallops and place them in a bowl for later use.

Raise the temperature under the skillet to high until the liquid reduces to about 1/2 cup; then reduce the heat to low. Use a wire whisk to whip in the mustard. Cut the butter into 4 squares, and whisk them in, one square at a time. Return the scallops to the skillet and add the Tabasco sauce, salt, and black pepper.

Add the pasta to the boiling water and cook al dente. This won't take long because the pasta is very thin and cooks quickly. Remove the pasta, drain, and toss with the olive oil and parsley until coated. Arrange equal portions of pasta on each serving plate and spoon a generous amount of scallops and sauce over each bed of pasta. Serve hot. Serves 4.

Lagniappe: Scallops are quite wonderful to cook with—they are one of the few seafoods that do not need to be peeled, deveined, cleaned, or scaled. This recipe is easy and fast. Because the sauce will break down in the refrigerator, I don't recommend making it in advance or trying to store it.

Calories—487; Carb—54; Fat—14.1; Chol—143; Pro—36; Fib—.2; Sod—890

SCALLOPS JOSEPHINE

1 cup chopped fresh
  parsley
4 cloves garlic, halved
1/2 cup chopped green
  onions
8 large fresh mushrooms
1/4 cup chopped celery
1/4 cup ripe pitted
  California olives
1 small carrot, chopped
1/2 medium apple, cored
  and chopped

1 tbsp. chopped fresh basil
1 1/2 sticks unsalted butter
1 tsp. salt
1 tsp. black pepper
1/4 tsp. Tabasco sauce
1/4 tsp. nutmeg
2/3 cup seasoned bread
  crumbs
2 tbsp. olive oil
1 1/3 lb. fresh scallops

Preheat the oven to 450 degrees. Place the first nine ingredients in a food processor and chop at full power for about 2 minutes. The mixture should be very finely chopped. Add the butter, salt, black pepper, Tabasco sauce, and nutmeg. Process for about 2 minutes until completely blended. Mix in the bread crumbs and olive oil.

Making sure they are clean and all membranes are removed, place the scallops into individual casseroles or au gratin dishes. Generously cover the scallops with the sauce. Bake at 450 degrees for 15 to 18 minutes, or until the sauce is bubbling and nicely browned. Serve hot with plenty of hot French bread. Serves 4 to 6.

Lagniappe: This is an easy way to use scallops. You don't have to do anything to them, the sauce works all the magic. Although scallops are easy to cook, most people are afraid to cook with them for fear they will mess up. Anyone can do this dish—even non-cooks!

You can substitute 1 1/3 pounds of large, peeled and deveined shrimp for the scallops to make **Shrimp Josephine.** Likewise, you can use 1 pound of lump crabmeat, king crabmeat, or dungeness crabmeat to make **Crabmeat Josephine.** Let's not leave out crawfish! **Crawfish Josephine** is outstanding and can be made using 1 pound of peeled and deveined crawfish tails instead of the scallops. Well, that just about covers the waterfront. Enjoy!

Calories—652; Carb—35.5; Fat—49.5; Chol—150; Pro—31; Fib—2; Sod—1344

SCALLOPS PONCHATOULA

2 14-oz. cans asparagus
  spears
2/3 cup water chestnuts,
  sliced
6 large fresh mushrooms,
  sliced
1/2 cup ripe California
  pitted olives, sliced
2 large hard boiled eggs,
  sliced
1 1/3 lb. fresh scallops
1/2 tsp. salt
1/2 tsp. black pepper
1/4 tsp. white pepper

1/2 tsp. garlic powder
1/2 cup grated Swiss
  cheese
1/2 cup grated sharp
  cheddar cheese
1 10 3/4-oz. can condensed
  cream of mushroom soup
2/3 cup dry white wine
1 tbsp. Worcestershire
  sauce
1/2 tsp. Tabasco sauce
2/3 cup cracker crumbs
2 tsp. unsalted butter
paprika

Preheat the oven to 375 degrees. Butter a 3-quart casserole dish and place 1 can of asparagus spears on the bottom of the casserole. Cover with 1/3 cup of the sliced water chestnuts, 3 of the sliced mushrooms, 1/4 cup of the sliced olives, 1 sliced egg, 1/4 cup of Swiss cheese, and 1/4 cup of cheddar cheese.

Rinse, drain, and season the scallops with salt, pepper, and garlic powder. Place 1/2 of the scallops on top of the mixture just added to the casserole. In a separate bowl, mix together the soup, wine, Worcestershire sauce, Tabasco sauce, and parsley until smooth. Pour 1/2 of this soup mixture over of the scallops in the casserole.

Repeat the same layering process with the remaining half of the ingredients. Top the casserole with the cracker crumbs, dot with small pieces of butter, and sprinkle with paprika. Bake, uncovered, for 30 minutes at 375 degrees. Serves 4.

Lagniappe: Often we forget about fresh scallops in choosing our seafoods. They are practical to use because all you are buying is edible meat. There is no waste or mess. Seafood lends itself to all types of sauces, which stretches the budget for the entree.

This dish can be made in advance and refrigerated or frozen for later use. To reheat, just thaw in the refrigerator, uncover, and bake for 20 minutes at 325 degrees.

You can make **Crabmeat Ponchatoula** by substituting 1 pound of fresh lump crabmeat for the scallops. Another possibility is **Shrimp Ponchatoula,** which is made by substituting 1 1/3 pounds of peeled and deveined shrimp. Finally, **Crawfish Ponchatoula** is made by using 1 pound of peeled and deveined crawfish tails in the place of the scallops.

Calories—558; Carb—43; Fat—28; Chol—115; Pro—13; Fib—.5; Sod—1242

SCALLOPS TERRIOT

1/3 cup olive oil
1 1/2 lb. scallops, rinsed
and drained
2 cloves garlic, minced
1 tbsp. minced shallots
2 tbsp. finely chopped
celery
1 1/2 tsp. Cajun Seasoning
Mix (see index)
1 tbsp. fresh oregano leaves
(or 2/3 tsp. dried)

2/3 cup champagne
1/2 large fresh lemon, juice
only
1 tbsp. white
Worcestershire sauce
2 tbsp. minced green onion
tops
2 tbsp. minced fresh
parsley

Heat a large skillet over medium heat. Add the olive oil and, when it begins to smoke, add the scallops. Brown the scallops for about 3 minutes; then add the garlic, shallots, and celery. Sauté for 2 minutes. Blend in the **Cajun Seasoning Mix** and the fresh oregano leaves. Deglaze the pan by adding the champagne and stirring it around to absorb all the pan drippings.

Add the lemon juice and Worcestershire sauce and cook for about 2 minutes until the liquid is reduced by about half. Stir in the green onion tops and fresh parsley, then serve hot. Serves 4.

Lagniappe: This dish can be served with rice or the noodles of your choice. Be sure the noodles are cooked al dente, and just toss the **Scallops Terriot** with about 3 cups of noodles. If you prefer rice, just serve the scallops on a bed of cooked white rice. Be sure to use long grain rice—it has a lot less gluten so it won't be as gummy as short grain rice.

This is a quick recipe. I don't recommend making it in advance, nor do I recommend freezing it. Too many flavors would be lost by freezing this dish.

A note on the champagne: Either use a small bottle—it does not have to be the best quality available—or serve champagne to your guests, and just use your glass (2/3 cup) to cook with!

You can make **Shrimp Terriot** by using 2 pounds of fresh, peeled and deveined shrimp instead of the scallops. **Crawfish Terriot** requires 1 1/2 pounds of fresh, peeled and deveined crawfish tails; and **Crabmeat Terriot** requires 1 1/2 pounds of lump crabmeat (or king crab leg meat). Whatever you choose, it will be delicious!

Calories—353; Carb—9; Fat—19.2; Chol—56; Pro—29.3; Fib—.1; Sod—548

OYSTERS DAVID

1 cup olive oil
10 cloves garlic, peeled and crushed
2 tbsp. chopped shallots
1 qt. fresh oysters, drained
1 cup seasoned bread crumbs
1 cup cracker crumbs
1/2 cup chopped green onions
2 tsp. Cajun Seasoning Mix (see index)

1/2 cup grated parmesan cheese
1/4 cup grated romano cheese
1/2 tsp. Tabasco sauce
1 tbsp. Worcestershire sauce
1/4 cup minced fresh parsley

Preheat the oven to 500 degrees. Add the olive oil, garlic, and shallots to a cold, medium-sized, heavy saucepan and heat over medium heat until it begins to boil. Let the oil boil for 7 minutes.

While the oil is boiling, combine the oysters, bread crumbs, cracker crumbs, green onions, and **Cajun Seasoning Mix** in a large mixing bowl. Mix thoroughly, then blend the remaining ingredients into the mixture in the mixing bowl.

After the oil has boiled for 7 minutes, carefully pour it over the oyster mixture and stir in well. Pour the mixture into a large, greased casserole dish or 6 individual casseroles, and bake for 12 minutes at 500 degrees. Serve hot. Serves 6.

Lagniappe: You can prepare this dish up to the baking point, and refrigerate until you are ready to serve. Do not refrigerate for more than 2 days. I don't like to freeze this dish.

For those who don't like oysters, you can make **Broiled Shrimp David** by substituting 2 1/2 pounds of fresh, peeled and deveined shrimp for the quart of oysters.

This a rare case in which you add cold oil to a cold pot. I know that I always say to add cold oil to a hot pot, but there is an exception to every rule. In this case, it is easier to bring the olive oil to a boil in a cold pot than in a hot pot. You might want to strain the oil mixture before pouring it over the oysters to screen out the big pieces of garlic. I happen to like boiled garlic, so I leave mine in.

Calories—627; Carb—43; Fat—44; Chol—75; Pro—18.4; Fib— .4; Sod—1378

OYSTER FRITTERS

peanut oil (for frying)
2 cups oysters
2 cups all-purpose flour
1 tbsp. baking powder
1 tsp. baking soda
2 tsp. Cajun Seasoning Mix
  (see index)
1/4 tsp. nutmeg
2 large brown eggs, beaten

1 cup milk
1/4 tsp. Tabasco sauce
1 tsp. Worcestershire sauce
2 tbsp. unsalted butter,
  melted
1/2 cup finely chopped
  green onions
2 cloves garlic, minced
2 tbsp. minced parsley

Heat the oil in a deep fryer to 375 degrees. Drain the oysters on paper towels until most of their liquid is absorbed. Chop them and set them aside for later use.

In a large mixing bowl, combine the flour, baking powder, baking soda, **Cajun Seasoning Mix,** and nutmeg. Set aside. In another bowl, mix together the eggs, milk, Tabasco sauce, Worcestershire sauce, and butter until well blended. Slowly pour the egg mixture into the flour mixture, and blend in well. Fold in the chopped oysters, green onions, garlic, and parsley. Drop this batter by spoonful into the hot peanut oil and cook until golden brown, about 3 minutes. Remove and drain on paper towels. Serve hot. Serves 4.

Lagniappe: This is a great alternative to plain fried oysters. I recommend this recipe for the someone that does not like to bite into a whole oyster. You get the flavor of the oyster without the texture. This makes a great appetizer or entree—the choice is yours. Be sure to use peanut oil in this recipe. The peanut oil stays hotter and imparts a slight nutty flavor to the dish.

You can make the batter in advance and refrigerate it until you are ready to fry, but do not try to freeze it.

Calories—534; Carb—54; Fat—21; Chol—230; Pro—12.3; Fib—.4; Sod—320

CATFISH MELANSON

1 1/2 lb. catfish filets
1 1/2 tsp. Cajun Seasoning
  Mix (see index)
1 cup shell noodles,
  uncooked
3 tbsp. olive oil
1 cup chopped onion
2 cloves garlic, minced
1/4 cup chopped celery
1/2 medium red bell
  pepper, sliced in strips
1/4 cup dry white wine
3 tbsp. distilled white
  vinegar
1 tsp. sugar

1 tsp. hot dry mustard
1 tsp. minced fresh basil
  (or 1/4 tsp. dried)
1 tsp. chopped fresh
  rosemary (or 1/4 tsp.
  dried)
1/2 cup ripe California
  olives, pitted and sliced
1/4 cup shredded carrots
1 cup diced mozzarella
  cheese
1/2 cup grated Swiss
  cheese
1/4 cup minced fresh
  parsley

Rinse, clean, and drain the catfish filets; then pat them dry with paper towels. Cut the filets into bite-sized pieces. Season the fish with the **Cajun Seasoning Mix** and set it aside for later use. Cook the shell noodles al dente, according to package directions, and set aside for later use.

Heat a large, heavy skillet over medium heat. Add the olive oil and continue to heat until it begins to smoke. Carefully place the catfish pieces in the hot oil, and sauté until they become puffy and white, about 2 1/2 minutes. Be sure to move the fish around so they cook on all sides. Add the onions, garlic, celery, and red bell pepper; and sauté for 2 1/2 more minutes.

In a small mixing bowl, combine the wine, vinegar, sugar, hot dry mustard, basil, and rosemary. Pour this liquid mixture into the skillet and stir in well. Cook for about 4 minutes; then reduce the heat to low-medium and add the cooked shell noodles, olives, carrots, and cheeses. Cover and cook over low-medium heat for about 2 1/2 minutes. Stir in the parsley, and serve. Serves 6.

Lagniappe: Here is another one-dish meal—and what a meal it is! This is quick, easy, and fairly inexpensive (I almost said cheap). Catfish is a great fish to cook with because it cooks quickly and has a great deal of flavor. It is unfortunate that most people only eat it fried, because it is magnificent in other dishes.

You can use this recipe to make **Crawfish Melanson** by substituting 2 pounds of peeled and deveined crawfish tails for the catfish. Sauté the crawfish for just 1 minute, then proceed with the recipe. Whether it's crawfish or catfish, I know you'll love this dish!

Calories—446; Carb—20; Fat—25; Chol—107; Pro—31; Fib—.8; Sod—634

BAKED CATFISH CHRISTINE

4 8-oz. catfish filets
1 tsp. salt
1/2 tsp. red pepper
1/4 tsp. black pepper
1/4 tsp. white pepper
1/2 tsp. onion powder
1 medium onion, thinly
sliced
1 clove garlic, minced
1 1/2 tbsp. butter, cut into
dots
1 cup mayonnaise

1/4 cup creole mustard
2 tbsp. fresh lemon juice
1/4 cup dry white wine
1/2 tsp. Tabasco sauce
1/2 tsp. Worcestershire
sauce
1/4 cup minced green
onions
1/4 cup minced fresh
parsley
lemon wedges

Preheat the oven to 350 degrees. Place the filets in a shallow baking dish. Combine the salt, peppers, and onion powder; then season the filets with the mixture. Cover the filets with the sliced onions and minced garlic; then bake at 350 degrees for 20 to 22 minutes, or until the fish flakes when touched with a fork.

While the fish is baking, blend together the mayonnaise, mustard, lemon juice, wine, Tabasco sauce, and Worcestershire sauce until smooth. When the fish is cooked, cover the filets with the mayonnaise mixture. Set the oven to broil, and place the the dish about 4 to 5 inches from the heat for 3 minutes. When it is nicely browned, remove from the oven, sprinkle with the green onions and parsley, garnish with lemon wedges, and serve. Serves 4.

Lagniappe: This is a quick and easy baked fish entree. You can bake the fish and cover it with the mayonnaise sauce; then refrigerate, covered, for up to 24 hours. Just broil for 3 minutes, top with green onions and parsley, and serve. Be sure to spoon plenty of sauce on top of the fish — it is divine. I don't recommend freezing this dish. Feel free to try the same recipe with other filets of fish, just substitute your favorite in the place of the catfish. This is good eating!

Calories — 596; Carb — 20; Fat — 34; Chol — 159; Pro — 43.4; Fib — .3; Sod — 1229

CATFISH ELOISE MARIE

2 lb. catfish filets
2 tsp. Cajun Seasoning Mix
  (see index)
1/3 cup minced carrots
2 tbsp. minced celery
2 cloves garlic, minced
1 medium onion, cut into
  1/4-inch strips
1 medium sweet red bell
  pepper, diced
1/4 cup diced green bell
  pepper
2 tbsp. olive oil
1/4 cup unsalted butter

1/3 cup brandy
1/2 tsp. minced fresh thyme
  (or 1/8 tsp. dried)
1/2 tsp. minced fresh
  oregano (or 1/8 tsp.
  dried)
1/2 cup chopped green
  onions
2 1/2 cups cooked white
  rice
1/4 cup minced fresh
  parsley
1/2 cup ripe California
  olives, pitted and sliced

Cut the catfish filets into bite-sized pieces. Season the pieces with the **Cajun Seasoning Mix** and place them in a large mixing bowl. Cover the fish with the carrots, celery, garlic, onions, and bell peppers.

Heat a large, heavy skillet over medium-high heat. When it is very hot, add the olive oil and let it begin to smoke; then add the butter and let it melt. As soon as it begins to smoke, add the catfish-vegetable mixture and cook at medium-high heat until the fish is browned on all sides, about 5 minutes.

Reduce the heat to low and carefully add the brandy. Strike a match and carefully bring it just close enough to the skillet to ignite the brandy. (There will be a puff of hot fire.) Do not jiggle the pan or stir; the flame will go out by itself. When it does, stir the contents of the skillet well. Add the green onions and cook for 1 minute. Mix in the rice, parsley, and olives and serve at once. Serves 6.

Lagniappe: Do not freeze this dish. You cannot refrigerate this dish after it is cooked without losing quality; but you can refrigerate the seasoned catfish for up to 48 hours before cooking it. It will actually enhance the flavor—the seasonings will have more time to blend together.

Cooking time is very brief and this is one dish that you will want to cook in front of your guests. Please do be vigilant with the flambé. If you have never done a flambé before, you may want to watch someone else cook this before you try.

Serve with a nice green vegetable. This is a rudimentary, yet quite sumptuous and flamboyant dish.

Calories—512; Carb—28; Fat—25; Chol—109; Pro—31; Fib—1.2; Sod—1014

FRESH FLOUNDER MEUNIERE

2 whole, fresh flounders,
  cleaned
1/2 cup all-purpose flour
1 tsp. Cajun Seasoning Mix
  (see index)
1/4 cup unsalted butter

1/2 fresh lemon, juice only
2 tbsp. unsalted butter,
  chilled
2 tbsp. minced fresh
  parsley
lemon wedges

Rinse the flounders with cold water, then pat them dry with a paper towel. In a large mixing bowl, combine the flour and **Cajun Seasoning Mix.** Dredge the flounders in the flour, taking care to coat the fish evenly. Heat a large skillet over medium-high heat. When hot, add the 1/4 cup of butter. When the butter begins to smoke, fry the fish for about 2 minutes on each side. Remove the fish and place them on warmed plates.

Add the fresh lemon juice to the skillet and blend it in with a wire whisk. Reduce the heat to low and whisk in the remaining butter, 1/2 tablespoon at a time. Pour half of the meuniere butter sauce on each fish, and sprinkle with parsley. Garnish with lemon wedges. Serve at once. Serves 2.

Lagniappe: What a great dish. This is the way seafood was meant to be cooked—fast, very fast! You don't want to do anything in advance with this recipe. It is simple and it is a dish for those who really like the taste of fish. We have a tendency to overcook seafood. Because seafood is mainly water, overcooking just evaporates the water that holds the flavors. That means texture, taste, and quality go out the door—or should I say out of the pot? You are left with a tasteless chunk of matter. To enjoy seafood, you must cook it right.

Calories—773; Carb—24; Fat—41.3; Chol—223; Pro—74; Fib—.2; Sod—534

STUFFED FLOUNDER BOURGEOIS

6 small whole flounders
1 recipe Stuffed Crabs,
  unbaked (see index)
2 tbsp. unsalted butter,
  melted

paprika
lemon wedges

Rinse, clean and scale the flounders. Cut off the heads (optional). Use a small, sharp knife to make a cut down the middle of the top side of the flounder. Create a pouch for the crab stuffing by cutting the fish away from the backbone on each side. Be careful not to cut all the way through the fish. Open the hole and generously stuff the crab mixture into the pouch. Place the stuffed fish in a lightly greased baking dish. Brush lightly with the melted butter and sprinkle with paprika. Bake at 375 degrees for 25 minutes, basting twice with melted butter and pan drippings. When cooked, the fish will flake easily and the flesh will be white and somewhat puffy. Serve hot with a few fresh lemon wedges. Serves 6.

Lagniappe: If you really want to go *bon vivant* on this dish, just spoon **Hollandaise Sauce** (see index) over the fish and sprinkle with a little red caviar. Now that is a dish fit for a king!

This recipe may be prepared in advance, and you can freeze the un-baked stuffed fish for later use. Wrap it well with plastic wrap and place it in a freezer bag. Label and date it; then freeze. Thaw the frozen fish in the refrigerator, and bake as above. If I am serving this for dinner guests, I do all my work in the morning and refrigerate, covered with plastic wrap, until I am ready to bake. It makes a nice meal that can be done with ease for a dinner party.

Calories—555; Carb—30; Fat—19.5; Chol—492; Pro—65; Fib—.7; Sod—1096

SKILLET FRIED FISH

2 lb. fish filets
1 1/2 tsp. Cajun Seasoning
    Mix (see index)
1 cup buttermilk
1 tsp. Dijon mustard
1/4 tsp. Tabasco sauce

1 cup seasoned bread
    crumbs
peanut oil (for frying)
lemon wedges
Tartar Sauce (see index)

Wash the filets and dry them with paper towels. Season the fish evenly with the **Cajun Seasoning Mix.** In a large mixing bowl, combine the buttermilk, mustard, and Tabasco sauce. Whisk these ingredients together with a wire whisk. Place the bread crumbs in a shallow pan or on a large platter.

Pour peanut oil into a heavy skillet to 1 inch deep. Heat over medium heat until it reaches about 375 degrees. Dip the fish filets into the buttermilk mixture; then coat with the bread crumbs, shaking off any excess crumbs. Fry the fish for about 2 minutes on each side, turning the fish carefully, so the oil does not splatter. Remove the fish from the skillet, and drain on paper towels. Serve with wedges of fresh lemon and **Tartar Sauce.** Serves 4.

Lagniappe: Don't do anything in advance. Fresh fish needs to be cooked and eaten right away. With this recipe, you can use whole filets or you can cut them into smaller pieces—whichever you prefer. Skillet fried fish will have a taste different from deep fried fish, but both are great. You can deep fry this recipe—just be sure to change the name!

Calories—525; Carb—30.6; Fat—19; Chol—87; Pro—54.3; Fib—.4; Sod—1451

REDFISH LACOMBE

4 6 to 8-oz. redfish filets,
  skinned
1/2 cup all-purpose flour
2 tsp. Cajun Seasoning Mix
  (see index)
1/2 cup cracker crumbs
1/2 cup French bread
  crumbs
1 cup finely chopped
  walnuts

2 large eggs, beaten
1/4 tsp. Tabasco sauce
2 tbsp. milk
1 tbsp. Worcestershire
  sauce
3 tbsp. olive oil
lemon wedges

Pat each filet with paper towels to dry. In a large bowl or platter, sift together the flour and 1 teaspoon of the **Cajun Seasoning Mix.** In another bowl or platter, mix together the cracker crumbs, bread crumbs, walnuts, and the other 1 teaspoon of **Cajun Seasoning Mix.** In a third bowl, combine the eggs, Tabasco sauce, milk, and Worcestershire sauce.

Heat a heavy skillet over medium heat. Preheat the oven to 375 degrees. Lightly dust the redfish with the seasoned flour, then dip it into the egg wash. Coat the fish with the walnut mixture, pressing lightly to make sure that a lot of the mixture adheres to the fish. When the skillet is hot, add the olive oil; and when it begins to smoke, add the crumb-covered fish filets. Sauté each side for about 2 1/2 minutes until the fish is nicely browned. Carefully remove the fish from the skillet, place them in a lightly greased baking dish or cookie sheet, and bake at 375 degrees for 4 to 6 minutes. Serve straight from the oven, garnished with a few lemon wedges. Serves 4.

Lagniappe: There is no need to toast the walnuts prior to using them because they will toast nicely during the baking process. The fish are dusted with flour first to create a barrier that seals in the fish juices and flavor.

You can prepare this dish up to the baking point, and refrigerate or freeze it for later use. Just thaw the fish in the refrigerator and bake for 5 to 7 minutes at 350 degrees. Serve with a colorful vegetable and potato or rice, and you've got a meal fit for a king. For variety, feel free to substitute any firm, quality fish filet that you like.

Calories—568; Carb—29; Fat—25; Chol—221; Pro—57; Fib—.3; Sod—662

FRIED SHARK BABIN

peanut oil (for frying)
1 1/2 lb. shark filets
3/4 cup flour
2 tsp. Cajun Seasoning Mix
   (see index)
1/4 tsp. nutmeg
1 tsp. dried sweet basil
1 tsp. baking powder

3/4 cup beer
2 tsp. vinegar
1 tsp. Worcestershire sauce
1/2 tsp. Tabasco sauce
Tartar Sauce or Jude's
   Special Seafood Sauce
   (see index)

Preheat the oil to 375 degrees in a deep fryer. Rinse the shark filets and pat them dry with paper towels. Cut the filets into bite-sized pieces. In a large mixing bowl, combine the flour, **Cajun Seasoning Mix,** nutmeg, basil, and baking powder. Blend the beer, vinegar, Worcestershire sauce, and Tabasco sauce into the flour mixture. Coat the shark pieces with the batter; then drop them into the hot oil. Fry until golden brown. Remove and drain on paper towels. Serve warm with **Tartar Sauce** or **Jude's Special Seafood Sauce.** Serves 4.

Lagniappe: Can you imagine how much **Shark Babin** they could have made with the shark in *Jaws* if a Cajun had been in the story? This is a great, uncomplicated batter for any fish—not just shark. Feel free to use 1 1/2 pounds of the fish of your choice to make **Fried Fish Babin.** Shark meat is really nice to cook with. It is firm, easy to handle, and quite tasty. Go ahead, try it—it won't bite!

Calories—391; Carb—20; Fat—11; Chol—70; Pro—34; Fib—.1; Sod—552

RED SNAPPER ALICE

2 qt. water
1 tbsp. salt
1 lemon, sliced
10 whole black
   peppercorns
1 tbsp. chopped fresh basil
1 rib celery, chopped
1 small onion, coarsely
   chopped
1/2 tsp. Tabasco sauce
2 8 to 10-oz. red snapper
   filets

1 7-oz. jar whole straw
   mushrooms
1/2 lb. boiled medium
   shrimp, peeled and
   deveined
1/4 cup ripe California
   olives, drained and sliced
1 tsp. minced fresh basil
1 recipe Hollandaise Sauce
   (see index)
paprika
lemon wedges

In a poacher or a large saucepan, bring the water to a hard boil. Add the salt, lemon, black peppercorns, celery, and onion and boil for 1 minute. Add the Tabasco sauce and red snapper, and reduce to a low simmer. Poach for 15 minutes; then remove the filets, drain well, and place each on a serving plate. Drain the mushrooms well; then fold them with the shrimp, olives, and fresh basil into the warm **Hollandaise Sauce.** Pour equal amounts of sauce over each snapper filet. Sprinkle with paprika and garnish with two or three lemon wedges. Serve at once. Serves 4.

Lagniappe: Just as I was finishing up this book, I discovered whole straw mushrooms. I really like them, so I added this and a few other recipes that use this great product. I think you will be pleased with the beauty and unique taste of these little gems. This is what I call "speedy gourmet." It is an elegant meal that has wonderful flavor. I hope you enjoy!

Other than making the **Hollandaise Sauce,** I wouldn't do anything in advance. You can make the sauce about 1 hour before you need it. In the poaching liquid and the sauce, I think fresh basil is preferable, but if you can't find fresh, you can substitute dried basil. Use about 1 teaspoon of dried basil in the poaching liquid and about 1/4 teaspoon in the sauce.

Calories—593; Carb—5; Fat—39.1; Chol—520; Pro—66.3; Fib—.5; Sod—1340

FRESH SWORDFISH WITH CAPER SAUCE

4 6 to 8-oz. swordfish
  steaks, about 1-inch
  thick
1 1/2 tsp. Cajun Seasoning
  Mix (see index)
3 tbsp. unsalted butter
3 tbsp. minced shallots
1 clove garlic, minced
3 tbsp. minced celery
1/2 cup diced yellow bell
  pepper
1 tbsp. minced fresh basil
  (or 1 tsp. dried)

2 tsp. minced fresh thyme
  (or 1/2 tsp. dried)
1/2 cup dry vermouth
1/4 cup fresh lime juice
1 tbsp. white
  Worcestershire sauce
1/4 tsp. Tabasco sauce
1/4 cup capers, drained
2 tbsp. unsalted butter,
  cold
2 tbsp. minced fresh
  parsley
lemon wedges

Season the swordfish steaks with the **Cajun Seasoning Mix.** Heat a heavy skillet over medium-high heat. When it is hot, melt the butter; when it begins to smoke, cook the steaks for about 5 minutes on each side. They should turn white and firm. Remove the steaks, and place them on a warm platter for later use.

Add the shallots, garlic, celery, and yellow bell pepper to the hot skillet, and sauté for about 3 minutes. Add the basil and thyme and sauté for 1 more minute. Deglaze the skillet with the wine, lime juice, Worcestershire sauce, and Tabasco sauce, making sure the pan drippings are absorbed into the liquid. Cook for about 3 more minutes. The sauce should thicken slightly. Stir in the capers, turn the heat to medium, and swirl in the cold butter—1/3 tablespoon at a time. Add the fresh parsley, stir, and spoon generous amounts of this sauce over the swordfish steaks. Garnish with lemon wedges and serve. Serves 4.

Lagniappe: This is another dish that must be made just prior to serving. You can do all the prep work in advance, and actual cooking time is under 15 minutes. Swordfish is readily available all over the country.

You won't find many old Cajuns cooking swordfish, but I contend that any culture that looked at a "mudbug" and said, "Laissez les bon temps rouler! Let's eat it," would definitely eat swordfish. My grandmother always used to say, "Cher, we eat what we can get, and cher, then we make it taste good!" I think my grandmother would have cooked swordfish, shark, salmon, or whatever she could have gotten fresh. Today, the world is at our fingertips. If we don't take advantage of it, we will miss out on some unique dishes. (End of sermon.)

Calories—401; Carb—6.6; Fat—36.1; Chol—240; Pro—102; Fib—.7; Sod—1446

TROUT MARTAIZE

1 1/2 qt. water
2 cups dry white wine
1 lemon, sliced
1 tbsp. salt
1 medium onion, coarsely
 chopped
5 whole black peppercorns
3 whole bay leaves
1 rib celery, cut in 3 pieces

1 sprig fresh parsley
1/4 tsp. red pepper
4 8-oz. trout filets
1 recipe Hollandaise Sauce
 (see index)
2 tbsp. minced fresh chives
1 tbsp. minced fresh
 parsley

In a poacher or large saucepan, bring the water and wine to a boil. Add the next eight ingredients and let them boil for 2 minutes. Reduce to a simmer and add the trout. Poach for 12 minutes, then carefully remove the trout and drain. Place each filet on a serving plate and cover each with **Hollandaise Sauce.** Sprinkle with the chives and parsley; then serve hot. Serves 4.

Lagniappe: Fish is so very easy to cook, yet so often it is bypassed because people are afraid to try. I guess they look at a recipe and say, "It can't be that easy!" It really is easy—give it a try.

 You can make your **Hollandaise Sauce** in advance, and let it sit at room temperature for up to 1 hour. The rest of the recipe is so easy that you can do it just before serving. If you don't want to use wine, just increase the water to two quarts.

Calories—663; Carb—6.2; Fat—53.3; Chol—378; Pro—139; Fib—.3; Sod—961

CAJUN SEASONING MIX

1/4 cup salt
1/4 cup paprika
2 tbsp. cayenne pepper
2 tbsp. onion powder
1 1/2 tbsp. garlic powder
1 tbsp. finely ground black
    pepper
1 tbsp. white pepper
2 tsp. sweet basil
1 tsp. dry mustard
1 tsp. chili powder

1/2 tsp. ground bay leaves
1/2 tsp. filé powder
1/4 tsp. ground cloves
1/4 tsp. ground thyme
1/4 tsp. rosemary
1/8 tsp. ground ginger
1/8 tsp. cumin powder
1/8 tsp. ground tarragon
1/8 tsp. ground nutmeg
1/8 tsp. ground allspice

Combine all ingredients in a mixing bowl and mix thoroughly. Store in a tightly covered glass jar for use as needed.

Lagniappe: I decided to create one seasoning mix that would work as the single Cajun spice mixture in many dishes. This is an excellent seasoning for any dish that could use a little Cajun flavor.

You will notice that the amount of salt in my seasoning mix is minimal. If you are on a salt-free diet, just cut out the salt and use the rest of the ingredients. This mixture keeps well for up to 6 months if it is kept cool, dry, and covered. This mixture is used often throughout this book—a nice big jar of this also makes an excellent gift for your favorite Cajun cook.

Calories—5.1; Carb—1; Fat—.2; Chol—0; Pro—.2; Fib—Trace; Sod—187

MEUNIERE SAUCE

1/2 cup unsalted butter
2 tbsp. all-purpose flour
2 tbsp. finely chopped
green onions
2 tbsp. fresh lemon juice
3/4 tsp. salt
1 tbsp. Worcestershire
sauce

1/2 tsp. Tabasco sauce
1/4 tsp. black pepper
1/4 tsp. white pepper
3 tbsp. finely chopped fresh
parsley

Over medium heat, melt the butter. Add the flour and cook for 3 minutes, stirring constantly. Stir in the green onions and lemon juice. Add the salt, Worcestershire sauce, Tabasco sauce, black pepper, and white pepper. Mix in well. Add the parsley and heat for one more minute. Serve at once over cooked seafood. Makes about 1 cup of sauce.

Lagniappe: This is a basic Cajun French sauce that is used over seafood. Use it as recommended in recipes or be creative and serve it over your own creations. It is simple but captivating.

Calories—33; Carb—1.3; Fat—3.2; Chol—8.3; Pro—.3; Fib— Trace; Sod—121

JUDE'S SPECIAL SEAFOOD SAUCE

1 1/2 cups catsup
1 cup mayonnaise
3 tbsp. horseradish
2 tsp. Tabasco Sauce

1 clove garlic, finely
minced
1/2 fresh lemon, juice only

With a wire whisk or electric mixer, mix together all the ingredients until smooth. Chill until ready to use. Makes about 3 cups of sauce.

Lagniappe: This is my favorite sauce for boiled crawfish or shrimp. I think it really brings out the taste of both. This sauce is great for all boiled seafood, and also may be used for fried seafood instead of or in addition to tartar sauce.

If the sauce is too spicy for you, reduce the amount of Tabasco sauce first. If it is still too spicy, reduce the horseradish. It will store in the refrigerator for 4 or 5 days, as long as it stays cold and tightly covered.

Calories—28; Carb—3.2; Fat—1.3; Chol—1.3; Pro—.2; Fib—Trace; Sod—116

TARTAR SAUCE

2 cups mayonnaise
1/2 cup diced sweet pickles
2 tbsp. minced onion
2 tbsp. chopped stuffed
olives
1 tbsp. minced fresh
parsley

1 tbsp. white wine vinegar
1/2 tsp. cream of tartar
1/2 tsp. prepared mustard
1/2 tsp. Tabasco sauce
1/4 tsp. dried basil
1/4 tsp. black pepper

Mix all ingredients together thoroughly in a large mixing bowl. Pour the tartar sauce into a container with a tight lid, and refrigerate until ready to use. Makes about 2 3/4 cups.

Lagniappe: This sauce may be made 2 or 3 days in advance. Just keep it well refrigerated and tightly covered. This is a great sauce for all fried seafood. It does not have to be made in advance to be used, although a few hours in the refrigerator allow the flavors to blend together better.

Calories—48; Carb—3.6; Fat—3.8; Chol—3; Pro—.2; Fib—.1; Sod—103

Poultry

CHICKEN ETOUFFEE

1 stick unsalted butter
2 medium onions, chopped
1/4 cup thinly sliced celery
3 cloves garlic, minced
1 small red bell pepper,
    diced
8 5-oz. chicken thighs,
    skinned
1 1/2 tsp. Cajun Seasoning
    Mix (see index)
3 tbsp. all-purpose flour

2 tbsp. tomato paste
1/4 tsp. Tabasco sauce
1 tsp. Worcestershire sauce
1 1/2 cups chicken stock,
    chicken broth or water
1 cup chopped green
    onions
1/2 cup minced fresh
    parsley
cooked long grain white
    rice

Heat a large, heavy skillet over medium heat until it is hot. Melt the butter until it begins to smoke, then sauté the onions, celery, garlic, and red bell pepper for about 5 minutes, stirring often. While the vegetables are sautéing, season the thighs with the **Cajun Seasoning Mix.** Add them to the skillet after the vegetables have sautéed for 5 minutes. Brown the chicken thighs nicely, cooking about 5 minutes per side; then remove the thighs and set aside for later use.

Add the flour to the skillet and stir it in well. Cook for about 4 minutes, stirring constantly. Blend in the tomato paste, Tabasco sauce, and Worcestershire sauce. Add the chicken stock and stir until the sauce begins to thicken. Add the cooked chicken thighs, cover, and cook for 12 minutes. Remove the cover, add the green onions and parsley, and cook uncovered for 3 more minutes. Serve hot over cooked rice. Serves 8.

Lagniappe: This recipe loves to be made ahead of time and either refrigerated or frozen for later use. Cook the dish entirely, except for adding the green onions and parsley, before you freeze or refrigerate. When you are ready to reheat, just remove from the freezer, thaw in the refrigerator, and cook covered for 5 minutes over medium heat. Add the green onions and parsley and cook three more minutes; then you are ready to serve. This makes an excellent Cajun T.V. Dinner. In a dish that can go in the freezer, place a bed of rice and a chicken thigh, and cover with sauce. Cover with a good plastic wrap and freeze. To reheat, just punch a few holes in the plastic wrap, and pop it in the microwave to heat.

I chose to use thighs in this dish because étouffée is usually an economical meal. You can use chicken legs (I'd recommend 2 per serving), or you can use breasts (cut in half). With chicken breasts, the cost of the meal will go up dramatically. This is indubitably one of the best Cajun dishes around!

Calories—187; Carb—9.3; Fat—15.9; Chol—50; Pro—6.9; Fib—.4; Sod—293

CHICKEN CUTLET NANCY

2 whole boneless chicken
  breasts, skinned
1/4 cup flour
1 tsp. Cajun Seasoning Mix
  (see index)
3 tbsp. peanut oil
1 tbsp. minced shallots
2 cloves garlic, minced
1/2 cup chopped sweet red
  bell pepper
1/2 cup thinly sliced
  carrots

1/4 cup thinly sliced celery
1/4 cup chopped green
  onions
4 large mushrooms, sliced
3/4 cup dry white wine
1 cup chicken stock or
  chicken broth
1/2 tsp. Tabasco sauce
3 cups cooked white rice
1 tbsp. minced fresh
  parsley

Cut each chicken breast in half. Place a large piece of plastic wrap over your cutting board. Place a half chicken breast in the center of half of the plastic wrap, and fold the other half over to cover the chicken. Using a kitchen mallet, pound each cutlet until it has increased in size by about 1/3.

In a large mixing bowl, combine the flour and **Cajun Seasoning Mix;** then dredge the chicken in the mixture. Heat a large, heavy skillet over medium-high heat. When it is hot, add the peanut oil; when the oil begins to smoke, sauté the shallots and garlic for 1 minute. Add the chicken cutlets, two at a time, and fry for 2 1/2 minutes on each side. Place the chicken on a warm plate and set it aside for later use.

Add the bell pepper, carrots, celery, green onions, and mushrooms to the skillet and sauté for 5 minutes. Stir in the wine, chicken stock, and Tabasco sauce, scraping the bottom of the pan to dissolve the pan drippings. When the mixture comes to a boil, reduce the heat to simmer, return the chicken to the skillet, and simmer for 12 minutes. Serve each cutlet on a bed of cooked white rice covered with generous amounts of the vegetables. Garnish with a little freshly chopped parsley. Serve at once. Serves 4.

Lagniappe: Chicken breasts are easy to cook with and most people—even my oldest child—like them. Therefore, this dish is usually a big hit. This is a fast-paced recipe that must be cooked just before serving. If you are really pressed for time, it is possible to cook the recipe in advance up to the point of returning the chicken to the skillet; and store it in the refrigerator for up to 24 hours. When you are ready to serve, just bring the mixture back to a simmer and add the chicken. Cook the remainder as the recipe directs. Another option would be to do all the cutting, chopping, and pounding ahead of time, and start the recipe just before serving. Cooking time is around 20 minutes. Be prepared for rave reviews on this one!

Calories—468; Carb—48.7; Fat—15.5; Chol—73.3; Pro—33; Fib—1.1; Sod—1001

CHICKEN JOSEPH BOREL

1 3-lb. whole chicken fryer
1/2 cup all-purpose flour
2 tsp. Cajun Seasoning Mix
  (see index)
1/4 cup peanut oil
1 10 3/4-oz. can condensed
  cream of mushroom soup
1/2 cup chopped green
  onions
1 tbsp. Worcestershire
  sauce

1/4 tsp. Tabasco sauce
2 tsp. minced fresh basil
2 tbsp. minced fresh
  parsley
1 7-oz. jar whole straw
  mushrooms
1 tsp. fresh lemon juice
1/4 tsp. nutmeg
1/4 cup brandy
1 1/4 cup sour cream
cooked white rice

Clean the chicken and cut it into serving pieces. I prefer to take the skin off, but that is a matter of individual taste. Pat the chicken dry with paper towels. In a large bowl, mix together the flour and **Cajun Seasoning Mix,** then dredge the chicken in the seasoned flour. Heat a heavy skillet over medium-high heat; then add the peanut oil. When the oil begins to smoke, fry the chicken until it is browned on all sides. Remove the chicken from the skillet and set it aside, catching all the drippings to add back into the dish with the chicken.

In a large saucepan over medium heat, combine the soup, green onions, Worcestershire sauce, Tabasco sauce, and basil and bring it to a boil. Add the chicken with its drippings, and let the soup simmer over a low heat for 20 minutes. Stir in the parsley, straw mushrooms, lemon juice, and nutmeg. Simmer for 3 more minutes. Blend in the brandy and sour cream, and heat until the sauce thickens somewhat. Serve hot over noodles or mashed potatoes. Serves 6.

Lagniappe: This is a quick chicken stew that uses mushroom soup as a base. The addition of brandy to the dish gives it a nice flavor without being overpowering. The sour cream mellows the sauce and gives it a rich texture. I use those whole straw mushrooms in this dish, because it needed something catchy to set it off.

You can make this dish in advance and refrigerate it, but I do not recommend freezing it. To reheat, just heat on the stove on low-medium until the chicken is heated through.

Calories—642; Carb—25; Fat—36; Chol—187; Pro—60; Fib—.4; Sod—991

BREAST OF CHICKEN "AH-B"

1/2 stick unsalted butter
1 1/2 tsp. Cajun Seasoning
  Mix (see index)
2 10 to 12-oz. chicken
  breasts, halved
3 cloves garlic, minced
1 tsp. minced shallots
1 small red bell pepper,
  diced

1 1/2 cups small green
  peas, cooked and drained
1 7-oz. jar whole straw
  mushrooms, drained
2 tbsp. minced fresh
  parsley

Heat a large, heavy skillet over medium heat until hot; then add the butter. While the butter is heating, season the chicken breasts with the **Cajun Seasoning Mix** and place them on a cutting board. Cover them with plastic wrap and pound each one about 3 times with a kitchen mallet. When the butter begins to smoke, sauté the chicken breasts on one side for about 5 minutes. Add the garlic, shallots, and red pepper; turn the chicken over; then sauté for about 5 minutes, until the breast is cooked through. Add the peas, straw mushrooms, and parsley and cook, stirring carefully, for 5 more minutes. Place the chicken on serving plates and cover with the vegetable mixture. Serve hot. Serves 4.

Lagniappe: When it comes to speedy cooking, chicken breasts are hard to beat. The end product is always appetizing and appealing. This is a dish that has to be cooked just prior to eating. You'll find it very quick and quite effortless; but I don't recommend trying to make it in advance.

Calories—318; Carb—12.3; Fat—15.7; Chol—106; Pro—31.7; Fib—2.4; Sod—521

CHICKEN KEITH

2 10-oz. chicken breasts
1 tsp. salt
1/2 tsp. onion powder
1/2 tsp. garlic powder
1/2 tsp. cayenne pepper
1/4 tsp. sweet basil
1/4 tsp. white pepper
1 large yellow bell pepper,
  cut in thin strips
1 small onion, quartered
1/8 cup chopped celery
2 tbsp. soy sauce

3 tbsp. dry white wine
2 tsp. Worcestershire sauce
1/4 tsp. Tabasco sauce
2 tsp. cornstarch
2 tbsp. canola oil
2 tbsp. peanut oil
2 tsp. minced ginger root
3 cloves garlic, minced
1 1/2 cups broccoli florets
1 cup snow peas
cooked white or brown rice

Remove any excess skin or fat from the chicken. In a bowl, combine the salt, onion powder, garlic powder, cayenne pepper, basil, and white pepper. Season the chicken with the spice mixture.

In a heavy skillet over medium heat, sear the chicken on both sides for about 7 minutes, until it is nicely browned and cooked through. While the chicken is cooking, combine the bell pepper, onion, celery, soy sauce, wine, Worcestershire sauce, Tabasco sauce, cornstarch, and canola oil in a large bowl. Once the chicken is cooked, cut it into bite-sized pieces and mix it into the vegetable mixture.

Wipe the skillet with paper towels and return it to medium-high heat. When the skillet is hot, add the peanut oil. Let the oil lightly coat the bottom of the skillet; then add the chicken-vegetable mixture, ginger, and garlic. Cook for 3 minutes, stirring a few times. Stir in the broccoli and snow peas, and cook for 5 minutes. Serve immediately over a bed of white or brown rice. Serves 4.

Lagniappe: This dish cannot be made entirely in advance, but you can cut the vegetables, prepare and season the chicken, and cook the rice beforehand. The rest of the dish can be cooked in about 15 minutes. Don't let the long list of ingredients scare you—this is a simple and delicious recipe.

You can make **Pork Keith** by substituting 20 ounces of pork tenderloin for the chicken. Season it the same way, but slice the tenderloin into 1-inch pieces before cooking them. The sliced tenderloin will only require 5 minutes to cook instead of 7.

Calories—336; Carb—13.8; Fat—17.6; Chol—73; Pro—31; Fib—2.4; Sod—1225

CHICKEN BREAST EUPHEMIE

2 12-oz. chicken breasts, boned and skinned
1 1/2 tsp. Cajun Seasoning Mix (see index)
1/4 cup olive oil
2 medium onions, finely chopped
1/2 cup finely chopped celery

1/2 cup sauterne wine
1/2 tbsp. paprika
1 cup sour cream
1/4 tsp. Tabasco sauce
1 tbsp. minced fresh parsley

Wash the chicken thoroughly and dry it with paper towels. Season the chicken with the **Cajun Seasoning Mix** and set it aside. Heat a large, heavy skillet over medium-high heat. When it is hot, add the olive oil. When it smokes, sauté the onions and celery for about 5 minutes until they are browned. Add the chicken and sauté it for about 3 minutes per side. Stir in the sauterne wine, allowing the wine to absorb the pan drippings to thicken the liquid. Reduce the heat to medium and add the paprika. Cover and cook for 5 minutes, shaking the pan often to prevent sticking.

In a bowl, combine the sour cream, Tabasco sauce, and fresh parsley. Turn the heat down to low, remove the cover, and stir in the sour cream mixture. Let the sauce cook over low for 2 more minutes; then serve. Serves 4.

Lagniappe: You can serve this over the noodles of your choice, long grain white rice, brown rice, or with potatoes. I don't recommend making this dish in advance because the cream sauce will begin to break apart when reheated. The chicken should be brown and tender, and the sauce should be light and fresh. This is "company cooking" that is simple enough for everyday fare.

Calories—389; Carb—7.4; Fat—26.8; Chol—93; Pro—29; Fib—.4; Sod—335

CHICKEN AGNES

1 16-oz. pkg. thin egg
noodles
1/2 stick butter, melted
2 tbsp. minced fresh
parsley
1/2 tsp. black pepper
2 12-oz. whole chicken
breasts
2 tbsp. olive oil
2 tbsp. unsalted butter
1 15-oz. can tomato sauce
1 tbsp. Worcestershire
sauce

1/2 tsp. Tabasco sauce
1 tsp. salt
1 16-oz. carton cottage
cheese
1 8-oz. pkg. cream cheese,
cut into squares
1 cup sour cream
1/2 cup chopped sweet red
bell pepper
1/2 cup minced green
onions
2 cloves garlic, minced

Preheat the oven to 375 degrees. Cook the noodles al dente according to the package directions. Rinse with hot water and drain. When the noodles are drained, put them in a large mixing bowl, pour the melted butter over them, and add the parsley and black pepper. Toss lightly and set it aside.

Cut the chicken into strips that are 1/2 inch wide and 2 inches long. Heat a heavy skillet over medium-high heat; then add the olive oil and butter. When it begins to smoke, sauté the chicken breast strips for about 5 to 7 minutes until the chicken is nicely browned. Add the tomato sauce, Worcestershire sauce, Tabasco sauce, and salt; and simmer for 4 minutes. Pour the mixture over the noodles in the mixing bowl, and add the remaining ingredients. Toss until mixed, pour into a 4-quart casserole, and bake at 375 degrees for 25 minutes. Serve hot. Serves 6 to 8.

Lagniappe: This is a great one-dish meal. It is a true crowd pleaser that is quite simple to make. Serve it with French bread and a nice green salad. You can make this dish in advance and either refrigerate or freeze it as long as you cover it tightly. To reheat, just thaw in the refrigerator, and bake at 350 degrees for 15 minutes, or until it is heated through.

Calories—840; Carb—69; Fat—38; Chol—178; Pro—45.4; Fib—.4; Sod—1397

CHICKEN SEAN

1 1/2 lb. skinned chicken
  breasts
3 tbsp. olive oil
1 medium onion, cut in
  wedges
1 medium bell pepper, cut
  in strips
4 cloves garlic, minced
1/2 cup sliced celery
2 tbsp. all-purpose flour
1/2 cup red wine vinegar
1 cup dry white table wine
1 tsp. salt
2 medium tomatoes,
  skinned and diced

1 tsp. minced fresh thyme
  (or 1/3 tsp. dried)
2 tsp. minced fresh basil
  (or 2/3 tsp. dried)
1 tsp. minced fresh sage (or
  1/4 tsp. dried)
1 tbsp. Worcestershire
  sauce
1/2 tsp. Tabasco sauce
1 cup ripe California olives,
  chopped in half
  lengthwise
cooked white rice or
  cooked al dente noodles

Cut the chicken breasts into 3-inch strips. Heat a large, heavy skillet over medium-high heat. When it is hot, add the olive oil and heat until it begins to smoke; then add the chicken and cook for 5 minutes. It should be nicely browned. Add the onions, bell pepper, garlic, and celery; then sauté for 5 more minutes over medium-high heat, stirring often. Add the flour and cook, stirring constantly, for 4 minutes. Add the vinegar, wine, salt, and tomatoes. Lower the heat to medium, add the remaining ingredients (except for the rice and/or noodles) and cook for 4 minutes. Serve hot, right from the skillet, over cooked white rice or noodles. Serves 6.

Lagniappe: This recipe is named for my spicy little nephew, Sean. He may be young, but he pondered the ingredients, quizzed me on my choices, and finally granted me his approval. You can make this dish in advance and refrigerate or freeze it—just be sure to cover it tightly. To reheat, thaw in the refrigerator, and cook over low-medium heat until the chicken is heated through. It is a great recipe for a quick meal.

Using boneless chicken breasts makes the job all the easier. If I am only going to use the breast meat, and don't have a need for the rest of the chicken, I come out ahead by buying the boneless breasts. When you overlay speed and ease, the boneless skinless breast wins by a mile. This one's for you, Scooby!

Calories—289; Carb—10.3; Fat—20.2; Chol—49; Pro—19.6; Fib—1.4; Sod—870

CHICKEN CASSEROLE ZAUNBRECHER

1 lb. chicken breast meat
1 10 3/4-oz. can condensed cream of mushroom soup
1 10 3/4-oz. can cream of onion soup
1 tsp. Cajun Seasoning Mix (see index)
1/2 cup diced red bell pepper

1/4 cup chopped onion
2 tbsp. minced celery
1 clove garlic, minced
1/4 cup dry white wine
1/4 tsp. Tabasco sauce
2 tbsp. minced fresh parsley
2/3 cup uncooked white rice

Preheat the oven to 350 degrees. Cut the chicken into bite-sized pieces. Mix all ingredients together thoroughly in a large mixing bowl. Pour the mixture into a lightly greased 2 1/2-quart casserole, and bake for about 1 hour until the rice is tender and perfect. Serve hot, straight from the oven. Serves 4.

Lagniappe: This is one those great "can-can" dishes—it is almost as easy as pouring 2 cans together. You can put it into the oven and forget about it. Just in case you do forget about it, you can freeze or refrigerate it after baking. To reheat, just thaw in the refrigerator and heat at 350 degrees for about 7 minutes, or until it is hot.

You can use this recipe to make **Sausage Zaunbrecher** by substituting 1 1/4 pounds of smoked rope sausage (beef, pork, chicken, turkey or mixed). This is a quick and easy version of jambalaya. Using raw rice makes the dish appealing to those who always have problems with cooking the rice. Please don't let the ease of this dish fool you. If you try it, I know you will be pleased.

Calories—431; Carb—33.2; Fat—14.8; Chol—94; Pro—34.2; Fib—.6; Sod—1794

CHICKEN CHRISTINE NOELIE

3 tbsp. olive oil
2 10-oz. chicken breasts,
  skinned
1 1/2 tsp. Cajun Seasoning
  Mix (see index)
3 cloves garlic, minced
3 tbsp. minced celery
3 tbsp. finely chopped
  turnip
3 tbsp. finely chopped
  carrot
3 tbsp. unsalted butter
1 cup chopped green
  onions
2 firm red tomatoes, cut in
  wedges
1/2 medium yellow bell
  pepper, sliced in strips
1/2 red bell pepper, diced
1/3 cup dry white wine
6 large fresh mushrooms,
  sliced
3 cups cooked white long
  grain rice
2 tbsp. minced fresh basil
  (or 1 tsp. dried)
1/2 tsp. Tabasco sauce
1/4 tsp. black pepper
1/4 cup ripe California
  olives, pitted and sliced
  in half
1/2 cups walnuts, lightly
  roasted
1/2 cup minced fresh
  parsley

Heat a very large, heavy skillet over medium-high heat until it is hot; then add the olive oil. While the skillet is heating, cut the chicken into bite-sized pieces, then season them with the **Cajun Seasoning Mix.** When the olive oil begins to smoke, sauté the chicken pieces for 2 minutes, stirring and shaking the skillet often. Add the garlic, celery, turnip, and carrot. Sauté for 2 more minutes, then add the butter. When the butter is melted, add the green onions and tomatoes. Sauté for 1 minute, then add the yellow and red bell pepper and sauté for another minute. Stir in the wine to absorb the pan drippings. Stir in the rice and fresh basil, coating them with the gravy. Add the remaining ingredients, stir in well; then serve, straight from the skillet. Serves 6 to 8.

Lagniappe: Serve this dish with a modest salad, hot fresh bread, and a nice dry white wine. Eat this dish directly after cooking. It is full of crisp vegetables that will lose their freshness if refrigerated or frozen. Total cooking time is well under 10 minutes, so it doesn't take very long anyway. It is mandatory to chop everything prior to cooking because there is not enough time once you get started. The one exception, of course, is the parsley. Chop the parsley just before using it. It loses too much of its flavor if chopped and left to sit. Roll the parsley into a tight ball and cut with a chef's knife.

To roast the walnuts, just heat your skillet and drop the walnuts in. Shake the pan to keep the walnuts moving until you smell a nice toasted aroma; then cook for one more minute.

Calories—414; Carb—35; Fat—21; Chol—65; Pro—22.7; Fib—1.6; Sod—698

CHICKEN LIVERS MARSEILLES

1 1/2 lb. fresh chicken livers
1 1/2 tsp. Cajun Seasoning Mix (see index)
1/2 stick unsalted butter
3 cloves garlic, sliced
2 tbsp. sliced shallots
1 tbsp. whole fresh basil leaves
1 tsp. whole fresh rosemary leaves

1/2 cup all-purpose flour
1/2 cup dry vermouth
2/3 cup chicken stock or chicken broth
1/4 cup chopped green onions
2 tbsp. minced fresh parsley

Clean, drain, and dry the chicken livers. Season them with the **Cajun Seasoning Mix,** and set them aside for later use. Heat a large, heavy skillet over medium heat. When it is hot, melt 1/2 of the butter (that's 1/4 stick) until it begins to smoke. Sauté the garlic, shallots, basil, and rosemary for 2 minutes; then remove them from the skillet and set aside to use later.

Return the skillet to the heat and add the remaining 1/4 stick of butter. While the butter melts, dredge the chicken livers in the flour, shaking off any excess flour. Sauté the livers in the butter after it has begun to smoke again. Cook for about 2 1/2 minutes, browning all sides of the livers. Remove the livers carefully, and place them on a warm platter for later use.

Return the herb mixture to the skillet, and add the wine and stock to deglaze the skillet, making sure the pan drippings are dissolved. Cook until the sauce thickens nicely. Mix in the green onions and parsley. Carefully, return the livers to the skillet and cook, shaking the skillet often, for 1 minute. Serve immediately. Serves 4.

Lagniappe: I am often asked what I would serve with this dish. My answer is never the same because it depends on my mood. Served over cooked noodles is nice; on a bed of rice is superb; with a baked potato is noble; topping stiff mashed potatoes is spectacular; and of course, alone with plenty of hot fresh bread is divine. I guess I am trying to tell you to serve them with the starch of your choice and a green vegetable, like broccoli or asparagus, to add color to the plate.

You can make this dish in advance and refrigerate it, but do not freeze it. Cooked liver breaks apart easily after it has been frozen—leaving you with a tasty mush. I prefer to serve the dish right after it has been cooked. I use white wine (vermouth) in this dish, but you can substitute a nice burgundy or bordeaux for a scrumptious twist!

Calories—451; Carb—16; Fat—22.2; Chol—1115; Pro—45; Fib—.2; Sod—449

POULET MADOLYN

2 large chicken breasts
2 tsp. Cajun Seasoning Mix
  (see index)
3 tbsp. olive oil
3 tbsp. unsalted butter
2 cloves garlic, minced
1/4 cup minced carrots
3 tbsp. minced celery
1 tbsp. minced shallots

1/4 cup sliced water
  chestnuts
1 medium white onion, cut
  in wedges and separated
1 small red bell pepper, cut
  in strips
2/3 cup cognac
cooked long grain white
  rice or noodles

Remove the skin and bones from the chicken breasts. Cut them into bite-sized pieces; then season them with the **Cajun Seasoning Mix** and set aside. Heat a heavy skillet over medium-high heat until hot, then add the olive oil. When the olive oil is hot, add the butter, let it melt and begin to smoke. Sauté the garlic and carrots for 30 seconds;

then add the seasoned chicken breast pieces. Cook, stirring, for about 3 minutes to brown all sides.

Add the celery, shallots, water chestnuts, and white onion; sauté for 3 minutes. Add the red bell pepper, reduce the heat to low, and carefully add the cognac. Strike a match away from the skillet, then tilt the pan a little and bring the match just close enough to ignite the cognac. Be careful at this stage; there will be a burst of flame when the cognac ignites. Let the dish burn itself out. Serve at once over cooked white rice or noodles cooked al dente. Serves 6.

Lagniappe: I would not advocate doing anything in advance other than cutting the vegetables and chicken. The entire recipe has a cooking time of less than 10 minutes, so you will find it both easy and quick.

You should plan on eating all the chicken at one time, but if there are leftovers, you can refrigerate or freeze them for another day. Be forewarned, they just aren't as delectable after refrigeration. This is a dazzling dish that is superb for guests, but uncomplicated enough for everyday fare. With an epicureal quality not often found in such elementary fare, this dish will add zeal to any repast.

Calories—231; Carb—5; Fat—15; Chol—65; Pro—18.6; Fib—.5; Sod—252

CHICKEN CREPES SHANE

2 tbsp. olive oil
1 1/2 tsp. Cajun Seasoning
  Mix (see index)
2 whole chicken breasts,
  skinned and washed
1/2 cup chopped green
  onions
2 tbsp. minced fresh
  parsley

2 tbsp. minced celery
4 large mushrooms, sliced
1 10 3/4-oz. can condensed
  cream of mushroom soup
1 10 3/4-oz. can condensed
  cream of celery soup
1/2 tsp. Tabasco sauce
1 recipe Crepes (see index)
1 cup grated Swiss cheese

Preheat the oven to 350 degrees. Heat a heavy skillet until hot, then add the olive oil. While the oil is heating, season the chicken breasts with the **Cajun Seasoning Mix.** When the oil smokes, fry the chicken over medium-high heat for about 3 minutes on each side. Remove the chicken and chop it into small pieces.

In a large saucepan, combine the chicken, green onions, parsley, celery, mushrooms, soups, and Tabasco sauce and heat over medium heat until it begins to bubble. Spoon generous amounts of the mixture into the middle of each crepe, sprinkle with the grated Swiss cheese, and either fold the crepes over or roll them. Place the stuffed crepes on a lightly greased baking pan. Bake at 350 degrees for 20 minutes and serve hot. Serves 6.

Lagniappe: You can make these crepes in advance and either freeze or refrigerate them until you are ready to serve them. Don't keep them in the refrigerator for more than 2 days. To serve, just thaw in the refrigerator and bake at 300 degrees for about 10 minutes, or until hot.

This is an uncomplicated dinner. I like to serve this with fresh asparagus with a lemon butter or hollandaise sauce and, of course, fresh hot French bread. Crepes always look so appealing and imaginative, but now you see that making them is not so laborious as it seems.

Calories—498; Carb—30; Fat—27.4; Chol—245; Pro—32.4; Fib—.7; Sod—1297

CHICKEN AND SAUSAGE AGUILLARD

1 1/2 lb. rope smoked turkey sausage, sliced

2 large chicked breasts, skinned

1 1/2 tsp. Cajun Seasoning Mix (see index)

1/2 stick unsalted butter

2 cups dark brown sugar

1 1/2 cups light brown sugar

1/2 cup vinegar

1/2 cup port wine

2/3 tsp. Tabasco sauce

1 tbsp. Worcestershire sauce

1 large onion, cut in wedges and separated

1 17-oz. can pineapple chunks, drained

1 medium red bell pepper, cut in chunks

Heat a large, heavy skillet over medium-high heat until it is hot, then fry the sausage until browned. Remove the sausage from the skillet and set it aside.

Cut the chicken into bite-sized pieces and season them with the **Cajun Seasoning Mix.** In a clean skillet, melt the butter until it begins to smoke; then sauté the chicken, stirring often, for about 4 minutes until it is browned and cooked through. Add the brown sugars and cook for about 2 minutes—until it begins to smell like caramel. Blend in the vinegar, wine, Tabasco sauce, and Worcestershire sauce; and cook until the sauce has dissolved the sugar. Add the sausage and the remaining ingredients and cook for 5 minutes at medium-high, then reduce to a low simmer. Let the dish stand at room temperature for 12 to 15 more minutes; then serve hot in a casserole or au gratin dish with plenty of sauce. Serves 6.

Lagniappe: This dish is a takeoff on an old barbecue sauce that my grandmother used to make. I made it sort of contemporary by using a few suggestions I picked up in cooking schools around the country. It makes a nice indoor barbecue for all those rainy days that we get in Louisiana.

You can thicken the sauce with a little cornstarch in water (or arrowroot) to make a sweet sauce to serve over cooked white rice. You can make this dish completely in advance and refrigerate or freeze it for later use. Thaw it in the refrigerator, then heat over medium heat until it is hot.

You can serve this as a main dish or as an hors d'oeuvre. It is grand gala food. Be sure to notice the onion, bell pepper, and pineapple in the dish; they are most zippy.

Calories—500; Carb—90; Fat—19.9; Chol—100; Pro—28.5; Fib—.5; Sod—820

BREAST OF CHICKEN KEBABS

1 medium fresh pineapple
1/4 cup chopped onion
1/4 cup red wine vinegar
1 tbsp. peanut oil
1 tbsp. soy sauce
1 tbsp. Worcestershire
  sauce
2 tbsp. sugar
2 cloves garlic, minced

1/2 tsp. Tabasco sauce
2 tsp. cornstarch
1 whole chicken breast
1/2 tsp. Cajun Seasoning
  Mix (see index)
1 medium red bell pepper
1 medium green bell
  pepper
8 firm red cherry tomatoes

Trim the pineapple and cut it into 1 1/2-inch square chunks. Put 3 of the pineapple chunks with the onion in a food processor or blender, and chop at full power until it is liquified. Add the vinegar, peanut oil, soy sauce, Worcestershire sauce, sugar, garlic, and Tabasco sauce. Blend for 1 more minute. Pour the liquid into a small saucepan and add the cornstarch. Cook, stirring often, until the sauce thickens; then remove from the heat.

Cut the chicken breast into 1-inch pieces, then season them with the **Cajun Seasoning Mix.** Cut the red and green bell peppers into 1-inch pieces and remove the stems from the cherry tomatoes. Thread four 14-inch skewers with a red bell pepper piece, a piece of chicken, a green bell pepper piece, a pineapple chunk, a chicken piece, a cherry tomato, and so on, until you have filled each skewer. Cook the kebabs on an uncovered gas or charcoal grill over a hot fire for about 10 minutes. Baste the kebabs often with the sauce and carefully turn them about 4 times. Serve right off the grill. Serves 4.

Lagniappe: These kebabs and their sauce can be made in advance and refrigerated until you are ready to grill them. You can also cook these kebabs under the broiler in the oven by placing them about 6 inches under the heat source and basting with the sauce for about 15 minutes. Be sure to turn the kebabs several times. I usually make the kebabs the day before I plan on cooking them, and marinate them in the basting sauce overnight. It gives them a greater flavor. Feel free to change the vegetables on the kebabs to whatever you like.

Calories—242; Carb—34.2; Fat—6.1; Chol—37; Pro—15.5; Fib—3.5; Sod—366

BOP CHICKEN

1 3-lb. young chicken fryer
1 tbsp. Tabasco sauce
2 tsp. Cajun Seasoning Mix
  (see index)
1/2 cup pure cane syrup
1 tbsp. Worcestershire
  sauce

1/2 cup cracker crumbs
1/2 cup seasoned bread
  crumbs
1/4 cup corn flakes,
  crushed

Wash and clean the chicken; then cut it into serving pieces and pat them dry with paper towels. Preheat the oven to 400 degrees. Place the chicken in a large mixing bowl with the Tabasco sauce. Move the pieces around until all parts of the chicken are coated; then season with the **Cajun Seasoning Mix.** Combine the syrup and Worcestershire sauce and pour it over the seasoned chicken. Stir the chicken pieces until they are all coated with the syrup mixture. Let the chicken marinate in the syrup mixture for about 7 minutes.

In a large mixing bowl, mix together the cracker crumbs, bread crumbs, and crushed corn flakes. Roll the marinated chicken in the crumb mixture with enough pressure to ensure that plenty of the crumb mixture sticks to the chicken. Lightly grease a shallow baking pan and place the breaded chicken in it. Bake at 400 degrees for about 25 minutes, turning the chicken at about halfway through to brown the other side. Serve hot. Serves 4 to 6.

Lagniappe: You can prepare this chicken in advance up to the baking point. The "Bop" came from the name my brothers and I had for cane syrup. For some unknown reason, we called it "Bop". So "bop" it is. The combination of sweet and pepper in this recipe gives it quite a unique taste.

Calories—806; Carb—51; Fat—26; Chol—257; Pro—87; Fib—.3; Sod—1229

BROILED CHICKEN FONTENOT

1 2 1/2 to 3-lb. chicken
  fryer
1 1/2 tsp. Cajun Seasoning
  Mix (see index)
1/2 cup olive oil
4 cloves garlic, minced
2 tbsp. minced shallots
2 tbsp. fresh whole

rosemary leaves (or 2 tsp.
  dried)
1/4 cup red wine vinegar
1 tsp. hot dry mustard
1 tbsp. sugar
1 tsp. salt
1 tsp. black pepper
1/2 tsp. Tabasco sauce

Cut the chicken into serving pieces. Wash, then dry the chicken with paper towels. Remove the skin if you like, then season with the **Cajun Seasoning Mix** and set it aside for later use.

Heat a small, heavy skillet over high heat. When it is hot, add the oil and heat until it begins to smoke. Sauté the garlic, shallots, and rosemary for 3 minutes over high heat. Remove from the heat, let the oil cool for 1 minute, then carefully stir in the wine vinegar. Mix the remaining ingredients into the seasoned oil. Place the seasoned chicken in a baking pan. Pour the oil mixture over the chicken and cover. The longer you let the chicken sit in the oil before cooking, the more flavorful it will be. When you are ready to cook, set the oven to broil and place the chicken about 5 inches from the heat. Cook for about 12 to 14 minutes per side, basting often with the seasoned oil. Serve hot. Serves 4.

Lagniappe: This basting sauce can be used on other meats as well. Sautéing the garlic, shallots, and rosemary brings out their flavors and blends them into the chicken. You can broil in advance and refrigerate, but I prefer to refrigerate before broiling—you get fresher results. The oil and chicken can be refrigerated for up to 48 hours prior to cooking.

Calories—814; Carb—7.7; Fat—48.8; Chol-255; Pro—83.3; Fib—.2; Sod—1051

ROAST CORNISH HENS CLYDE

4 1-lb. Rock Cornish hens
1 tsp. Cajun Seasoning Mix
(see index)
2 tbsp. unsalted butter,
melted
1/4 tsp. Tabasco sauce

1 tsp. Worcestershire sauce
2 tsp. fresh whole rosemary
leaves
1 recipe Baked Eggplant
Emilie, unbaked stuffing
only (see index)

Preheat the oven to 475 degrees. Wash the hens and pat them dry with paper towels. Season them with the **Cajun Seasoning Mix,** then arrange them in a heavy baking dish so they are not touching each other. In a small bowl, combine the melted butter, Tabasco sauce, and Worcestershire sauce; then brush the hens with the mixture. Sprinkle the hens liberally with half of the fresh rosemary leaves. Bake for 15 minutes, then remove them from the oven and allow them to cool enough to be handled.

Reduce the oven temperature to 400 degrees. Stuff each bird with **Baked Eggplant Emilie** stuffing, and truss the legs together. Brush each hen with the seasoned melted butter and sprinkle with the remaining half of the rosemary. Put the extra eggplant mixture in a casserole dish, and place it in the oven with the hens. Bake for 35 to 40 minutes. Remove from the oven and cut the truss strings. Either serve whole or split the birds in half. Serve on a bed of the extra eggplant mixture. Serves 4 whole.

Lagniappe: I would only recommend serving whole hens if you do not have much else to serve. A half bird is quite sufficient — especially if it's served with plenty of stuffing. This is a wonderful dish for company, but it is superb for Sunday dinner with the family as well — if anyone still eats Sunday dinner with the family.

You can prepare the hens in advance, bake for all but about 10 minutes, then refrigerate or freeze for later use. Be sure to wrap the hens tightly for refrigeration or freezing. If you freeze them, just defrost them in the refrigerator; then bake at 375 degrees for about 15 minutes. Remember that, as with any stuffing, you want to be sure that it is handled properly. Keep it chilled until you are ready to serve.

Calories — 1858; Carb — 34.5; Fat — 94.6; Chol — 610; Pro — 218; Fib — 3; Sod — 1848

TURKEY AU SHERRY

4 turkey cutlets (about 1
  1/4 lb.)
1 tsp. Cajun Seasoning Mix
  (see index)
2/3 cup finely chopped
  onion
1/4 cup minced celery
2 cloves garlic, minced

8 large mushrooms, sliced
2/3 cup cream sherry
1 tbsp. fresh lemon juice
1/4 tsp. Tabasco sauce
1/2 tsp. black pepper
2 tbsp. minced fresh
  parsley
2 tbsp. olive oil

Preheat the oven to 375 degrees. Season the turkey cutlets with the
Cajun Seasoning Mix. Lightly butter the bottom and sides of a shallow 3-quart baking dish. Place the turkey cutlets on the bottom of the
baking dish. Cover them with the onions, celery, garlic, and mushrooms. Combine the sherry, lemon juice, and Tabasco sauce and pour
it over the vegetables. Sprinkle the black pepper and parsley over the
contents of the dish, then drizzle the olive oil over it. Bake uncovered at
375 degrees for 30 minutes. Serve hot with the sauce from the pan on
the side. Serves 4.

Lagniappe: You can put this dish together in advance and store it in
the refrigerator for up to 48 hours before baking it. Keep it tightly covered until you are ready to bake. Do not cook in advance. In order to
experience the full *élan* of the dish, eat it right after it is cooked. I recommend fresh hot bread to soak up the juices. This is quite a savory
and sensible dish.

*Calories—324; Carb—7; Fat—10.6; Chol—48; Pro—46.6; Fib—
.9; Sod—277*

ALMOND TURKEY

4 turkey cutlets (about 1
   1/4 lb.)
1 1/4 tsp. Cajun Seasoning
   Mix (see index)
1/4 cup all-purpose flour
1/2 stick unsalted butter
1 cup slivered almonds
1 cup chopped green
   onions

1/4 tsp. Tabasco sauce
2 tbsp. minced fresh
   parsley
1 tbsp. white
   Worcestershire sauce
1/2 cup sauterne wine

Season the turkey with 1 teaspoon of the **Cajun Seasoning Mix.** In a medium-sized mixing bowl, mix the remaining 1/4 teaspoon with the flour. Lightly dredge the turkey in the seasoned flour and set aside for later use.

Heat a large skillet over medium-high heat. When the skillet is hot, add the butter and let it melt. As the butter begins to smoke, fry the turkey cutlets until they are golden brown, about 2 1/2 minutes per side. Remove them from the skillet and keep them on a warm plate for later use. Add the almonds and green onions to the skillet and sauté for 5 minutes until the almonds become nicely browned. Stir in the remaining ingredients. Return the turkey to the skillet and simmer over low-medium heat for 3 to 5 minutes, or until the turkey is tender. Serve hot. Serves 4.

Lagniappe: This dish is magnificent served with a potato or a sauced noodle side dish. It would also complement any rice casserole. Do not prepare this recipe in advance. The turkey looks and tastes best right from the skillet. Cooking time is minimal for a dish of such gastronomical delight.

Look for turkey cutlets in your supermarket. If you can't find them, ask the poultry manager to either order some or cut some from fresh breast of turkey. These cutlets are white turkey meat that has been sliced to allow for quick cooking. There is very little fat in this meat, yet the taste is great. If you are trying to cut down on cholesterol, just substitute margarine or olive oil for the butter in the recipe.

Calories—526; Carb—15.9; Fat—29.7; Chol—78; Pro—52.2; Fib—1.7; Sod—357

TURKEY SKILLET FRED LAWRENCE

1 1/4 lb. turkey cutlets
1 1/4 tsp. Cajun Seasoning
  Mix (see index)
6 green onions
1/2 stick unsalted butter
1 tbsp. minced shallots
3 cloves garlic, minced
1 1/2 cups chicken stock or
  chicken broth
1 tsp. minced fresh basil
  (or 1/4 tsp. dried)
1 16-oz. pkg. frozen sweet
  peas

1 small red bell pepper, cut
  in strips
6 fresh mushrooms, sliced
1/4 cup shredded carrots
1/4 cup ripe California
  olives, pitted and sliced
2 tbsp. cornstarch
1 tbsp. fresh lemon juice
1/4 tsp. Tabasco sauce
1/3 cup dry white wine
cooked white long grain or
  brown rice

Spread out the turkey cutlets on half of a long piece of plastic wrap on top of your cutting board. Fold the other half of the wrap over the cutlets and pound them with a kitchen mallet until they have increased in size by 1/3. Cut the turkey into strips about 3 inches long and 1 inch wide. Season the turkey with the **Cajun Seasoning Mix.** Cut the green onions into pieces 3 inches long, then cut each piece lengthwise into four 3-inch slivers.

Heat a large, heavy skillet over medium heat. When it is hot, melt the butter until it begins to smoke. Add the turkey and brown on both sides for about 3 minutes. Add the green onion, shallots, and garlic and sauté them with the turkey for about 3 more minutes. Add the chicken stock, basil, and frozen peas and bring the liquid to a boil. Reduce the temperature to simmer for about 10 minutes. Add the red bell pepper, mushrooms, carrots, and olives; and continue simmering for 3 more minutes.

Blend together the cornstarch, lemon juice, Tabasco sauce and white wine until the cornstarch is dissolved. Add the mixture to the skillet and the sauce should begin to thicken. Serve hot over the cooked white or brown rice. Serves 6.

Lagniappe: Turkey cutlets make this dish easy because they require almost no preparation. Sometimes you might find them referred to as turkey tenderloin. They are just raw turkey breast meat sliced into thin cutlets. You can use this recipe to make **Chicken Skillet Fred Lawrence** by using 1 1/4 pounds of fresh, boneless and skinless chicken breast. Pound the chicken breast until it is about 3/8-inch thick before cutting it into strips. Follow the rest of the recipe as directed.

You can make this dish in advance and refrigerate, but I don't recommend freezing it. You can also be a little inventive and mix a little wild rice with the brown or white rice. It makes a dazzling dish.

Calories—334; Carb—18; Fat—13.5; Chol—53; Pro—36; Fib—3.7; Sod—574

TURKEY HAMIC

4 turkey cutlets (about 1 1/4 lb.)

1 1/2 tsp. Cajun Seasoning Mix (see index)

1/4 cup all-purpose flour

1/4 cup seasoned bread crumbs

2 tbsp. olive oil

2 tbsp. unsalted butter

1 cup julienned carrots (cut into thin strips about 2 inches long)

1 cup julienned yellow squash, unpeeled

1/2 cups julienned celery

1/4 cup diced red bell pepper

1 tbsp. minced fresh basil (or 1 tsp. dried)

1 7-oz. jar whole fresh straw mushrooms, drained

1 cup champagne

1 cup chicken stock or chicken broth

1/2 cup heavy whipping cream

1/2 cup minced fresh parsley

Season the turkey with 1 teaspoon of the **Cajun Seasoning Mix** and combine the other 1/2 teaspoon with the flour and bread crumbs in a medium-sized mixing bowl. Lightly dredge the turkey in the flour mixture; then set it aside for later use.

Heat a large skillet over medium-high heat. When the skillet is hot, add the olive oil, let it start to smoke, then melt the butter. Just as the butter begins to smoke, add the turkey cutlets and fry them until they are a golden brown, about 2 1/2 minutes per side.

Stir in the remaining ingredients, except for the cream and parsley. Cover the skillet, reduce the heat to low-medium, and let the dish simmer for 8 to 10 minutes until the turkey is tender. Remove the turkey and the vegetables from the skillet and place them on a warm plate. Raise the heat to medium and bring the sauce to a boil. Stir in the cream and parsley until the sauce thickens—but do not allow it to boil again. Spoon the sauce over the cutlets and vegetables. Serve hot. Serves 4.

Lagniappe: This dish is splendid to serve with a potato dish, rice casserole or a sauced noodle dish. Because the vegetables are cooked with the meat, you only need a starch, and perhaps a green salad, with plenty of hot fresh bread to make an sumptuous meal.

Do not cook this dish in advance. The turkey is at its best straight from the skillet. Cooking time is minimal and the resulting dish qualifies as an epicureal repast. Using cutlets allows you the bounty of turkey without the time requirement. It is a great idea that I'm sure will be a boon for the turkey industry!

Calories—539; Carb—21.4; Fat—27.6; Chol—105; Pro—52.1; Fib—1.4; Sod—1047

PAN FRIED TURKEY

1/4 cup peanut oil
4 turkey cutlets (about
  1 1/4 lb.)

3 tsp. Cajun Seasoning Mix
  (see index)

Heat a large, heavy skillet (I recommend a black iron skillet) over high heat. When it is hot, add the peanut oil and heat it until it smokes. Season the cutlets generously with the **Cajun Seasoning Mix,** pushing the seasoning into the meat with your fingers.

Add the cutlets to the skillet, one at a time, until all four are in the pan. Allow the oil to heat up slightly between each addition to the skillet. Cook the cutlets about 1 1/2 minutes on each side. Be sure to have your stove hood fan on because this will smoke quite a bit. Remove the cutlets from the skillet, place them on a plate, cover with foil, and set in a 170-degree oven until you are ready to serve. Remove the skillet from the heat as soon as the last cutlet is removed. Serve soon after cooking. Serves 4.

Lagniappe: I really like this dish. It uses an old Cajun technique called "pan frying." In the old days, the houses had large windows, no air conditioning, but plenty of cross breeze. While the dinner was cooking, the house filled with smoke. All the windows and doors were opened, and out went the smoke and offending odors. I would not advise cooking this dish indoors unless you have a great kitchen vent. After you remove the oil from the heat, let it cool. When it is completely cool, put about 4 or 5 paper towels into the oil. They will soak it up and make cleaning up easier. Never pour the oil down your drain.

The outside of the cutlets will be very dark (blackened), but the turkey will be quite juicy and will not taste burnt at all. It will also not be as spicy hot as you might imagine. There is nothing you can do in advance for this recipe, but it cooks so quickly that you won't need much preparation time. Some might call this dish "Blackened Turkey," but I opt to use the name my grandmother gave it. Either way, it is good eating. Bon appetit!

Calories—216; Carb—.8; Fat—10; Chol—45; Pro—45.3; Fib—0; Sod—560

Meats

PERFECT ROAST

1 6 to 7-lb. beef roast
3 cloves garlic, quartered
1/2 large shallot bulb,
  chopped into 9 pieces
1/2 green bell pepper, cut
  into 9 pieces
2 tsp. Cajun Seasoning Mix
  (see index)
1 cup dry hearty burgundy
  wine

1 cup beef stock, beef
  broth, or water
1 large onion, sliced in thin
  strips
1/4 cup diced red or green
  bell pepper
2 tbsp. minced fresh
  parsley

Stuff the roast with the garlic, shallot, and bell pepper. Push the **Cajun Seasoning Mix** into the holes containing the vegetables. Set the oven to broil, and cook for 15 to 20 minutes. Don't worry if it looks burned—it will just make the gravy darker. Reduce the temperature to 300 degrees, and cook uncovered for about 25 minutes per pound, or until the roast is tender.

When cooked, remove the roast and add the onion, bell pepper, and parsley. Deglaze the pan drippings by adding the burgundy wine and the beef stock. Stir over low heat until all the drippings are dissolved to give body and flavor to the gravy. Slice the roast just before you are ready to serve. Spoon a little gravy on top each the slice. Serve warm. Serves 8.

Lagniappe: I included this recipe for everyone who wants to cook a roast, but really doesn't know how. It is not difficult, but it is a premier dish that every cook must know how to create. Although the cooking time is out of the quick range, the recipe definitely falls into the easy category.

For variety, you can use other liquids to deglaze the drippings. Sometimes, I use a cup of strong coffee instead of the beef stock, it has a unique flavor and a splendid color. I also use red wine vinegar to give a little punch to the gravy. When I use the red wine vinegar, I substitute 1/2 cup of vinegar for half of the beef stock. When nothing else is available, I use plain water and the gravy comes out fine. The choice of liquids is yours. The point is that a liquid is necessary to deglaze the pan drippings (lift them into the liquid to make a glaze or a somewhat thickened gravy).

You might consider substituting a hot pepper for the bell pepper used to stuff the roast. You cannot imagine how scrumptious this is. Use tabasco peppers, jalapeno peppers, or cayenne peppers (leave the seeds in the cayenne) to add zest and intensity to your beef. This roast will win you raves with your family or your guests. Give it a try.

Calories—790; Carb—4.8; Fat—33.3; Chol—331; Pro—115.4; Fib—.3; Sod—504

TENDERLOIN OF BEEF CREOLE

1 1/2 lb. beef tenderloin, whole and trimmed
1 1/2 tsp. Cajun Seasoning Mix (see index)
1/4 cup unsalted butter
1 cup chopped green onions
2 tbsp. minced shallots
1 clove garlic, minced
2 tbsp. finely minced turnip

1/2 cup cognac
1 tsp. fresh thyme (or 1/4 tsp. dried)
1/4 tsp. Tabasco sauce
1 cup beef stock or beef broth
2 tbsp. Creole mustard
2 tbsp. unsalted butter, very cold
2 tbsp. minced fresh parsley

Cut the tenderloin into 4 steaks of about 6 ounces each. Season the steaks with the **Cajun Seasoning Mix** and set them aside. Heat a heavy skillet over medium-high heat. When it is hot, add the butter. When it begins to smoke, cook the seasoned steaks for about 3 minutes on each side for medium rare, or 4 minutes for medium. Remove the steaks from the skillet. Place them on a warm platter or in the oven at 170 degrees, covered loosely with foil.

Add the green onions, shallots, garlic, and turnip to the skillet and sauté for 3 minutes. Remove from the heat and carefully add the cognac. Return to the heat and flambé by lighting the cognac with the flame from the heat or a match. Be careful because cognac produces a hot flame. Do not do anything but let the flame burn itself out.

When the fire is out, stir in the thyme. Add the Tabasco sauce and beef stock, and bring to a boil. Cook until the liquid is reduced by about half. The remaining sauce should be somewhat thick. Use a wire whisk to blend in the Creole mustard, then swirl in the butter, 1/2 tablespoon at a time. Do not allow the sauce to boil again. Stir in the parsley, and serve the steaks with generous amounts of the hot creole sauce. Serves 4.

Lagniappe: Beef tenderloin is an excellent beef to serve for taste and for health. It is low in saturated fats and calories. It cooks quickly and is quite tender (hence the name *tenderloin*). Sauces that complement beef tenderloin are not heavy or overpowering. They need to have depth and class without weighing you down.

Again, let me caution you about flambé. It is pretty, and you cannot get the unique flavor without the flame, so do be careful. Alcohol flames get quite hot—do not try anything fancy like lifting or pouring the flame. Just gently shake the pan and let the flame die by itself. You get all of the flavor and all of the credit (credit for not burning down the place, that is!)

Calories—543; Carb—5.6; Fat—35; Chol—194; Pro—50; Fib—.4; Sod—572

TENDERLOIN OF BEEF WITH CHANTERELLES MUSHROOMS

2 tbsp. olive oil
2 tbsp. unsalted butter
1 lb. fresh chanterelles
   mushrooms, cut in half
2 tsp. minced fresh shallots
1 clove garlic, minced
12 2 to 3-oz. slices beef
   tenderloin
3/4 cup beef stock or beef
   broth

1/4 cup dry burgundy wine
1/4 tsp. Tabasco sauce
1 tbsp. fresh sage (or 1/4
   tsp. dried)
1 leaf fresh mint (or a pinch
   dried)
1 tsp. salt
1 tsp. black pepper

Heat a large skillet over medium heat. When it is hot, add the olive oil, heat it, then add the butter. When the butter is melted, sauté the mushrooms, shallots, and garlic for about 5 minutes until the mushrooms are lightly browned. Remove from the heat, place the mushrooms in a bowl, and set them aside for later use.

Reheat the skillet; then cook the slices of beef over medium heat for 3 minutes on each side. Remove the beef from the skillet to a warm plate. Use a paper towel to soak up about half of the grease in the skillet; then put it back on the heat. Add the broth, wine, and Tabasco sauce. Turn the heat up to high and bring it to a boil. Reduce the sauce by half; then add the remaining the ingredients. Turn the heat down to medium, add the mushroom mixture, and heat until it is hot. Spoon the sauce over the tenderloins and serve at once. Serves 6.

Lagniappe: This is elegant dining for guests. The price is quite reasonable for dinner for six, and the look is quite special. You may substitute oyster mushrooms, or even regular mushrooms if chanterelles are not available. I don't recommend doing any of this in advance, and I definitely don't recommend freezing this recipe. Make it, then serve it.

Calories—398; Carb—3.2; Fat—17.6; Chol—102; Pro—33.7; Fib—.7; Sod—557

BEEF TENDERLOIN DEBBIE

1 bunch green onions
1 large firm red tomato
3 tbsp. unsalted butter
1 tbsp. minced shallots
3 cloves garlic minced
3 tbsp. minced celery
1 1/4 lb. heavy beef
tenderloin, trimmed
1 1/2 tsp. Cajun Seasoning
Mix (see index)
1/3 cup cognac
1/2 medium orange or red
bell pepper, sliced in
strips

2 7-oz. jars whole straw
mushrooms, drained
1 tbsp. minced fresh
oregano (or 1 tsp. dried)
1/2 tsp. fresh thyme (or 1/8
tsp. dried)
1/2 tsp. Tabasco sauce
1/4 tsp. black pepper
1/2 cup minced fresh
parsley
cooked white rice or
noodles cooked al dente

Cut the green onions into 3-inch pieces, then slice them lengthwise in half. Peel the tomato, remove the seeds, dice it, and set both vegetables aside for later use. Heat a very large, heavy skillet over medium-high heat. When it is hot, melt the butter until it begins to smoke, then sauté the garlic, shallots, and celery for 2 minutes, stirring and shaking the skillet often.

While the garlic and vegetables are sautéing, slice the tenderloin into strips about 1/4 inch thick. Season well with the **Cajun Seasoning Mix.** After the 2 minutes, add the seasoned tenderloin to the skillet and sauté for 2 more minutes. Deglaze the skillet by adding the cognac, shaking it around, and stirring with a spoon. Carefully put a lit match just over the skillet to flambé. Be careful, there will be a big burst of flame. Flambé, shaking the pan a little, until the flame goes out. Add the green onions, tomato, orange bell pepper, straw mushrooms, oregano, and thyme and sauté for 2 minutes. Stir in the Tabasco sauce, black pepper, and parsley. Serve at once over cooked white rice or noodles. Serves 6.

Lagniappe: Serve this dish with an unpretentious salad, fresh hot bread, and a dry red wine. This dish is best if served right after it is cooked. It is easy, filled with a wide variety of flavors, and most tasty. Because total cooking time is under 10 minutes, it isn't necessary to cook in advance and refrigerate. However, everything must be chopped in advance of cooking because the dish moves fast. The one exception is, of course, the parsley. Chop the parsley just before using it. It loses too much of its flavor if chopped and left to sit. Just roll the parsley into a tight ball and cut it with a chef's knife.

If you are not familiar with the straw mushroom, I assure you that you will be pleased with them. Although they come in a jar, the quality is remarkable. They get their name from where they grow, not how they look. They grow in straw beds. Flavorful and quite pretty, they add ambience to your recipe. The same can be said for the orange bell pepper. It is relatively new on the scene, quite flavorful, and attractive. All in all, I think you will find this dish entertaining, delectable, and stunning.

Calories—280; Carb—7; Fat—15.7; Chol—97; Pro—28.5; Fib—.8; Sod—228

QUICK POTATO PIE

1 lb. ground chuck
1 medium onion, chopped
1/2 cup minced celery
3 cloves garlic, minced
1 medium bell pepper, diced
1 tsp. minced fresh basil
1/2 tsp. chopped fresh rosemary
1/2 cup chopped green onions
1 15-oz. can tomato sauce
1 1/2 tsp. Cajun Seasoning Mix (see index)
1/4 tsp. Tabasco sauce
1 17-oz. can whole kernel corn, drained

1 17-oz. can green beans, drained
2 large white baked potatoes, warm
1/2 stick salted butter
1/2 cup milk
1/2 tsp. black pepper
1/2 tsp. salt
vegetable oil spray
1/2 cup grated American cheese
1/2 cup grated Swiss cheese
1/4 cup grated sharp cheddar cheese
paprika

Preheat the oven to 375 degrees. Heat a large, heavy skillet over medium-high heat. When it is hot, add the ground chuck and cook until the meat is browned, about 2 minutes. Add the onion, celery, garlic, bell pepper, basil, rosemary, and green onions; and sauté with the meat for about 4 more minutes. Stir in the tomato sauce, **Cajun Seasoning Mix,** Tabasco sauce, corn, and green beans. Cook, stirring often, for 7 minutes.

Peel the two baked potatoes and mash them with the butter, milk, pepper, and salt in a large mixing bowl. Use an electric mixer or a wire whisk to whip the mashed potatoes until they are light. Spray the bottom and sides of a 2 1/2-quart casserole with the vegetable oil spray. Pour the ground meat mixture into the casserole. Spread the mashed potatoes evenly over the meat mixture, sprinkle the grated cheeses over the potatoes, and lightly dust with paprika. Bake at 375 degrees for 15 to 20 minutes, or until the potatoes are golden brown and all the cheese has melted. Serve hot. Serves 4.

Lagniappe: This is an easy way to put your whole meal into one dish. You've got your meat, vegetables, gravy, and cheese—all in one delicious dish. Pop it in the oven, and you've got an instant meal. You can make this dish in advance and refrigerate it, but I don't recommend freezing it. The potatoes just don't freeze well. Reheat in the microwave covered loosely with wax paper, or put it back into the oven at 300 degrees for about 15 to 20 more minutes until it is hot.

Calories—496; Carb—52.5; Fat—45.1; Chol—195; Pro—56.6; Fib—3.6; Sod—1518

GOOD OLE MEATLOAF

3 tbsp. peanut oil
1 small onion, chopped
2 ribs celery, chopped
3 cloves garlic, minced
1 small bell pepper, diced
1/2 cup chopped green
  onions
1 tbsp. minced fresh basil
  (or 1 tsp. dried)
1/4 tsp. crushed red pepper
1 1/3 lb. ground round
1 1/3 tsp. Cajun Seasoning
  Mix (see index)

1/4 tsp. Tabasco sauce
1 tbsp. Worcestershire
  sauce
2 large brown eggs, beaten
1/2 cup cornflakes
1/2 cup cracker crumbs
1/4 cup seasoned bread
  crumbs
1/4 cup catsup
1/4 cup chili sauce

Preheat the oven to 400 degrees. Heat a heavy skillet over medium heat. When it is hot, heat the peanut oil until it starts to smoke, then add the onion, celery, garlic, bell pepper, and green onions. Sauté for 4 minutes, then add the basil and red pepper and sauté for 1 more minute. Remove from the heat and set aside for later use.

In a large mixing bowl, season the ground round with the **Cajun Seasoning Mix,** Tabasco sauce, and Worcestershire sauce. Work in the remaining ingredients and the sautéed vegetables with your hands. Shape the meatloaf and place it in a large loaf pan. Bake at 400 degrees for about 40 minutes. Allow it to cool slightly before you cut it. Cut it into 1/2 to 1-inch thick slices and serve hot. Serves 4.

Lagniappe: This is a splendid tangy-tasting meatloaf. It is even good cold. You can make it completely in advance, and refrigerate or freeze it until you are ready to use it. To reheat, just defrost in the refrigerator and bake at 300 degrees for about 10 to 12 minutes. Meatloaf also reheats well by the slice in the microwave—you don't have to reheat the whole loaf for one serving.

Calories—594; Carb—34.6; Fat—26.5; Chol—283; Pro—56.3; Fib—1; Sod—1141

CASSEROLE DE PROVINCE

2 tbsp. olive oil
1/4 cup butter
1 small yellow bell pepper,
   cut in strips
1 small red bell pepper,
   diced
1 small orange bell pepper,
   chopped
1 large onion, chopped
2 stalks celery, minced
3 cloves garlic, minced
1/2 cup beef stock or beef
   broth
1 14 3/4-oz. can stewed
   tomatoes

1 4-oz. can tomato sauce
1/2 tsp. Tabasco sauce
2 tsp. Cajun Seasoning Mix
   (see index)
2 lb. ground round
8 large mushrooms, sliced
1 12-oz. pkg. twisted
   macaroni, cooked al
   dente
1 cup grated mozzarella
   cheese
1 cup grated sharp cheddar
   cheese

Preheat the oven to 375 degrees. Heat a large, heavy skillet over medium-high heat. When it is hot, heat the oil and butter until they begin to smoke; then sauté the peppers, onion, celery, and garlic for about 6 minutes until they are lightly browned. Add the stock, tomatoes, tomato sauce, and Tabasco sauce; reduce the heat to medium and let the sauce simmer.

Season the ground round with the **Cajun Seasoning Mix.** Gradually stir the seasoned meat into the hot sauce, stirring constantly until all the meat is in the sauce. Add the mushrooms and cooked macaroni and cook for 1 minute. Remove from the heat, and fold in the the mozzarella cheese. Pour into a 3-quart casserole and top with the cheddar cheese. Bake at 375 degrees for 25 minutes. Serve hot. Serves 6.

Lagniappe: This is an easy casserole that can be made in advance, baked, and stored in the refrigerator or freezer. To reheat, just defrost it in the refrigerator and bake for 15 minutes at 350 degrees. This is a one-dish meal—a real treat that is easy to do. Serve with a nice salad and fresh hot bread.

Calories—814; Carb—55; Fat—38; Chol—240; Pro—68; Fib—1.5; Sod—895

EGGPLANT CASSEROLE LA LANDE

1 lb. ground chuck
2 medium eggplants,
 peeled and diced
1 1/2 cups chopped fresh
 bread
1 medium onion, finely
 chopped
1/3 cup chopped bell
 pepper
2 cloves garlic, minced
1/4 cup minced fresh
 parsley

1 1/2 tsp. Cajun Seasoning
 Mix (see index)
1/2 tsp. chopped fresh
 thyme (or a pinch dried)
1 large egg, slightly beaten
1/2 tsp. Tabasco sauce
1 tbsp. Worcestershire
 sauce
1/4 cup catsup
1 1/4 cups cracker crumbs
paprika

Preheat the oven to 350 degrees. Combine all the ingredients, except for the cracker crumbs and paprika, and pour the mixture into a 2-quart casserole. Cover with the cracker crumbs and sprinkle lightly with paprika. Bake at 350 degrees for one hour. Serves 6.

Lagniappe: Is this easy or what? You don't have to cook the meat. You don't have to boil the eggplant. All you do is mix it together and bake it. You can make this dish in advance and either refrigerate or freeze it for later use. Completely cook it, allow it to cool, then wrap it tightly and freeze or refrigerate. I use about 3 layers of plastic wrap and, as always, I label and date it.

It is important to date everything that you put into the freezer. When you are searching for items to use, you can check the dates to avoid guessing how long something has been in the freezer. If you are going to freeze this dish, I advise using individual casserole dishes so you can pull out just the number of servings you need. The casserole makes a marvelous stuffing, or it can be sliced like a meat loaf after it cools somewhat.

Calories—441; Carb—33.4; Fat—20; Chol—123; Pro—31; Fib—19; Sod—616

BAKED EGGPLANT EMILIE

2 medium eggplants
1 tbsp. salt
2 tbsp. olive oil
1 lb. ground round
2 slices raw bacon, finely
  chopped
1 cup chopped onion
1/2 cup chopped celery
1 tsp. fresh rosemary leaves
  (or 1/4 tsp. dried)
1/2 cup chopped bell
  pepper

2 cloves garlic, minced
6 slices bread, toasted
1/2 tsp. Tabasco sauce
1 tsp. Worcestershire sauce
3 tbsp. dry vermouth
1/2 cup beef stock or beef
  broth
2 tsp. Cajun Seasoning Mix
  (see index)

Preheat the oven to 375 degrees. Place the whole eggplants in a large saucepan, cover them with water, and add the salt. The eggplants will float, so use enough water to cover them if they were submerged. Bring to a boil over high heat for 7 minutes. While they are boiling, turn them over once or twice with a spoon. Remove the eggplants from the water, and let them cool enough to be handled. Cut them in half, and scoop out the pulp with a melon scoop, leaving about 1/4-inch of pulp around the husk. Reserve the pulp and the husk for later use.

Heat a large, heavy skillet over medium-high heat. When it is hot, add the olive oil and tilt the skillet to spread the oil over the entire bottom of it. Add the ground round, bacon, onion, celery, rosemary, and eggplant pulp; then brown the meat for about 3 minutes over medium-high heat. Add the bell pepper and garlic, cook for 3 more minutes, then remove from the heat.

Chop the toasted bread into small pieces and add it, with the remaining ingredients, to the eggplant mixture. Blend together well, and stuff the mixture into the eggplant husks. Place in a lightly greased baking dish, and bake for 25 minutes at 375 degrees. Serve hot. Serves 4 as an entree or cut in half for a side dish.

Lagniappe: If you don't want to bake the mixture in the eggplant husk, you can pour it into individual casseroles or a 2-quart baking dish. I like to serve it in the husk because it looks so distinguished.

You can make this dish in advance and either refrigerate or freeze it.

If you freeze it, bake the dish completely and wrap it tightly. Defrost it in the refrigerator, and bake at 350 degrees for about 12 minutes. If you are going to refrigerate it for less than 48 hours, do not bake it in advance. Put the recipe together, stuff the husks, then cover and refrigerate them. Bake as above.

Calories—623; Carb—34; Fat—28; Chol—152; Pro—69; Fib—3; Sod—1431

STUFFED TURNIPS DANIELLE

8 large turnips
1 recipe Eggplant Casserole
  La Lande, unbaked (see index)

Wash the turnips and cut off the greens and roots. Scrub lightly to remove all dirt. Place the turnips in a steamer or a large pot with a little water on the bottom. Cover and steam for about 15 minutes. While turnips are steaming, prepare the eggplant casserole according to the recipe. When the turnips are steamed and cooled enough to handle, scoop out the center of each turnip, leaving about 3/8 inch of turnip around the sides.

Preheat the oven to 350 degrees. Finely chop the removed turnip pulp and mix it into the eggplant casserole dish. Stuff the turnip shells with as much of the eggplant mixture as possible. Top each turnip with the cracker crumbs from the eggplant casserole dish, sprinkle with paprika, and bake for one hour at 350 degrees. Serve hot. Serves 8.

Lagniappe: This dish lends itself well to advance preparation. You can prepare and bake the dish, allow it to cool, then refrigerate or freeze it for later use. To reheat, just defrost in the refrigerator and bake for 10 minutes at 375 degrees. Stuffed turnips make a nice entree or a great side dish.

You can make **Stuffed Bell Pepper Mire** by substituting 8 large bell peppers (the color of your choice) for the turnips. Wash the bell peppers, cut off the tops, and remove the seeds. Steam the peppers for only 5 minutes; then stuff and bake them just as you would the turnips.

Calories—373; Carb—36.5; Fat—15.3; Chol—923; Pro—25.2; Fib—2.3; Sod—579

STUFFED ACORN SQUASH DORALIZE

4 whole acorn squash
1/2 lb. ground chuck
1/2 lb. mild country
  sausage
1 cup chopped fresh French
  bread
1/3 cup diced bell pepper
3 cloves garlic, minced
1/2 cup minced fresh
  parsley

1/4 cup minced celery
1 1/2 tsp. Cajun Seasoning
  Mix (see index)
1 tsp. minced fresh basil
1/2 tsp. Tabasco sauce
1 tbsp. Worcestershire
  sauce
1 1/2 cups cracker crumbs
paprika

Preheat the oven to 375 degrees. Cut each squash in half. Scoop out the seeds and stringy pieces with a spoon. Place the squash halves flat side down in a baking pan. Add enough water to fill the pan to about 1 inch. Bake at 375 degrees for 15 minutes. Remove from the oven, pour off the water, and let the squash cool enough to be handled.

Raise the oven temperature to 450 degrees. Scoop most of the pulp out of the squash, leaving about 3/8 inch around the shell. Place the pulp in a large mixing bowl with the remaining ingredients, except for the 1 cup of the cracker crumbs and the paprika. Mix together well. Stuff each squash shell with the stuffing mixture. Top with the 1 cup of cracker crumbs, and dust with paprika. Bake at 450 degrees for 15 minutes; then reduce the heat to 375 and bake for 25 more minutes. Remove and serve at once. Serves 8.

Lagniappe: You can make this recipe completely in advance, then refrigerate or freeze it for later use. Should you freeze it, be sure to defrost it in the refrigerator; then bake at 350 degrees for about 15 minutes until it is hot.

Stuffed acorn squash makes a nice entree, especially if you can find some squash with mixed coloring. It is a truly sublime side dish as well. You will find this dish in the meat section of the book because this is where it belongs (a rather strong statement, don't you think?). The country sausage adds a definite tang to this recipe.

Calories—446; Carb—49; Fat—19; Chol—53; Pro—19.7; Fib—2.8; Sod—641

LAMB CHOPS GERMAIN

4 large lamb chops, about
1-inch thick
1 1/2 tsp. Cajun Seasoning
Mix (see index)
2 tbsp. olive oil
2 tbsp. unsalted butter
2 cloves garlic, minced
1 tbsp. minced shallots
1 tbsp. minced celery
2 tbsp. chopped fresh sage
(or 1 tsp. dried)

1 tbsp. chopped fresh
rosemary (or 1/2 tsp.
dried)
1/2 cup hearty burgundy
wine
1/2 cup beef stock or beef
broth
1 tsp. Dijon mustard
2 tbsp. unsalted butter,
chilled

Season the lamb chops with the **Cajun Seasoning Mix.** Heat a heavy skillet over medium heat. Once it is hot, heat the olive oil to the smoking point, then swirl in the butter until it melts. Add the garlic, shallots, celery, sage, and rosemary; then sauté for 1 minute before adding the lamb chops. Sauté the lamb chops for 4 minutes on each side, then remove them to a warm plate. Add the wine and broth to the skillet, raise the temperature to high, and bring it to a boil. Scrape the bottom of the pan to dissolve any meat drippings.

When the liquid is reduced by half, lower the heat to low-medium and whip in the mustard with a wire whisk. Cut the chilled butter into 4 pieces, and whisk in one piece at a time to produce a thickened sauce. Glaze the lamb chops with the sauce and serve the remainder of the sauce on the side. Serve warm. Serves 4.

Lagniappe: The technique of adding liquid to a skillet in which a meat has cooked is called *deglazing.* It is the dissolving of the pan drippings that gives the sauce its taste. You can use almost any liquid to deglaze. You are actually dissolving starches and sugars from the meat into the sauce, thus producing a somewhat thick, brown sauce with a sweet taste. Lamb is really wonderful to cook. It should never be cooked more than medium rare—it begins to toughen when it is overcooked. If cooked right, the meat is quite tender and the flavor is lovely.

Calories—498; Carb—2.8; Fat—25.8; Chol—49.5; Pro—1.1; Fib—.3; Sod—335

LAMB CHOPS ANDREE

2 tbsp. unsalted butter
4 lamb chops, about 3/4-inch thick
1 tsp. Cajun Seasoning Mix (see index)
1 small onion, thinly sliced
2 cups seedless green grapes
1 cup whole ripe California olives
2 cups chicken stock or chicken broth

1 cup dry white wine
3 tbsp. cornstarch
1/4 cup cold water
1/2 tsp. Tabasco sauce
2 tbsp. crushed fresh mint leaves
2 tbsp. light brown sugar
2 tbsp. honey
2 tsp. vanilla extract
1/4 cup finely chopped green onion tops

Heat a large skillet over medium heat. When it is hot, melt the butter and let it begin to sizzle. Fry the chops for 3 minutes on each side; then place them on a warm plate, sprinkle with the **Cajun Seasoning Mix,** and keep warm until you are ready to serve.

Sauté the onion, grapes, and olives in the skillet for 5 minutes. Add the stock and wine, and bring them to a boil, allowing the liquid to reduce by half. In a bowl, combine the cornstarch, water, Tabasco sauce, mint, sugar, honey, and vanilla. Stir until the cornstarch is dissolved. Pour the mixture into the skillet, and stir until the sauce thickens. Arrange a bed of rice on each plate, place a lamb chop in the center of the rice, and cover it generously with the sauce. Sprinkle with green onion tops. Serve hot. Serves 4.

Lagniappe: This is a pretty dish. Get everything ready before you start to cook because the recipe moves quite fast. This is a nice dish to introduce someone to lamb. The grape-mint sauce brings out the wonderful flavor of the lamb. To keep the chops warm while you finish cooking, just put them in a 170-degree oven until you are ready for them—they should stay hot without continuing to cook.

Calories—660; Carb—34.5; Fat—36; Chol—151; Pro—57.7; Fib—2.7; Sod—1264

LAMB CHOPS OAKLEY

8 3 to 3 1/2-oz. trimmed rib
lamb chops, about 3/4-
inch thick
1 1/2 tsp. Cajun Seasoning
Mix (see index)
2 tbsp. olive oil

1/2 stick unsalted butter
3 cloves garlic, minced
2 medium white onions,
sliced and separated
2 tbsp. minced celery
2/3 cup brandy

Season the lamb chops with the **Cajun Seasoning Mix** and set aside. Heat a heavy skillet over medium-high heat. Heat the olive oil until it is hot, then melt the butter until it begins to smoke. Add the garlic and sauté for 30 seconds before adding the seasoned lamb chops. Brown the chops for about 3 minutes on each side. Remove the chops to a platter and keep warm.

Add the onions and celery to the skillet, and sauté for 3 minutes. Return the chops to the skillet, reduce the heat to low, and carefully add the brandy. Strike a match away from the skillet; then, while tilting the pan slightly, lite the brandy. Be careful at this stage. Let the dish burn until it burns itself out. Immediately serve the chops covered with sautéed onion rings. Serves 4.

Lagniappe: I would not encourage doing anything in advance for this dish. It has a cooking time of less than 10 minutes, so it is quick as well as easy. You should plan on eating all of the chops at one sitting—they just aren't as scrumptious as leftovers. This is a flashy dish that is excellent for company but easy enough for everyday fare.

Calories—560; Carb—5.5; Fat—34; Chol—189; Pro—63.7; Fib—.3; Sod—892

DEBBIE'S RED BEANS

1 stick unsalted butter
1 small onion, chopped
3/4 cup chopped green
  onions
2 cloves garlic, minced
1/4 cup finely chopped
  celery
1 1/2 cup chopped ham
3 15-oz. cans New Orleans-
  style red kidney beans

1 tbsp. Worcestershire
  sauce
1 tsp. salt
1/2 tsp. Tabasco sauce
1/2 tsp. black pepper
1/2 tsp. garlic powder
1/2 to 1 cup cold water
2 tbsp. minced fresh
  parsley
cooked white rice

Heat a large saucepan over medium heat. When it is hot, add the butter and heat until it begins to smoke. Add the onion, green onion, garlic, and celery; then sauté for 5 minutes over medium heat. Add the ham and sauté for 4 more minutes. Pour the beans and their liquid from the cans into the saucepan and stir through.

Add the remaining ingredients, except for the water and parsley. Adjust the consistency of the liquid to your preference by adding the water, 1/4 cup at a time, until you get the thickness you want. Cook, uncovered, for 10 minutes over low-medium heat; then blend in the parsley and serve over cooked white rice. Serves 6.

Lagniappe: This is one of my wife's first recipes. The first time I ate this, I couldn't believe that she made it with canned beans. I thought she was lying (or kidding). When you sit down to eat, it is really hard to tell this from the long, soak-the-beans-all-night recipe. In fact, I think this recipe is better—at least to my tastes. Timewise, this is really quick and easy. Compare for yourself, and let me know what you think.

You can make this dish in advance and refrigerate it for up to 3 days. Just heat over low heat for about 15 to 18 minutes until the beans are heated through. You can freeze the dish, but the onions loose their sweetness, texture, and taste. I only recommend freezing the leftovers (if there are any) for later use.

This recipe is in the meat section because it is a main dish, not a vegetable. You may substitute sausage for the ham, but the sausage should be cooked and drained of excess grease beforehand. It should be eaten with a green salad and plenty of fresh hot bread.

Calories—485; Carb—44.7; Fat—23.3; Chol—77; Pro—24.3; Fib—6.8; Sod—2067

PORK JAMBALAYA

1 ripe red tomato
1 lb. smoked pork rope sausage
1 lb. pork tenderloin
1 tbsp. peanut oil
1 cup chopped ham
2 tsp. Cajun Seasoning Mix (see index)
1 large onion, finely chopped
1 medium bell pepper, diced
1/2 cup minced celery
3 cloves garlic, minced
1/2 tsp. Tabasco sauce
1 tbsp. Worcestershire sauce
1/2 cup beef stock or beef broth
3 cups cooked white long grain rice
1 cup finely chopped green onions
1/4 cup minced parsley

Skin the tomato, remove the seeds, dice it, and set it aside for later use. Cut the rope sausage into slices about 1/2 inch thick. Cut the pork tenderloin into bite-sized pieces. Heat a large, heavy skillet over medium-high heat. When it is hot, add the peanut oil, tilt the skillet to coat the bottom, and heat until it begins to smoke. Add the sausage and fry until it is browned, about 3 minutes. Add the pork tenderloin and fry another 3 minutes until it is browned.

Stir in the ham, fry for 1 minute, then season with the **Cajun Seasoning Mix.** Blend in well, then add the onions, bell pepper, celery, garlic, tomato, and Tabasco sauce to the skillet and sauté for 5 minutes. Stir in the Worcestershire sauce and the beef stock or broth to dissolve the brown spots on the skillet bottom. Mix in the rice, then add the green onions and parsley and cook, stirring often, for 2 more minutes. Serves 6.

Lagniappe: This is an old Cajun treasure. I have tried to speed it up while maintaining the substance. Cooking at high temperatures helps by quickly blending the flavors together. The dish is contains a fair amount of grease, but it is spread throughout the dish and is part of the nature of jambalaya. Traditionally, jambalaya was made from whatever was left in the icebox. It is a concoction of more than one meat that always includes rice. Jambalaya is most often eaten as a main dish. This is true backwoods eating!

Almost every Cajun household had their favorite jambalaya. I always liked the pork mixture. You can use this recipe to create your own version by changing the meats—it doesn't really matter which three meats you choose. You can make it in advance and refrigerate or freeze it. In fact, I usually cook extra (up to the addition of the rice) and freeze it for some very quick jambalaya. When I am ready to use it, I just heat it in the microwave until the mixture is hot, then stir in the rice, green onions, and parsley. I cover with a little plastic wrap, punch about 3 holes in the top, microwave it, then serve.

Calories—468; Carb—33.4; Fat—25.6; Chol—69; Pro—24; Fib—1.6; Sod—438

NOODLES LA LOUISIANE

2 tbsp. unsalted butter
1 cup diced ham
1/2 lb. smoked spicy
  andouille pork sausage,
  sliced
1 medium onion, diced
1 small red bell pepper,
  diced
2 cloves garlic, minced
8 large fresh mushrooms,
  sliced
2 1/2 cups beef stock or
  beef broth
1/4 cup dry white wine
1/4 tsp. Tabasco sauce
1/2 tsp. salt
1/2 tsp. black pepper
1 10-oz. pkg. colored
  corkscrew noodles
1/2 cup pecans, toasted
1/4 cup minced fresh
  parsley
1/2 cup sour cream

Heat a 3 or 4-quart saucepan over medium-high heat until it is hot; then heat the butter until it begins to smoke. Add the ham and sausage, sauté for 3 minutes, then add the onions, red bell pepper, and garlic. Sauté for 3 more minutes before adding the mushrooms. Sauté for 2 minutes, then add the rest of the ingredients, except the pecans, parsley, and sour cream. Bring to a boil for about 7 to 9 minutes; most of the liquid should be absorbed. Remove from the heat and stir in the remaining ingredients. Return to the heat for 1 more minute, stirring often. Serve hot. Serves 4.

Lagniappe: This recipe has many possibilities. I like to mix and match with different meats. I really like to use leftover meats to make a sort of noodle jambalaya. I've made it with andouille and shrimp, oysters and ham, chicken and sausage, and scallops and sausage. The possibilities are endless. Go ahead and create your own personal version!

Toasting pecans is a breeze. Heat a skillet over medium heat and add the pecans when the skillet is hot. Shake the skillet and move the pecans around for about 4 minutes, until the air is filled with the smell of toasted pecans; then pour them onto a plate that can take the heat. Once, at a demo in a bookstore, I poured the pecans onto a plastic plate. When I was ready to use them, I discovered a nice plate with pecans melted into it. Needless to say, I learned to warn people to pour the pecans into a plate that can take the heat!

Calories—712; Carb—61.4; Fat—37.8; Chol—152; Pro—33; Fib— 1.8; Sod—1934

TENDERLOIN OF PORK FAYE

1 1/2 lb. pork tenderloin
1 1/2 tsp. Cajun Seasoning
 Mix (see index)
3 tbsp. unsalted butter
3 cloves garlic, minced
1 tsp. grated gingerroot
1 17-oz. can sliced peaches
 in heavy syrup
1/4 cup water
1/4 tsp. Tabasco sauce

2 tbsp. minced fresh
 parsley
1 tsp. minced fresh basil
 (or 1/4 tsp. dried)
2 tsp. cornstarch
1 8-oz. can sliced water
 chestnuts, drained
cooked long grain white
 rice

Cut the pork tenderloin into four 6-ounce steaks and season them with the **Cajun Seasoning Mix.** Heat a heavy skillet over medium heat. When it is hot, melt the butter until it begins to smoke, then sauté the garlic, gingerroot, and pork tenderloin. Sauté the pork steaks for about 4 minutes on each side, then remove them from the skillet to a warm plate.

Add the syrup from the peaches to the skillet with the water, Tabasco sauce, parsley, basil, and cornstarch. Cook, stirring often, until the sauce thickens. Add the peaches and water chestnuts, reduce the heat, and simmer for 2 minutes, stirring often. Return the pork to the skillet and simmer for about 2 more minutes. Serve over cooked long grain white rice. Serves 4.

Lagniappe: Although this dish is best if served right after it is cooked, it can be refrigerated or frozen for later use. Because it is speedy and uncomplicated as well as lavish and eye-catching, this makes a very nice dish for company. When I freeze it, I usually put the dish completely together and tightly cover it with plastic wrap. To serve, I just punch a few holes in the plastic wrap to allow the steam to escape, and microwave it until it is heated.

You can use fresh peaches if you like. Peel three medium-sized peaches, place the peelings in about 1 cup of water and boil for about 5 minutes. Remove the skins, add 1/4 cup of sugar, and heat until the sugar is dissolved. Use this liquid in the place of the canned peach liquid and the 1/4 cup of water.

Calories—425; Carb—8.4; Fat—27.6; Chol—79; Pro—23; Fib—1.2; Sod—408

TENDERLOIN OF PORK ELLA MARIE

1 1/2 lb. pork tenderloin
2 tsp. Cajun Seasoning Mix
  (see index)
3 tbsp. minced carrots
3 tbsp. minced celery
4 cloves garlic, minced
2 medium onions, sliced in
  1/4-inch rings and
  separated
1 medium sweet red bell
  pepper, cut in strips

1/4 cup olive oil
2 tbsp. unsalted butter
1/2 cup brandy
1 tsp. minced fresh basil
1/2 cup minced green
  onions
3 cups cooked white rice
1/4 cup minced fresh
  parsley

Cut the tenderloin into steaks about 1/2-inch thick. Place them between pieces of plastic wrap; then pound them with a kitchen mallet
until they increase in size by one half. Cut the pounded pork into
3-inch strips about 1/4 inch thick. Season with the **Cajun Seasoning
Mix,** place the meat in a large mixing bowl, and cover it with the carrots, celery, garlic, onions, and bell pepper. Let it stand until you are
ready to cook.

When you are ready to cook, heat a large, heavy skillet over
medium-high heat. When it is very hot, add the olive oil, let it begin to
smoke, then add the butter. As soon as the butter melts, add the pork-
vegetable mixture. Cook over medium-high heat for about 5 to 7 minutes, until the pork is browned on all sides.

Reduce the heat to low, and carefully add the brandy. Strike a match
and bring it carefully to the skillet to light the brandy. There will be a
burst of hot fire. (If you have never worked with a flambé, you may
want to watch someone else cook this dish before you try it.) Do not
shake the pan or stir while the fire is burning. When the flame burns
itself out, stir the pork well and add the green onions. Cook for 1
minute, mix in the cooked rice, parsley, and toasted walnuts. Serve at
once. Serves 6.

Lagniappe: Do not freeze this dish. You cannot refrigerate this dish after it has been cooked without damaging its quality, but you can refrigerate the seasoned pork for up to 3 days before cooking. Allowing the seasonings to blend together in the refrigerator before cooking will actually improve the flavors. Cooking time is very short, and this is one of those dishes you will want to prepare in front of an audience.

Please do be careful with the flambé. Served with a nice green vegetable, this is an elementary, but exquisitely eye-catching dish. The taste will complete the spectacle.

Calories—534; Carb—32.1; Fat—29.2; Chol—114; Pro—34.3; Fib— .7; Sod—677

TENDERLOIN OF PORK ETOUFFEE

1 stick unsalted butter
2 medium onions, chopped
1/2 cup thinly sliced celery
4 cloves garlic, minced
1 small red bell pepper, diced
1 2-lb. pork tenderloin
2 tsp. Cajun Seasoning Mix (see index)
3 tbsp. all-purpose flour
1/4 tsp. Tabasco sauce

1 tsp. Worcestershire sauce
1 tsp. paprika
1 1/2 cups beef stock, beef broth, or water
3/4 cup chopped green onions
1/4 cup minced fresh parsley
cooked long grain white rice

Heat a large, heavy skillet over medium heat. When it is hot, melt the butter until it is hot enough to smoke, then add the onions, celery, garlic, and red bell pepper. Sauté for about 5 minutes, stirring often. While the vegetables are sautéing, cut the tenderloin into round steaks about 3/4 inch thick, and season them with the **Cajun Seasoning Mix.** When the 5 minutes are up, add the pork to the skillet. Brown for about 3 minutes per side; then remove the pork to a warm plate for later use.

Add the flour to the skillet and stir it in well. Cook for about 5 minutes, stirring constantly. Blend in the Tabasco sauce, Worcestershire sauce, and paprika. Add the beef stock, and stir until the sauce begins to thicken. Return the pork tenderloin to the skillet, cover, and cook for 12 minutes. Remove the cover, add the green onions and parsley, and cook uncovered for 3 more minutes. Serve hot over cooked rice. Serves 8.

Lagniappe: What a great recipe to make ahead of time. Cook the dish up to the point of adding the green onions and parsley before freezing or refrigerating. When you are ready to serve, just remove from the freezer, defrost in the refrigerator and cook covered for 5 minutes over medium heat. Add the green onions and parsley, cook three more minutes, then serve.

I suggest long grain rice because it will not "gum up" as much as the short grain. The long grain has less gluten (starch) and, therefore, does not stick together as readily as the short grain.

Calories—366; Carb—8.7; Fat—26; Chol—79; Pro—225; Fib—1.6; Sod—392

TENDERLOIN OF PORK THOMAS

1/4 cup olive oil
1 lb. pork tenderloin, cut into strips
1 1/4 tsp. Cajun Seasoning Mix (see index)
1 large onion, chopped
3 cloves garlic, minced
2 tbsp. minced celery
2 tbsp. minced fresh sage (or 1 tsp. dried)
2 tbsp. minced fresh rosemary leaves (or 1 tsp. dried)

1/2 cup minced apple
2 tbsp. finely minced carrots
1/4 tsp. Tabasco sauce
3 tbsp. marsala wine
1 cup cherry tomatoes, halved
1/2 cup ripe pitted California olives, halved
5 large fresh mushrooms, cleaned and sliced
1/4 cup chopped green onion

Heat a heavy skillet over high heat. When it is hot, add 1/2 of the olive oil and heat it. While the oil is heating, season the pork strips with the **Cajun Seasoning Mix.** When the oil starts to smoke, add the pork strips, brown them on all sides, then remove them to a warm platter for later use.

Add the remaining 1/2 of the olive oil and heat it. As it starts to smoke, add the onion, garlic, and celery to the skillet and sauté for 3 minutes. Reduce the heat to medium; then add the sage, rosemary, apple, and carrots. Sauté for 3 more minutes, add the remaining ingredients, and stir constantly for about 2 minutes. Return the cooked tenderloin strips to the skillet, and heat for about 30 seconds. Serve at once. Serves 4.

Lagniappe: This dish can be served over rice or noodles. It also is nice to top a baked potato or in a nest made of mashed potatoes piped through a pastry bag. Don't do anything in advance other than the chopping, mincing, and slicing. This is a quick dish that should not need to be made in advance.

The nice thing about tenderloin of pork is the extremely low fat content. Pork is an excellent meat that can be quite good for you if you avoid the pieces that have a high fat content. As you can see, one pound of pork tenderloin goes a long way when combined with all the vegetables.

Remember to use California olives rather than imported olives because the the taste and quality is far superior. Don't be tricked by the notion that imported is better—they are not! Do a taste test; you will be amazed.

Calories—346; Carb—8.6; Fat—25.5; Chol—69; Pro—22; Fib—1.4; Sod—387

TENDERLOIN OF PORK NICOLE MARIE

1 1/2 lb. pork tenderloin
1/2 cup peanut oil
2 tsp. Cajun Seasoning Mix
(see index)
2 cloves garlic, minced
1/4 cup minced celery
1 large white onion,
chopped
1 medium red bell pepper,
diced
2/3 cup madeira wine
(preferably sercial)
1 large fresh tomato,
skinned, seeds removed,
and diced

8 large fresh mushrooms,
quartered
3 cups cooked white long
grain rice
1 tbsp. minced fresh sage
(or 1/2 tsp. dried)
1/2 tsp. Tabasco sauce
1/4 tsp. black pepper
1/4 cup capers
1/2 cup sliced almonds,
toasted
1/2 cup finely chopped
green onions
1/2 cup minced fresh
parsley

Remove the excess fat from the pork tenderloin and cut it into strips. Heat a very large, heavy skillet over medium-high heat until it is hot; then add the peanut oil. Season the pork with the **Cajun Seasoning Mix.** When the oil begins to smoke, sauté the seasoned pork for 2 minutes, stirring often and shaking the skillet. Add the garlic, celery, onion, and red bell pepper; sauté for 2 more minutes, then stir in the wine to dissolve the pan drippings.

Add the diced tomato and quartered mushrooms, sauté for 1 minute, then add the rice and sage. Stir to coat the rice with the sauce, then stir in the remaining ingredients. Sauté for 2 minutes and serve straight from the skillet. Serves 8.

Lagniappe: Serve this dish with a modest salad, hot bread, and a dry red wine. Eat it shortly after cooking. It is full of fresh vegetables that will lose their characteristics if refrigerated or frozen. Total cooking time is under 10 minutes, so there is little reason to cook it ahead of time. It is essential that you chop everything prior to starting to cook because there is not enough time to do it as you cook. The one exception is, of course, the parsley. Mince the parsley just before adding it to the dish. Remember that chopping parsley causes it to give up the oils that hold its essence. If chopped and left to sit for too long, the parsley looses its punch.

I toast the almonds before I get started with the recipe by dropping them in a heated skillet, and shaking the pan to keep them moving until I smell that toasted nutty fragrance. That smell signals that the almonds are almost done. I usually cook them for 1 minute after I first sniff that nice toasted almond bouquet.

Calories—326; Carb—10.8; Fat—22.5; Chol—62; Pro—19; Fib— 1.0; Sod—461

PINEAPPLE PORK CHOPS

3 tbsp. peanut oil
4 large pork chops, about 1 inch thick
2 tsp. Cajun Seasoning Mix (see index)
1 small onion, quartered and separated
1 small bell pepper, cut in strips

1 cup beef stock or beef broth
1 cup dry burgundy wine
2 tbsp. soy sauce
2 tbsp. red wine vinegar
1/2 tsp. Tabasco sauce
3 tbsp. dark brown sugar
2 tbsp. cornstarch
1/4 cup cold water

1 clove garlic, minced
1 stalk celery, cut
  diagonally in 1/2-inch
  pieces
1 1/2 tsp. ground ginger
  root
1 15-oz. can pineapple
  chunks

1/2 tsp. cloves
1/4 cup minced fresh
  parsley
2 tbsp. minced green onion
  tops
cooked white rice

Preheat the oven to 170 degrees. Heat a large, heavy skillet over medium-high heat. When it is hot, heat the peanut oil until it begins to smoke. Season the pork chops with the **Cajun Seasoning Mix,** then fry them for 4 minutes on each side until nicely browned. Remove the chops to a warm plate, cover loosely with foil, and place in the pre-heated oven.

Add the onion, pepper, garlic, celery, ginger root, and pineapple chunks (reserve the liquid) to the skillet and sauté for 4 minutes. Raise the heat to high; add the stock, wine, vinegar, pineapple juice, and Tabasco sauce; and bring to a boil. Boil for 2 minutes, reduce the heat to medium, and stir well.

In a medium-sized mixing bowl, mix together the brown sugar, cornstarch, water, and cloves until the cornstarch is dissolved. Pour the mixture into the simmering skillet. Mix in well until the sauce begins to thicken, then stir in the parsley and green onions. Add the chops and cook for 1 minute. Serve the chops and cooked white rice covered with generous amounts of the sauce. Serve hot. Serves 4.

Lagniappe: This is the Cajun version of a sweet and sour pork dish. A sweet sauce goes well with pork, and adding a little Cajun spice makes the dish divine. Don't do anything in advance, it really is easy enough to do just before serving. If you like pork, this is worth trying.

Calories—643; Carb—10.5; Fat—41.9; Chol—190; Pro—61.8; Fib—.9; Sod—497

PORK CHOPS ASHLEY

4 1-inch-thick center-cut
   pork chops (about 1 1/2
   lb.)
2 1/2 tsp. Cajun Seasoning
   Mix (see index)
1/4 cup peanut oil
1 cup chopped onion
1/2 cup chopped celery
3 cloves garlic, minced
1 medium bell pepper,
   diced

2 tbsp. all-purpose flour
1 1/4 cups zinfandel wine
1/2 lb. whole oyster
   mushrooms
1/2 tsp. Tabasco sauce
1/2 cup minced green
   onions
1/4 cup minced parsley
cooked white rice

Clean and trim the pork chops, and season them with the **Cajun Seasoning Mix.** Heat a large, heavy skillet over high heat. Once it is hot, heat the peanut oil until it starts to smoke, then cook the chops for 2 1/2 minutes on each side. Remove them from the skillet and set them aside for later use.

Reduce the heat to medium and add the onions, celery, garlic, and bell pepper. Sauté for 2 minutes, then add the flour and cook for 5 more minutes, stirring constantly. Blend in the wine to make a sauce that should begin to thicken. Mix in the mushrooms, Tabasco sauce, green onions, and parsley. Return the pork chops to the pan. Cover and cook for 5 minutes over medium heat. Serve hot over cooked white rice. Serves 4.

Lagniappe: This is a lively and uncomplicated meal if served with a green vegetable and a nice salad on the side. Don't forget the hot French bread. Serve the chop on a bed of rice and ladle the sauce over the chop and the rice. You can also use the noodles of your choice.

Do not make this dish in advance. It is so easy and quick to make that you will want to cook it just before eating. Cooking the pork over high heat sears the meat and holds in its natural juices. You will find the pork to be succulent and luscious.

Calories—646; Carb—10.8; Fat—41.3; Chol—191; Pro—62; Fib—.8; Sod—496

PORK CHOPS LEMOINE

1 tbsp. peanut oil
4 pork chops, about 1 inch
  thick
1 tsp. salt
1/2 tsp. black pepper
1/4 tsp. white pepper
1/2 tsp. garlic powder
1 cup tomato sauce
1/2 cup catsup

2 tbsp. Worcestershire
  sauce
1/2 tsp. Tabasco sauce
1/2 tsp. sweet basil
1/2 tsp. prepared mustard
1 clove garlic, minced
1 small onion, finely
  chopped

Heat a heavy skillet over medium-high heat. When it is hot, add the peanut oil and brown the chops on both sides. Combine the salt, pepper, and garlic powder in a bowl and equally season the four chops. Combine the remaining ingredients and pour them over the chops. Cook until the sauce bubbles, reduce the heat to low, then cook for 15 more minutes. Serve hot. Serves 4.

Lagniappe: This is a quick pork dish. cooking over high heat ensures that the meat is completely cooked while sealing in the juices. The taste is delicate and tender. You can serve this over rice, potatoes, or noodles. The sauce is wonderful!

Calories—636; Carb—4.8; Fat—40.5; Chol—188; Pro—61; Fib—.2; Sod—495

ROQUEFORT STUFFED PORK CHOPS

4 8-oz. center cut pork
  chops, about 2 inches
  thick
4 oz. Roquefort cheese
1 tbsp. unsalted butter,
  melted

1 tbsp. Worcestershire
  sauce
1 tsp. fresh lemon juice
2 tsp. Cajun Seasoning Mix
  (see index)

Set the oven to broil. With a small, sharp knife, cut a slit in the center of the side of each pork chop to make a pocket to hold the cheese. Stuff each chop with one ounce of cheese, then press the opening closed with your fingers.

Place the chops on a broiler pan and brush them with a mixture of the melted butter, Worcestershire sauce, and lemon juice. Broil for 8 minutes on one side, turn the chop over, brush with the butter mixture, then broil for 7 minutes on other side. Remove from the oven and brush with the remaining butter mixture. Sprinkle both sides of the chops with the **Cajun Seasoning Mix,** then serve. Serves 4.

Lagniappe: You can stuff the chops in advance, wrap them, and refrigerate until you are ready to broil them. This has quite a nice blending of flavors. This recipe is simple, easy, and so delicious! Serve these chops with a potato dish, a vegetable, and some hot bread.

Calories—761; Carb—2.1; Fat—43.4; Chol—288; Pro—85.9; Fib—0; Sod—980

GRILLED SPARE RIBS

1 cup dry red wine
1 cup red wine vinegar
2 lemons, juice only
2 tbsp. Worcestershire
  sauce
1 1/2 tsp. salt
1 tsp. black pepper

1/2 tsp. Tabasco sauce
5 lb. spare ribs
1/2 cup Pickapeppa sauce
1/2 cup A-1 sauce
1/2 cup Heinz-57 sauce
1/4 cup Worcestershire
  sauce

In a large mixing bowl, combine the wine, vinegar, lemon juice, 2 tbsp. of the Worcestershire sauce, salt, pepper, and Tabasco sauce. Put the ribs in a large container, and pour the liquid mixture over the ribs. Let the ribs marinate overnight (or for up to 48 hours).

When you are ready to cook, place the ribs on a charcoal grill over low heat. Baste the ribs with the marinade every five minutes for about 35 minutes. While the ribs are cooking, combine 1/4 cup of the marinade with the remaining ingredients to make a second basting sauce. When the 35 minutes have passed, baste with the new basting sauce every five minutes for the next 25 minutes. Serve hot, right off the grill. Serves 6.

Lagniappe: I know this recipe takes longer than 30 minutes, but you really can't grill outdoors in less than an hour. I think it is apparent that this is really an easy outdoor grilling recipe. The marinades contain all the seasoning the meat needs.

You can also use this recipe to make **Grilled Chicken** by substituting 2 whole fryers, split in half, for the ribs. To make **Grilled Pork Chops,** just substitute 4 pounds of chops for the ribs. Be sure to get center cut pork chops. It is worth the slight difference in price because you get more meat, less fat, and less waste.

Calories—1415; Carb—5.1; Fat—105; Chol—418; Pro—101; Fib—0; Sod—944

BAKED HAM STEAK PITRE

1 center cut smoked ham
   steak, about 3/4-inch
   thick
10 whole cloves
1/2 cup light brown sugar
3 tbsp. honey
1/2 cup pineapple juice

1 tbsp. prepared yellow
   mustard
1/4 tsp. nutmeg
1/4 tsp. cinnamon
1/4 tsp. orange peel spice
1/4 cup minced fresh
   parsley

Preheat the oven to 425 degrees. Trim most of the heavy fat from the ham. Score the ham about every 3 inches and stick a whole clove in the center of each cut. Place the ham in a baking dish large enough to allow it to sit level.

In a large bowl, combine the remaining ingredients, except for the parsley, until well blended. Pour the mixture over the ham; then bake, uncovered, for about 45 minutes. Baste the ham often with the sauce. Remove from the oven, sprinkle with fresh parsley, and serve. Serves 4.

Lagniappe: This is a great way to enjoy good ham without having to fool with the whole ham. I like ham, but I don't like to eat it for 2 weeks straight—I can only create so many recipes for leftover ham! This way, you get the taste and pleasure of real ham without the problem of leftovers.

You can prepare the ham and the sauce, and let them sit in the refrigerator until you are ready to bake. When you are ready, just bake as directed above, and serve. You can use the recipe with a whole ham to make a wonderful **Honey Mustard Glazed Baked Ham.** Just make the sauce and use it to baste throughout the baking of the whole ham. Your ham will be a golden brown and have a deliciously unique flavor.

Calories—384; Carb—48.4; Fat—12.4; Chol—66; Pro—20.9; Fib—.2; Sod—1515

VEAL MARIE ELENA

1 1/2 cup cracker crumbs
1/2 cup romano cheese
1/4 cup parmesan cheese
1/4 cup finely minced fresh
   parsley
2 tsp. Cajun Seasoning Mix
   (see index)

2 tbsp. finely minced green
   onion tops
1 lb. boneless veal sirloin
1/4 cup all-purpose flour
1/4 cup unsalted butter,
   melted
2/3 cup toasted walnuts,
   chopped

Preheat the oven to 375 degrees. In a large mixing bowl, combine the cracker crumbs, cheeses, parsley, 1 teaspoon of the **Cajun Seasoning Mix,** and green onions until well blended; then set aside for later use.

Cut the veal steak into 4 equal pieces; then pound with a kitchen mallet to increase the size by 1/3. Season the veal with the other 1 teaspoon of **Cajun Seasoning Mix** and coat with the flour. Pour the melted butter onto a large platter. Dip the flour-coated veal into the butter; then press the meat into the cracker crumb mixture until coated. Put the coated veal in a baking dish, and drizzle the remaining melted butter over the veal. Bake for 25 to 30 minutes at 375 degrees. Do not turn the meat because it will make the coating soggy. Serve at once. Serves 4.

Lagniappe: Do not refrigerate or freeze after cooking, but you can prepare the veal up to the baking point and refrigerate until you are ready to cook. This crunchy veal is quick, easy, and tasty.

You can use this same mixture to coat other meats. If you use 4 large center cut pork chops in place of the veal, you will have **Pork Chops Marie Elena.** Just cook at 400 instead of 375 degrees for the same amount of time.

Calories—791; Carb—36.7; Fat—61.2; Chol—152; Pro—42.7; Fib—.5; Sod—994

VEAL SCALLOPINI EUPHEMIE BOREL

2 tbsp. olive oil
2 tbsp. unsalted butter
1 tbsp. minced shallots
2 cloves garlic, minced
3 tbsp. minced celery
1 tsp. chopped fresh
  oregano (or 1/4 tsp.
  dried)
1 1/2 lb. veal scallopini
1 1/3 tsp. Cajun Seasoning
  Mix (see index)

1/4 tsp. Tabasco sauce
1/3 cup cream sherry
1 tbsp. fresh lime juice (or
  lemon juice)
2/3 cup heavy whipping
  cream
3 tbsp. minced green onion
  tops
1/4 cup minced fresh
  parsley

Heat a large skillet over medium-high heat. When it is hot, heat the olive oil until it smokes, then swirl in the butter until it melts. When the butter starts to smoke, add the shallots, garlic, and celery and sauté for 2 minutes. Stir in the oregano, veal, and **Cajun Seasoning Mix.** Sauté the veal for about 2 to 3 minutes until it is nicely browned on both sides. Remove the veal to a warm plate and set aside for later use.

Add the Tabasco sauce, cream sherry, and fresh lime juice to the skillet. As it steams, shake the pan lightly and stir well to dissolve the pan drippings. Allow this mixture to reduce by half, then lower the heat to low-medium and stir in the heavy cream. Allow the cream to simmer, stirring constantly; then mix in the green onions and parsley. Return the veal to the skillet and let it simmer in the sauce for about 2 minutes. Serve at once. Serves 4.

Lagniappe: This is a rapid dish that really must be eaten right after cooking to get the full effect of the grand flavors. Do not do anything in advance but chop the vegetables. This will be a triumph at any meal or dinner party. I like to serve this dish with either creamed potatoes or al dente cooked noodles. The cream sauce is great on both.

Calories—638; Carb—6.9; Fat—7.1; Chol—223; Pro—46.6; Fib—.2; Sod—340

VEAL SANDERFORD

2 tbsp. olive oil
4 1/2-inch-thick veal chops
  (about 1 lb.)
1 tsp. Cajun Seasoning Mix
  (see index)
1 small red bell pepper,
  sliced in strips
2 large ripe peaches,
  peeled and pitted
2 cups chicken stock or
  chicken broth
1 tbsp. white
  Worcestershire sauce

1/2 cup dry white wine
2 tbsp. sugar
1 tbsp. light brown sugar
2 tbsp. cornstarch
1/4 cup cold water
1/4 tsp. Tabasco sauce
1 tsp. fresh ground ginger
1/2 tsp. nutmeg
2 tbsp. minced fresh
  parsley
1 tbsp. minced green onion
  tops
cooked white rice

Preheat the oven to 170 degrees. Heat a large, heavy skillet over medium heat. When it is hot, heat the olive oil until it begins to smoke; then fry each chop for 2 1/2 minutes on each side. Remove the meat to a warm plate, season both sides of each chop with the **Cajun Seasoning Mix,** cover loosely with foil, and put into the 170-degree oven. (This should keep the chops hot without continuing to cook them.)

Add the red pepper strips to the skillet and reduce the heat to low-medium. Slice each peach into six wedges and add them to the skillet. Sauté for 3 minutes. Add the stock, Worcestershire sauce, and white wine to the skillet and bring to a hard boil over high heat. Let the mixture boil for 2 minutes, then reduce the heat to medium.

In a small bowl, stir together the sugars, cornstarch, water, Tabasco sauce, ginger, and nutmeg until the cornstarch is dissolved. Pour the mixture into the skillet and stir until the sauce begins to thicken. Mix in the parsley and green onions. Return the chops to the skillet, let them sit in the sauce for 1 minute, then serve over cooked white rice with plenty of sauce and about 1/2 peach per plate. Serves 4.

Lagniappe: Veal chops are made to be served with fruit. Peaches are an excellent complement to meats—and veal is no exception. I would not recommend making any part of this dish in advance. It is quick and easy. If you try to make the sauce without frying the chops in the skillet, it will be missing the flavor of the veal drippings. If you cook the veal ahead of time, you will sacrifice the depth and taste of good veal. This is a great dish for company that is easy enough for everyday fare.

Calories—407; Carb—15.5; Fat—31.6; Chol—101; Pro—33.2; Fib—.5; Sod—616

SAUCE DE BARBECUE

1 stick unsalted butter
1 medium onion, minced
1 clove garlic, minced
1/2 cup minced celery
4 cups catsup
3 cups red wine vinegar
1/2 cup Worcestershire
  sauce
1/2 cup dark brown sugar

1/4 cup light brown sugar
1 tsp. salt
1 tsp. black pepper
1 large lemon, juice only
1 tsp. onion powder
1 tsp. Tabasco sauce
1 cup water
1/4 cup mustard

In a large saucepan over medium heat, melt the butter. Add the onion, garlic, and celery. Sauté for 7 minutes, then add the remaining ingredients. Bring to a boil, then reduce to simmer for 18 minutes. The sauce will be ready to use on your choice of meat, or you can refrigerate until you are ready to use. Makes about one quart of sauce.

Lagniappe: This is a barbecue sauce for any type of meat. This sauce can be made in advance, covered, and stored in the refrigerator for up to 1 week. You can reduce everything by half to make just a pint, or you can double it to make more. If I have any leftover sauce, I freeze it for later use. This is a good, easy, all-around barbecue sauce.

Calories—43; Carb—7.6; Fat—1.6; Chol—4.2; Pro—.4; Fib—Trace; Sod—213

Vegetables

ARTICHOKES CHAD THOMAS

1/4 cup olive oil
2/3 cup finely chopped
   onions
1/2 cup diced carrots
1/4 cup minced celery
1 clove garlic, minced
1 15-oz. can artichoke
   bottoms, cut in half
1/2 tsp. salt
1/2 tsp. black pepper

1/4 tsp. Tabasco sauce
1 tsp. fresh lemon juice
1 tsp. minced fresh sage (or
   1/4 tsp. dried)
1 tsp. minced fresh mint
   (or 1/4 tsp. dried)
1 cup beef stock or beef
   broth
1/4 cup dry red wine

Heat a large, heavy skillet over medium-high heat. When it is hot, heat the oil until it smokes; then add the onions, carrots, celery, and garlic. Sauté for 5 minutes; then add the artichoke bottoms, salt, black pepper, and Tabasco sauce and sauté for 3 more minutes. Reduce the heat to medium, add the remaining ingredients, and simmer for 5 minutes, stirring a few times. Serve hot. Serves 4.

Lagniappe: Artichokes are not your average vegetable, that's what makes them interesting. They are a little expensive, but they have a unique taste that goes well with almost any dish. This is a very colorful recipe that can brighten up a dull plate. You can make it in advance and refrigerate for up to 8 hours, but do not freeze. Reheat, covered with waxed paper, in a microwave; or in a saucepan over low heat for about 3 minutes.

Feel free to change the spice mixture. I like to use herbs that are easy to grow—both sage and mint grow well all over the country. Remember to bring your herbs inside before winter so you can have fresh herbs all year long. Plant the herbs in clay pots and set them in those plastic drain pans from your garden center for the duration of the winter. I happen to have a bay window in my kitchen that is perfect for holding fresh herbs. I always have fresh herbs unless I get caught by an early freeze. Don't count on the weatherman to warn you. When the temperatures drop into the lower forties, bring them in!

Calories—189; Carb—15.5; Fat—13.8; Chol—0; Pro—3.7; Fib—1.8; Sod—571

FRESH BRUSSELS SPROUTS DANIEL

2 qt. water
2 tsp. salt
5 black peppercorns
1 bay leaf
2 tbsp. vegetable oil
1 1/3 lb. fresh brussels
   sprouts, washed and
   trimmed
3 tbsp. unsalted butter

1/4 cup diced onions
1 tbsp. red wine vinegar
1/4 cup toasted slivered
   almonds
1/2 tsp. salt
1/2 tsp. black pepper
1/8 tsp. Tabasco sauce
2 tbsp. fresh parsley

In a large saucepan or stock pot, boil the water, salt, peppercorns, and bay leaf over high heat. When the water is at a full boil, add the vegetable oil and brussels sprouts and cook over high heat for 9 minutes. Remove the sprouts from the water and drain.

Heat a large saucepan (you can rinse and dry the one you just used) over medium-high heat. When it is hot, heat the butter until it begins to smoke. Add the onions, sauté for 1 minute, then add the brussels sprouts and sauté, constantly shaking the pan, for 4 minutes. Stir in the red wine vinegar and almonds, and cook for 1 minute. Season with the salt, black pepper, and Tabasco sauce; then add the parsley. Cook, shaking the pan, for 1 more minute. Serve hot. Serves 4.

Lagniappe: I put the bay leaf into the water to boil the sprouts because the flavor of bay leaf intensifies that of the brussels sprouts. I put 2 tbsp. of oil in the water with the sprouts to help to bring out the beautiful green color without destroying the vitamins or flavor of the vegetable. I think this may be one of my favorite vegetables. They are pretty, tasty, and easy to use. Fresh brussels sprouts are reasonable in price and there is not much loss of bulk in the cooking process. This is an easy recipe that can add real zest to your dinner.

Calories—165; Carb—10.8; Fat—13.7; Chol—17; Pro—3.9; Fib—1.7; Sod—901

ASPARAGUS POYDRAS

1 lb. fresh asparagus	1/2 tsp. salt
1 qt. water	1/2 tsp. black pepper
2 tsp. salt	1/4 cup grated romano
5 whole black peppercorns	cheese
2 tbsp. vegetable oil	1/4 cup grated parmesan
1/2 stick unsalted butter	cheese
1 lemon, juice only	1 tbsp. minced fresh
1 tsp. Worcestershire sauce	parsley
1/4 tsp. Tabasco sauce	paprika

Clean the asparagus and chop off the hard ends. Heat the water, salt, and black peppercorns in a large pot over high heat until the water comes to a hard boil. Add the asparagus and vegetable oil; then bring the water back to a boil. Time exactly 3 minutes, then remove from the heat. Cover the pot with a lid and allow the asparagus to sit.

Turn the oven to broil. In a small saucepan over low heat, melt the butter; then mix in the remaining ingredients, except for the parsley and paprika. Remove the asparagus from the hot water and drain well. Place the asparagus in a baking dish and spoon the butter-cheese mixture over the asparagus. Top with the fresh parsley and paprika and place the dish about 6 inches under the hot broiler for 3 minutes. Serve at once. Serves 4.

Lagniappe: This is an alternative to serving asparagus with hollandaise sauce. The dish can be made in advance and refrigerated before broiling. You will lose a little bit of the freshness of the asparagus, but the quality is still quite acceptable.

To trim fresh asparagus, use a small paring knife to gently press on the the stalk where the color changes to green from white or purple. Where the knife goes in without resistance is the place to cut the bottom off. Be sure to save the asparagus bottoms to use in a wonderful vegetable stock. I keep a large jar in the freezer full of pieces of vegetables (like carrot ends, celery pieces, parsley stems, asparagus bottoms, etc.). When I am ready to make a beef stew, vegetable soup, or a stock, I have a variety of vegetables to enrich it. It is hard to beat the flavor that these vegetables give to mixed vegetable or meat stocks.

Calories—201; Carb—7.4; Fat—16.7; Chol—45; Pro—8.5; Fib—.3; Sod—1093

BROCCOLI AU GRATIN

1 3/4 lb. fresh broccoli
1 qt. boiling water
1/4 cup unsalted butter
1/4 cup all-purpose flour
1 1/2 cup evaporated milk
1 tsp. salt
1/2 tsp. white pepper
1/4 tsp. dry mustard
1/8 tsp. nutmeg
1/2 cup grated Swiss
  cheese

1/2 cup grated American
  cheese
1/2 cup sliced water
  chestnuts
2 tbsp. minced fresh
  parsley
1/2 cup grated sharp
  cheddar cheese
paprika

Cut the broccoli into serving-size pieces. Place the broccoli in a large mixing bowl, and pour the boiling water over it. Let it stand in the water until you are ready to use it.

Preheat the oven to 375 degrees. Heat a large saucepan over medium-high heat. When it is hot, melt the butter, then add the flour and cook, stirring with a wire whisk, for 4 minutes. Whisk in the milk over the medium-high heat, then mix in the dry seasonings. As the sauce thickens, add the Swiss and American cheeses, the water chestnuts, and the parsley. Stir until thoroughly mixed and the cheeses have begun to melt. Drain the broccoli and arrange it in a 2 1/2-quart casserole dish. Pour the sauce over the broccoli, sprinkle the top with the cheddar cheese, and top with paprika. Bake at 375 degrees for 25 minutes. Serve straight from the oven. Serves 6.

Lagniappe: To Americans, *au gratin* means "with cheese." However, *au gratin* actually refers to a casserole with a crust on top. It is interesting how this interpretation came about. In this country, the crust is usually made of a cheese, so the term evolved to encompass any casserole that contains cheese. Now you know the rest of the story. Whatever *au gratin* means to you, it is a great way to serve broccoli.

You will find the crunch from the water chestnuts in this dish a true delight (or at least I do). This casserole can be made in advance and refrigerated or frozen before baking. If you freeze it, defrost it in the refrigerator (never leave food out on the counter to thaw), then bake as directed above. What a treat!

Calories—298; Carb—21.2; Fat—21.9; Chol—73; Pro—28.5; Fib—1.8; Sod—774

QUICK CAULIFLOWER AU GRATIN

1 head fresh cauliflower   **1/4 tsp. Tabasco sauce**
1 8-oz. jar Cheez Whiz
1/4 cup finely chopped
** green onions**

Wash the cauliflower and cut it into florets. Remove the metal cap from the Cheez Whiz and microwave according to the directions on the jar. In a 2-quart casserole, arrange the cauliflower florets. Sprinkle the green onions over the cauliflower.

Remove the heated Cheez Whiz from the microwave carefully and stir in the Tabasco sauce. Cover the cauliflower and green onions with the Cheez Whiz. Cover the dish with plastic wrap, and punch about 8 holes into the wrap to let the steam escape. Microwave at high power for 4 minutes. Then reduce the setting and cook for 8 more minutes. Remove from the oven and let it stand for 2 minutes. Serve warm. Serves 6.

Lagniappe: This is an easy way to prepare au gratin. Kids will learn to eat cauliflower with this flavored cheese on top. You can make this dish in advance and refrigerate or freeze it. Only cook for 4 of the second 8 minutes before chilling. If you freeze it, let the dish thaw in the refrigerator; then cover as above and cook for 4 minutes. Let sit for 1 minute, then serve.

Calories—133; Carb—8.8; Fat—7.9; Chol—22; Pro—8.5; Fib—2.4; Sod—511

BAKED CABBAGE CASSEROLE

1 head cabbage	1/2 cup half and half
1 gallon water	1/4 tsp. Tabasco sauce
1 tbsp. salt	1 cup sharp cheddar cheese
1 10 3/4-oz. can condensed cream of onion soup	1 tbsp. chopped pimento

Preheat the oven to 375 degrees. Chop the cabbage into bite-sized pieces. Boil the water and salt in a large stock pot over high heat. Add the cabbage, cook for 3 minutes, then remove from the heat and drain in a colander.

In a medium-sized mixing bowl, mix together the soup, half and half, Tabasco sauce, and 1/2 cup of the cheese until smooth. Place about 1/3 of the cabbage on the bottom of a 2-quart casserole dish and cover it with 1/3 of the soup mixture. Repeat the process until all of the cabbage and soup mix are gone. Top with the remaining 1/2 cup of cheddar cheese, and sprinkle the pimento nicely over the cheese. Bake at 375 degrees for 20 minutes. Serve hot. Serves 4.

Lagniappe: Cabbage is a great fresh vegetable to serve. According to reports from the medical community, eating cabbage and members of the cabbage family has very significant health benefits. I eat cabbage because I like it!

This is an easy way to fix a cabbage casserole that is quite tasty. You can make it in advance and refrigerate it for up to 2 days without losing the great taste and nice texture. Be sure that it stays chilled in the refrigerator. To reheat, just put it back in the oven at 325 degrees for about 15 minutes. This casserole blends particularly well with pork and chicken entrees.

Calories—336; Carb—24.1; Fat—19.4; Chol—62; Pro—14.9; Fib—2.9; Sod—1592

CARROTS AUNT ALICE

1 lb. young carrots
3 tbsp. butter
1/2 cup light brown sugar
3 tbsp. sugar

1/2 tsp. salt
1/4 tsp. Tabasco sauce
1/8 tsp. fresh grated lemon
peel

Julienne the carrots to about 3 inches long. Heat a heavy, medium-sized skillet over medium heat. Combine all of the ingredients in the skillet, and stir until the sugar begins to melt. Cover the skillet, reduce the heat to low-medium, and cook for 15 minutes, shaking the pan often and stirring every 5 minutes. Serve hot. Serves 4.

Lagniappe: Carrots and sweetness go extremely well together. This recipe makes a dish that can brighten up any entree. Julienne the carrots to about the size and appearance of those large wooden kitchen matches that we used to use. The recipe is simple and easy, but don't put the heat too high—you want the sugar to caramelize, not burn.

Calories—257; Carb—44.4; Fat—9.3; Chol—25; Pro—1.2; Fib—1.8; Sod—1321

LEEKS BASIL

6 medium leeks
2 tbsp. peanut oil
2 tbsp. olive oil
1 clove garlic, minced
1 tbsp. minced fresh basil
(or 1 tsp. dried)

1 cup beef stock or beef
broth
1/4 tsp. Tabasco sauce
1/2 tsp. black pepper
3/4 tsp. salt

Trim, clean and cut the leeks in half lengthwise. Place a large, heavy skillet over high heat. When the skillet is hot, heat the oils until they begin to smoke; then brown the leeks on all sides, turning them carefully. Add the garlic and basil, sauté for 1 minute; then add the remaining ingredients and bring to a hard boil. After the liquid has boiled for 1 minute, reduce the heat to low and cover. Let the leeks simmer for about 15 minutes until they are tender. Serve hot. Serves 4.

Lagniappe: You can make this dish in advance and store it in the refrigerator for up to 2 or 3 days. I don't recommend freezing it because the onion flavor is lost in the freezing process. I would recommend cooking just before eating to get all of the true taste out of the dish. It is easy, and leeks are quite tasty.

Calories—237; Carb—25; Fat—14.6; Chol—0; Pro—3.4; Fib—2; Sod—662

EASY FRESH CORN ON THE COB

4 ears fresh corn,   **pepper**
  unshucked   **melted butter**
salt

Place the whole ears of corn in your microwave. Do not pull the silk out or shuck. Microwave for 5 minutes at full power. Turn the corn over and microwave for 4 more minutes at full power. Carefully remove the corn from the microwave (they will be very hot and full of steam), and allow them to cool for about 5 minutes. Slowly peel the husks to the bottom and wrap a paper towel around the base to make it easier to hold. Pull off the silk—it will come off very easily. If there is a damaged part, cut it off with a sharp knife (it will usually be at the very top). Salt and pepper to taste. Brush with melted butter to taste. Serve at once. Serves 4.

Lagniappe: It is hard to believe that it is so easy to cook corn, but it is. Try this method, and I bet you'll love it. The corn is so tender and juicy. I know this looks to good to be true, so try it and see for yourself!

Calories—232; Carb—41.2; Fat—8.3; Chol—17; Pro—5.5; Fib—2.2; Sod—604

CREAMY MUSHROOMS DARRELL

1 lb. fresh small
  mushrooms
2 slices bacon
3 tbsp. unsalted butter
1 medium yellow bell
  pepper, sliced in strips
1 cup sour cream
1/4 tsp. Tabasco sauce

2 tbsp. minced fresh chives
1 tsp. minced fresh basil
  (or 1/4 tsp. dried)
1 tsp. salt
2 cups cooked thin egg
  noodles, cooked al dente
1 tbsp. minced fresh
  parsley

Clean the mushrooms by brushing or wiping with a damp cloth. Heat a large skillet over medium heat. When it is hot, fry the bacon until it is crispy; then remove the bacon and set aside for later use.

Melt the butter in the skillet, then sauté the mushrooms and yellow bell pepper for 4 minutes. Crumble the bacon and add it to the mushrooms. Stir in the remaining ingredients, except for the noodles and parsley. Let the sauce coat the mushrooms and begin to bubble—but not boil—for about 2 minutes. Stir in the noodles and parsley until coated with the sauce. Serve at once. Serves 4.

Lagniappe: This makes a nice luncheon entree that is unique and not loaded with meat. Noodles are a great source of complex carbohydrates that are easy to use. *Al dente* simply means that the noodles still have a good deal of bounce in them. They still hold themselves together and they still have a yellow hue.

We do not wash the mushrooms with water because they are like a kitchen sponge, they absorb liquid and hold it. They then dump it back into the pan when heated, causing your sauce to have a lot of extra liquid and, frankly, be a failure. Therefore, just brush or wipe the mushrooms. They grow in a sterile medium, so a small amount of dirt won't hurt.

Calories—382; Carb—26.8; Fat—27.5; Chol—78; Pro—15.1; Fib—.8; Sod—661

GREEN BEANS RABALAIS

4 slices bacon
1 medium onion, finely
  chopped
1/2 cup minced red bell
  pepper
1 16-oz. can French cut
  green beans
1/4 cup catsup
1/4 cup chili sauce

1/4 tsp. Tabasco sauce
1 tsp. prepared yellow
  mustard
1 tbsp. Worcestershire
  sauce
1/2 tsp. salt
1/2 tsp. garlic powder
1/2 tsp. black pepper

Heat a large, heavy skillet over medium heat. When it is hot, fry the bacon slices until they are crisp. Remove the bacon, drain it on a few paper towels, and set it aside for later use. Add the onion to the hot bacon drippings in the skillet and sauté for 3 minutes. Add the bell pepper, sauté for 3 more minutes, then add the beans and sauté for 2 minutes. Reduce the heat to low.

Crumble the cooked bacon; then mix it together with the remaining ingredients in a small mixing bowl. Pour the well-blended mixture over the beans in the skillet. Continue to cook over low heat for about 20 minutes. Serve hot. Serves 4.

Lagniappe: This is almost like a barbecue sauce for green beans. It is quite nice. The red and green color combination is wonderful for almost any plate. You can cook this in advance and refrigerate it until you are ready to serve, but the red pepper is not quite as crispy after it has been chilled. Do not freeze this dish, you will lose too much quality.

I prefer to use freshly ground black pepper. There is a specific reason for using fresh ground. The black peppercorn retains a great deal of natural oil that is released at the cracking of the corn. As you might guess, the flavor is in the oil. Therefore, the more oil released, the greater the true flavor of the pepper. By using freshly ground pepper, we get the peak of flavor from our pepper.

Calories—200; Carb—17; Chol—13.4; Pro—17.8; Fib—1.9; Sod—1133

GREEN BEANS LOUISE

1 1/3 lb. fresh green beans
2 cups water
1 slice bacon
1 bay leaf
1/2 small onion, chopped
1 tsp. lemon juice
1 tsp. salt
5 black peppercorns

3 tbsp. unsalted butter
2 tbsp. minced fresh
  parsley
1 tbsp. minced fresh basil
  (or 1/4 tsp. dried)
1/2 tsp. black pepper
1/4 tsp. salt

Wash the green beans and cut off the ends. Break each bean into two pieces. In a large saucepan, combine the water, bacon, bay leaf, onion, lemon juice, salt, and peppercorns; then bring the water to a hard boil over high heat. Let the mixture boil for 1 minute, reduce the temperature to medium, and add the beans. Cook the beans for 10 minutes over medium heat.

Drain the beans, dry the saucepan, and return it to medium heat until it is hot. Melt the butter until it begins to smoke; then add the green beans and sauté them for 1 minute before adding the parsley and basil. Sauté for 3 more minutes, add the pepper and salt, then serve at once. Serves 4.

Lagniappe: As you have probably noticed, most of my recipes call for unsalted butter. I prefer unsalted butter because it is a better quality butter. It smokes at a higher temperature than regular butter, and you are able to control the exact amount of salt that you add to the dish. You may substitute margarine in all my recipes that call for butter, but remember that it will change the flavor of the dish. You can use a product called Butter Buds to give the dish the real butter flavor—you just can't sauté or fry in it. You must use some other oil, then add the Butter Buds for flavor after the cooking process is complete.

You can cook this recipe in advance, but I really don't know why you would. It is so quick and easy. Green beans will lose a lot of their quality and taste if they are not eaten right after cooking.

Calories—173; Carb—13.6; Fat—12.9; Chol—29; Pro—7.2; Fib—2.8; Sod—337

LOVELY LIMAS

1 cup water
1 lb. frozen lima beans
1 strip bacon, chopped
3 tbsp. unsalted butter
1/4 cup diced onions
2 tsp. sugar
3/4 tsp. salt

1/2 tsp. white pepper
1/8 tsp. Tabasco sauce
1/4 cup sour cream
1 tsp. all-purpose flour
 tbsp. minced green onion
    tops

In a medium-sized saucepan over high heat, bring the water to a boil. Rinse the frozen limas under cold water to separate them from each other; drain excess water. Add the limas with the chopped bacon to the boiling water. Bring the water back to a boil; then reduce the heat to medium, cover, and cook for 10 minutes.

Heat a small saucepan over medium-high heat. When it is hot, melt the butter until it begins to smoke; then sauté the onions for about 5 minutes, or until they are limp and clear. Add the sautéed onions to the limas along with the sugar, salt, pepper and Tabasco sauce. Blend in well. Cook the beans, uncovered, for 7 more minutes. Combine the sour cream and flour until blended; then pour it into the beans. Heat to the boiling point, but do not bring to a boil. Simmer for 2 minutes. Stir in the onion tops and serve hot. Serves 4.

Lagniappe: You can make these beans in advance and refrigerate them for up to 48 hours, but do not freeze them. Just reheat over low to the desired serving temperature, and serve. See the *Lagniappe* under **Field Peas New Iberia** for my lecture about using frozen beans and peas. I think you will really like the looks of this dish as well as the taste.

Calories—299; Carb—32.2; Fat—15.5; Chol—33.5; Pro—13.6; Fib—3.9; Sod—483

LIMA BEANS ST. JAMES

1 17-oz. can limas
1/2 cup dry vermouth
2 chicken bouillon cubes
1 slice bacon, chopped
1 medium onion, diced
1/2 cup diced green bell
  pepper
1/4 cup minced celery
1 clove garlic, minced
1 tbsp. Worcestershire
  sauce
1/4 tsp. Tabasco sauce

1/2 tsp. salt
1/3 cup grated monterey
  jack cheese
1/3 cup grated Swiss
  cheese
1/2 cup slivered almonds,
  roasted
1/2 cup seasoned bread
  crumbs
2 tsp. unsalted butter
paprika

Open the can of limas, and pour the liquid from the can into a small saucepan along with the dry vermouth, chicken bouillon, bacon, onion, green pepper, celery, garlic, Worcestershire sauce, Tabasco sauce, and salt. Bring the liquid to a boil over high heat until the liquid is reduced by half.

In a 1 1/2 or 2-quart casserole, place about 1/2 of the limas, cover with about 1/2 of the heated liquid, then 1/2 of the cheeses, and 1/2 of the almonds. Repeat the layering process, then spread the bread crumbs on top, dot with small pieces of the butter, and sprinkle with paprika. Bake at 375 degrees for 25 minutes. Serve hot. Serves 4.

Lagniappe: You can make this dish in advance and refrigerate it. Don't bake it completely before refrigerating. Remove from the oven with 10 minutes remaining to bake, allow to cool for a few minutes, then cover and refrigerate. When you are ready to serve, bake at 350 degrees for about 12 to 15 minutes.

I like this dish made with other types of beans as well. To make **Butter Beans St. James,** substitute a 17-ounce can of large butter beans for the limas. For **Navy Beans St. James,** use a 17-ounce can of navy beans; the rest of the recipe remains the same. I find that children like beans if they are prepared this way. I'm sure it has something to do with the cheese, but they seem prefer bean casserole to just plain beans. Some adults are like that too. I'm not saying they are childish — don't put words into my mouth!

Calories—486; Carb—48.5; Fat—29; Chol—42; Pro—25.9; Fib— 6.3; Sod—1149

FRENCH FRIED OKRA

peanut oil
1/3 cup all-purpose flour
1/3 cup yellow cornmeal
1 tsp. salt
1/4 tsp. red pepper
1/4 tsp. black pepper

1 lb. okra, cut in 1/2-inch slices
1 egg, beaten
1 cup milk
1/2 tsp. Tabasco sauce

Heat the peanut oil in a deep fryer to 375 degrees. In a paper sack or mixing bowl, combine the flour, cornmeal, salt, and red and black peppers. Mix well. Pour the sliced okra into the paper sack (or bowl) and coat well with the mixture.

In a large mixing bowl, combine the egg, milk, and Tabasco sauce. Remove the okra from the sack, taking care to shake off excess flour mixture, then soak the okra in the egg-milk mixture for 30 seconds. Return the okra to the flour mixture, and shake for 30 more seconds. Place the okra in the hot peanut oil and fry until it is golden brown. Drain on paper towels and serve at once. Serves 4.

Lagniappe: This is good Cajun eating. You can substitute fried okra for French fries or anytime you would like to add a little color and variety to a plate. They are easy to cook and quite tasty. Frying the okra removes all of its slime and gives it a unique flavor. The only negative aspect is that it does not keep well. You really must serve it soon after it is fried.

Calories—377; Carb—25.9; Fat—5.1; Chol—77; Pro—7.5; Fib— 1.5; Sod—632

CAJUN FRIED ONION RINGS

peanut oil	1 cup milk
2 large yellow onions	2 large eggs, lightly beaten
2/3 cup all-purpose flour	1 tbsp. Worcestershire
3 tsp. Cajun Seasoning Mix	sauce
(see index)	1/2 tsp. Tabasco sauce

Preheat the oil in a deep fryer or large saucepan to 375 degrees. Cut the onions into rings about 3/8 inch thick and spread them out so you can handle them easily. Put the flour and 2 tablespoons of the **Cajun Seasoning Mix** into a large paper or plastic bag; shake until the flour and seasonings are blended. Place about 1/4 of the onion rings into the bag and shake. Remove the onions to a large plate and repeat the process until all onions are lightly coated with flour.

In a large mixing bowl, combine the milk, eggs, Worcestershire sauce, and Tabasco sauce until blended. Place about 1/4 of the floured rings at a time into the milk mixture and let them soak. Return them to the flour bag and shake lightly until the onions are coated. Place them in the hot peanut oil and fry until they are a nice golden brown. Remove and set on paper towels to dry. Season to taste with the remaining **Cajun Seasoning Mix.** Serves 4.

Lagniappe: Fried onion rings are usually a hit with all kinds of foods. I like to use them as an appetizer or a vegetable. You can't really make this dish in advance. I would not even cut the onions because they loose so much of their natural juice (which helps the first coat of flour to stick) after being cut. You can't batter them in advance because the batter will become gummy and loose both texture and taste. They also must be eaten up completely because they are really no good when they are reheated. That's the downside. The upside is that they are so easy to fix that there is no real concern.

Remember to use peanut oil, it makes great onion rings. Don't plan on using the same peanut oil for other dishes; it loses it's effectiveness as an oil after one exposure to cooking. Therefore, use only as much oil as you think you are going to need.

Calories—349; Carb—25; Fat—24.2; Chol—148; Pro—8.3; Fib—.5; Sod—262

CREAM PEAS

1 16-oz. pkg. frozen green
  peas
2 tbsp. unsalted butter
1 tsp. minced shallots
3/4 cup chicken stock or
  broth
1/4 cup heavy whipping
  cream

1 tsp. all-purpose flour
1 tsp. sugar
1/2 tsp. salt
1/2 tsp. minced fresh basil
1/4 tsp. white pepper

Heat a 3-quart saucepan over medium heat. Place the frozen peas into a colander and run cold water over them to separate the peas. Drain well. Melt the butter in the hot skillet; then sauté the shallots for 1 minute. Add the peas and sauté for 3 minutes; then add the chicken stock and cook over medium heat for 9 minutes. Combine the cream, flour, and sugar until the flour is blended in. Pour the mixture into the pan of peas and bring to the boiling point, stirring often. Stir in the rest of the ingredients, and continue cooking until the sauce thickens nicely. Serve hot. Serves 4.

Lagniappe: Cream peas are a nice addition to any plate that needs the color or taste of sweet peas. They are a natural with any potato side dish and entree. You can make this dish completely in advance and refrigerate it (up to 48 hours) until you are ready to serve. Just reheat over low heat until the peas are warmed throughout. Do not freeze this dish.

Calories—161; Carb—18.5; Fat—7; Chol—17; Pro—7.4; Fib—4; Sod—441

GREEN PEAS AND RICE

3 tbsp. unsalted butter
1 medium onion, chopped
1/2 cup chopped bell
  pepper
1/4 cup minced celery
2 cloves garlic, minced
6 large mushrooms, thinly
  sliced
1 10-oz. pkg. frozen English
  peas, thawed
1/4 cup slivered toasted
  almonds

1/2 cup chopped green
  onions
1/4 cup ripe California
  olives, pitted and sliced
2 tbsp. chopped pimento
3 cups cooked long grain
  white rice
1 tsp. salt
1/2 tsp. Tabasco sauce
1/2 tsp. white pepper

Heat a large skillet over medium heat. When it is hot, add the butter. When the butter has melted and is beginning to smoke, sauté the onions, bell pepper, celery, and garlic for 3 minutes. Add the mushrooms, sauté for 2 minutes, then add the peas. Sauté for 1 minute before blending in the remaining ingredients; then sauté until the rice is hot. Serve at once. Serves 8.

Lagniappe: This is a green rice dish. The peas and the other vegetables really make this a beautiful dish. This is a sublime dish that is perfect to serve when you don't have a gravy or when you just need a vibrant side dish. You can make it in advance and either freeze or refrigerate it. To serve, either defrost in the refrigerator and heat in a skillet, or just put the frozen dish into the microwave covered with waxed paper, and heat.

Calories—208; Carb—28.7; Fat—8.9; Chol—13; Pro—5; Fib—2.3; Sod—689

FIELD PEAS NEW IBERIA

1 1/4 cup cold water
1 tsp. minced garlic
1/4 cup chopped onion
3/4 tsp. salt
1/2 tsp. black pepper
1 lb. fresh or frozen field
   peas with snaps
1 slice bacon, chopped
2 tbsp. butter

1/4 cup diced red bell
   pepper
2 large banana peppers, cut
   in long strips (or green
   bell peppers)
2 tsp. chopped fresh basil
1/4 tsp. Tabasco sauce
1 tbsp. minced fresh
   parsley

In a medium-sized saucepan over high heat, boil the water. Add the garlic, onion, salt, and black pepper. Let the mixture boil for 1 minute while you run cold water over the peas to separate them if they are frozen together. If the peas are fresh, just rinse them with cold water. Lower the heat to medium and add the peas, bacon, and butter to the boiling water. Bring the water back to boiling over medium heat, and cook at a rolling boil for 10 minutes. Add the bell pepper, banana pepper, basil, and Tabasco sauce; and cook for 9 more minutes at medium. Stir in the parsley; then remove from the heat and let the peas stand for 1 minute. Serve hot. Serves 4.

Lagniappe: Field peas are beans with a lot of depth. The stock they produce is quite tasty and can even be served as a gravy over rice. They retain their pretty color and create a stunning dish when combined with the peppers.

Don't be afraid to use quality frozen peas. They are quite good when you find a brand you can depend on. It is hard to beat the quality of fresh peas, unless you get them from a farmer's market or grow them yourself (or have a good friend with a farm!). Remember that, for the most part, frozen peas are picked and frozen the same day, capturing the peak of freshness. When peas go to market, they may be one or more weeks old. Which do you think is better? I don't know where we get the idea that freezing something necessarily makes it bad—it does not!

Oh well, I will get off the soap box and back to the kitchen. You can cook this dish in advance and refrigerate or even freeze it. Just defrost it in the refrigerator, and reheat over low heat until the peas are warm. Boy, you got extra *lagniappe* with this recipe!

Calories—235; Carb—28.3; Fat—10; Chol—21; Pro—12.7; Fib—4.2; Sod—482

JUST GREAT PEAS

1 17-oz. can green peas
2 tbsp. unsalted butter
1/4 tsp. Tabasco sauce
1/4 cup chopped green
  onions

2 tsp. sugar
1/4 cup finely chopped ham

Separate the peas from their liquid, reserving the juice. Heat a 2-quart saucepan over medium heat. When it is hot, melt the butter; then sauté the peas, Tabasco sauce, and green onions for 2 minutes. Add the sugar and 1/4 cup of the liquid from the pea can; then cook for 1 more minute. Add the ham, cook for 3 minutes, then serve hot. Serves 2.

Lagniappe: A recipe does not always have to be difficult to be good. I created this recipe when I had a little bit of leftover ham and didn't really know what to do with it. I liked the results of my experiment, so here it is. You can use frozen peas in this recipe if you just substitute 3/4 cup of chicken stock or broth (or water) for the liquid from the peas, and cook for 9 minutes after adding the liquid (instead of the 1 minute called for in the recipe). Peas add color to a plate and are quite tasty. Try them, you'll see!

Calories—369; Carb—15.1; Fat—49.4; Chol—50; Pro—18; Fib—8.1; Sod—395

SWEET PEAS BOGALUSA

1 10 3/4-oz. can cream of
  celery soup
1 cup grated Mexican-style
  Velveta cheese
1/2 cup grated Swiss
  cheese
2 17-oz. cans sweet peas
1/4 tsp. Tabasco sauce

1/2 cup salt
1 tbsp. sugar
1 tbsp. Worcestershire
  sauce
1 tsp. minced fresh parsley
1 tsp. white wine vinegar
1/2 cup slivered almonds
1/2 cup cracker crumbs

Heat the soup in a large saucepan over medium heat. Add the cheeses and continue to cook over medium heat. Blend in the remaining ingredients, except for the cracker crumbs. Place the mixture in a casserole dish and top with the cracker crumbs. Bake at 350 degrees for 25 minutes, or until the sauce begins to bubble around the edges. Serve hot. Serves 6.

Lagniappe: This is yet another very easy vegetable that tastes like you put more work into it than you did. It can be made in advance and stored in the refrigerator until you are ready to use it, but do not freeze it. I recommend refrigerating before baking; then bake just before you serve. Using the soup as a sauce base adds speed and provides a delicious quality product.

Calories—428; Carb—39.5; Fat—21.3; Chol—43; Pro—21.4; Fib—5.9; Sod—1326

POTATOES EDNA

1 gallon water
1 tbsp. salt
2 whole bay leaves
1 6-inch sprig fresh
    rosemary (or 1 tsp. dried)
1 1/2 lb. medium red
    potatoes, washed
5 strips uncooked bacon

1/2 tsp. Tabasco sauce
2 tbsp. unsalted butter
1/2 cup chopped green
    onions
1/2 cup diced red bell
    pepper
2 tbsp. minced fresh
    parsley

Boil the water in a large stock pot or 10-quart saucepan over high heat. Add the potatoes, salt, bay leaves, and fresh rosemary and cook for 14 minutes. Remove the potatoes, allow them to cool enough to be handled; then cut them into 1/4-inch slices.

Heat a large skillet over medium-high heat. When it is hot, fry the bacon until it is brown and crisp. Remove the bacon from the skillet; then add the Tabasco sauce and the butter. When the butter has melted, sauté the green onions and bell pepper for 2 minutes. Add the sliced potatoes and cook, shaking the pan often, for 4 minutes on one side then 6 minutes on the other. Crumble the cooked bacon and sprinkle the potatoes with it and the fresh parsley. Serve hot. Serves 4.

Lagniappe: The flavor of bacon is very pronounced in this potato dish. The potatoes are golden brown and the flavor is wonderful. This dish is especially good with pork or chicken. You can save a lot of time by boiling the potatoes in advance and letting them sit in the refrigerator until you are ready to use them.

Calories—226; Carb—37.5; Fat—22.5; Chol—36; Pro—22.7; Fib—1.7; Sod—787

CHEESY POTATOES

3 large white baking
potatoes (1 1/2 lb.)
3 tbsp. butter
3 tbsp. all-purpose flour
1 1/4 cup evaporated milk
1/2 tsp. Tabasco sauce
1/2 tsp. salt
1/4 tsp. white pepper

1/4 cup grated Swiss
cheese
1/4 cup grated monterey
jack cheese
1/4 cup grated gruyère
cheese
1 tbsp. minced fresh chives
1/4 tsp. paprika

Wash and scrub the potatoes, then stick each one with a fork. Wrap each potato in waxed paper and place them in the microwave. Microwave at full power for 6 minutes; then turn over and microwave for 6 more minutes at full power. Remove from the microwave and allow the potatoes to cool as you complete the recipe.

In a 4 or 5-quart saucepan over medium heat, melt the butter. Add the flour and cook, constantly stirring, for 3 minutes. Add the milk, Tabasco sauce, salt, and white pepper. Cook, stirring, for 2 minutes. Peel the potatoes, slice them very thinly crosswise; then add them to the sauce. Reduce the heat to low and cook for 3 minutes, stirring carefully. Fold in the cheeses until they have melted. Add the fresh chives and paprika and serve at once. Serves 4.

Lagniappe: This is a real treat. Potatoes and cheese really go well together. We made a light roux by mixing the flour with the oil (butter); then we made a light cream sauce called a béchamel sauce. We cooked the potatoes in the sauce and, by adding the cheese, we made a mornay sauce. This is an easy dish that represents several cooking techniques.

You can bake the potatoes up to 4 to 6 hours in advance. I don't like the color of baked potatoes if they are done much earlier than that—they begin to darken. In this nice white sauce, darkened potatoes would take away from the overall ambience. This is a great side dish for almost any entree.

Calories—454; Carb—50.6; Fat—24.5; Chol—70; Pro—15.4; Fib—1.5; Sod—455

SAUTEED POTATOES TERRIOT

1 gallon water
1 tbsp. salt
1 1/4 lb. medium red
    potatoes, washed well
12 peppercorns
3 tbsp. unsalted butter

1 clove garlic, minced
3/4 tsp. Cajun Seasoning
    Mix (see index)
2 tbsp. minced fresh
    parsley

Boil the water in a large stock pot or 10-quart saucepan over high heat. Add the potatoes, salt, and peppercorns; then bring the water back to a boil. Cook at a rolling boil for 14 minutes. Remove the potatoes from the water and allow them to cool enough to be handled. Peel the skin off and slice the potatoes about 3/8 inch thick.

Heat a heavy skillet over medium-high heat. When it is hot, melt the butter until it begins to smoke; then swirl in the garlic. Add the potatoes to the skillet and cook for 4 minutes, shaking the pan a few times. Turn the potatoes over to brown the other side. Sprinkle with the **Cajun Seasoning Mix,** add the parsley, and brown for 5 to 6 more minutes. The potatoes should be firm but tender and golden brown. Serve hot. Serves 4.

Lagniappe: This is another easy potato recipe that can replace a mundane baked potato. These potatoes will take on a nice crisp crust that is quite tasty. This is a great side dish to accompany any steak, chicken, or veal dish. It is pretty and tasty.

You can boil the potatoes in advance and store them in the refrigerator until you are ready to cook. In fact, you can boil them up to 3 days in advance. That makes the recipe even more of a breeze. The potatoes are easier to handle when they are cold rather than just cool enough to handle.

Calories—233; Carb—35.1; Fat—9.4; Chol—25; Pro—3.4; Fib—1.3; Sod—739

SAUTEED NEW POTATOES

1 1/4 lb. small new
  potatoes
1 tsp. salt
3/4 cup seasoned croutons
1 large egg, beaten
1 tbsp. water
1 tsp. Worcestershire sauce
1/2 tsp. Tabasco sauce

1/2 stick unsalted butter
1 clove garlic, minced
1 tbsp. minced fresh basil
  (or 1 tsp. dried)
1/4 cup finely chopped
  green onions
2 tbsp. minced parsley

Clean the new potatoes and place them in a large pot. Cover them with water and add the salt. Bring to a boil over high heat for 7 minutes; then remove the pot from the heat, leaving the potatoes in the water until you are ready for them.

Place the croutons in a food processor or blender and chop until they turn into crumbs. Pour the crumbs into a large mixing bowl or on a large platter. In another large mixing bowl, combine the eggs, water, Worcestershire sauce, and Tabasco sauce. Mix together well. Remove the potatoes from the water and drain. Drop the potatoes into the egg mixture, coat them well, then press them into the crumbs. Place the potatoes on a plate.

Heat a large skillet over medium-high heat until it is hot. Add the butter, let it melt and begin to smoke; then sauté the garlic, basil, green onions, and potatoes for about 5 to 7 minutes. Shake the pan to prevent sticking and to ensure browning on all sides. Serve straight from the skillet. Serves 4.

Lagniappe: This is a great substitute for the boring baked potato! Potatoes are an excellent choice as a starch, but all to often we don't use our imagination when serving potatoes. We either bake, boil, or mash them. This is a good example of just how interesting the potato can be.

The total preparation time for this dish is under 20 minutes, and you can do some of the steps in advance. The potatoes can be boiled, dipped into the egg mixture, and pressed into the crumbs in advance. You can cover and refrigerate them until you are ready to sauté. You can refrigerate the leftovers (if there are any), and reheat by warming them in a skillet for about 3 minutes. I don't recommend freezing them.

Using fresh herbs, if you can, is always preferable to dried. You get a crispness and fullness that you can't get from the dried herbs.

Calories—305; Carb—36.8; Fat—15.3; Chol—102; Pro—6; Fib—.3; Sod—452

TWICE BAKED POTATO

2 large baking potatoes, about 7 to 8 inches long
1/2 stick unsalted butter
3/4 cup chopped green onions
1 tbsp. minced celery
1 tsp. salt
1/2 tsp. black pepper
1/2 tsp. onion powder

1/4 tsp. Tabasco sauce
1/2 cup grated monterey jack cheese
1/2 cup grated Swiss cheese
2/3 cup sour cream
1/4 cup real bacon bits
2/3 cup grated sharp cheddar cheese

Wash and clean the potatoes well, cutting off any brown spots. Pierce each potato with a fork to allow steam to escape; then wrap them in waxed paper and put them into the microwave. Cook at full power for 8 minutes. Turn the potatoes over, and set the microwave to cook for another 8 minutes at full power. After 5 minutes, check the doneness of each potato by pressing with your finger. Be careful because they are extremely hot. If the potato is soft, it is cooked; if not, continue to cook for the remaining 3 minutes. Remove the potatoes from the microwave, cut them in half lengthwise, and allow them to cool enough to be handled.

Preheat the oven to 400 degrees. Heat a medium-sized skillet over medium heat. When it is hot, melt the butter until it begins to smoke, then sauté the green onions and celery for 4 minutes. Scoop the center of each potato half into the skillet. Mix in well, then remove from heat and fold in the remaining ingredients, except for 1/3 cup of the cheddar cheese. Spoon the potato mixture back into the four potato shells. Top each potato with the remaining cheddar cheese. Place the four halves into the 400-degree oven, and bake for 15 minutes. Serve hot. Serves 4.

Lagniappe: This is the ultimate potato. It is great as a substitute for a baked potato. I like it as an entree for lunch. You can add extra stuffing, such as seafood, meats, or vegetables. With additional ingredients, the potatoes are quite stuffed and look quite appealing.

You can make them in advance and either freeze or refrigerate until you are ready to serve them. I would not do the final baking before refrigerating or freezing. To serve, just place directly into the oven (frozen or not) at 400 degrees, and bake for 15 minutes.

Calories—608; Carb—46.3; Fat—38.5; Chol—97; Pro—24.1; Fib—1.8; Sod—889

QUICK DIRTY RICE
(Rice Dressing)

1 lb. ground chuck
1 lb. hot country sausage
1/2 lb. chicken livers
2 tsp. Cajun Seasoning Mix
  (see index)
1 large onion, finely
  chopped
1 medium bell pepper,
  diced
1/2 cup minced celery

3 cloves garlic, minced
1/2 tsp. Tabasco sauce
1 tbsp. Worcestershire
  sauce
3 cups cooked white long
  grain rice
1 cup finely chopped green
  onions
1/4 cup minced parsley

Heat a large, heavy skillet over medium-high heat until it is hot; then sauté the ground chuck, sausage, and chicken livers for about 3 minutes, stirring often, until browned. Blend in the **Cajun Seasoning Mix.** Add the onions, bell pepper, celery, garlic, and Tabasco sauce; then sauté for 5 more minutes. Mix in the Worcestershire sauce and rice, then add the green onions and parsley. Cook, stirring often, for 2 more minutes. Serve immediately. Serves 6.

Lagniappe: This dish is an old Cajun jewel that I have tried to speed up without losing its essence. Cooking at high temperatures helps keep everything crisp while quickly blending the flavors together. The liver will break apart and practically dissipate because of all the stirring. This is tradition in a contemporary mode. Don't let the name frighten you—it comes from the color the rice takes from the browned meats. If "dirty" food bothers you, you can call it by its cultured name—**Rice Dressing.**

You can make it in advance and either refrigerate or freeze it. In fact, I usually cook extra meat mixture, up to the addition of the rice, and freeze it for some very quick **Dirty Rice.** When I am ready to use it, I just defrost it in the microwave, and stir in the cooked rice, green onions, and parsley. I then cover it with plastic wrap, punch about 3 holes in the top, and microwave. Even Cajuns can use high tech cooking methods! If you are wondering why this recipe is in the vegetable section, it is because it is most often eaten as a side dish.

Calories—690; Carb—32.6; Fat—36.4; Chol—382; Pro—53; Fib—.7; Sod—1683

SPINACH SPAULDING

1 1/2 lb. fresh spinach
2 tsp. salt
1 1/2 cups cooked white long grain rice
1/2 cup grated Swiss cheese
1/2 cup grated sharp cheddar cheese
1/2 cup grated American cheese
2 large brown eggs, lightly beaten
1/2 cup half and half cream

1 tbsp. butter, softened
1/4 cup minced onions
2 cloves garlic, minced
2 tbsp. minced celery
1 tbsp. Worcestershire sauce
1/4 tsp. Tabasco sauce
1 tsp. salt
1 tsp. minced fresh basil (or 1/4 tsp. dried)
1/2 tsp. minced fresh sage (or 1/8 tsp. dried)
1/2 cup cracker crumbs

Preheat the oven to 375 degrees. Clean and trim the spinach, then place it in a large saucepot or stockpot. Cover with water to 1 inch over the spinach. Boil the spinach over high heat for 4 minutes. In a large mixing bowl, combine the remaining ingredients, except for the cracker crumbs. Mix until thoroughly blended.

Remove the spinach from the pot, drain it, and allow it to cool enough to work with. Chop the spinach a few times, then mix it into the mixing bowl. Butter a 2-quart casserole, pour the spinach mixture into the casserole, and sprinkle with the cracker crumbs. Bake for 20 minutes at 375 degrees. Serves 8.

Lagniappe: This is the way to disguise spinach for those who won't eat it—just don't tell them what it is. Sit back and watch, but don't laugh out loud because people get very angry if they are tricked by a cook!

This is a great casserole that can be made completely in advance and either frozen or refrigerated. To bring it back to life, just allow it to thaw in the refrigerator; then bake at 325 degrees until it is heated through, about 12 to 15 minutes.

This dish can be served as a vegetable or as the starch for the meal. You can make an entree out of it by adding 1 pound of lump crabmeat after you add the spinach. Fold the crabmeat in gently so you won't destroy the beautiful lumps in your **Lump Crabmeat Spaulding.** You can add 2 cups of baked or sautéed bite-sized pieces of chicken breast along with the spinach to create **Breast of Chicken Spaulding.** The possibilities are endless.

Calories—236; Carb—19.3; Fat—14.3; Chol—109; Pro—8.9; Fib—3.3; Sod—1600

SUMMER SQUASH SAUTE

1 lb. tender yellow summer
  squash
2 tbsp. butter
2 tbsp. olive oil

1 tbsp. minced shallots
1/2 tsp. salt
1/2 tsp. black pepper
1/8 tsp. cayenne pepper

Cut the squash into slices about 3/8 inch thick and set them aside. Heat a large, heavy skillet over medium heat. When it is hot, heat the butter and olive oil until they begin to smoke; then add the squash. Sauté the squash for 2 minutes; then add the remaining ingredients and sauté, stirring often, for about 5 more minutes. The squash should be crisp and tender. Serves 4.

Lagniappe: The only thing I would do in advance is slice the squash. Everything else happens so fast that this recipe is finished almost as soon as it is started. The pronounced yellow color of the dish really makes it a nice vegetable for many entrees.

Calories—162; Carb—11.4; Fat—13.5; Chol—17; Pro—1.3; Fib—1.4; Sod—291

YELLOW SQUASH CALHOUN

8 medium yellow summer
  squash
4 tsp. salt
3 cups water
1 lb. large shrimp,
  unpeeled
4 slices bacon, chopped
3 tbsp. unsalted butter
1 medium onion, chopped
2 cloves garlic, minced
2 tbsp. minced celery
3 tbsp. minced carrots
1 1/2 tsp. Cajun Seasoning
  Mix (see index)

1 1/2 cups chopped soft
  French bread
1 large brown egg, slightly
  beaten
1/4 cup minced fresh
  parsley
1 tsp. minced fresh basil
1/2 cup seasoned bread
  crumbs
1 tbsp. lightly salted butter,
  melted

Wash the squash and place them in a large pot. Cover them with water and add 2 teaspoons of the salt. Boil over high heat for 2 minutes; then remove from the heat. Let the squash sit in the water until you are ready for them.

In another pot, combine the 3 cups of water and the remaining 2 tsp. of salt. Bring it to a hard boil, add the shrimp and cook for exactly 3 minutes after the water returns to a boil. Drain the shrimp and let them cool. Remove the squash from the pot and cut off the stems. Cut each squash in half lengthwise and scoop out the pulp, leaving about 1/4 inch of pulp around the shell. Chop the pulp and set it aside. Peel the shrimp, coarsely chop them, and set them aside.

Preheat the oven to 400 degrees. Heat a skillet over medium-high heat. When it is hot, fry the bacon pieces until they are browned. Add the butter, and when it begins to smoke, sauté the onions, garlic, celery, and carrots for 4 minutes. Add the reserved squash pulp, sauté for 3 more minutes; then mix in the shrimp and **Cajun Seasoning Mix.**

Combine the remaining ingredients, except for the seasoned bread crumbs and melted butter. Fold this mixture into the skillet and mix it in well. Spoon the stuffing mixture into the squash shells. Mix the bread crumbs into the melted butter, then sprinkle over each stuffed squash half. Place the squash in a baking dish and bake at 400 degrees for about 20 to 25 minutes until golden brown. Serve hot. Serves 8.

Lagniappe: This dish may be made in advance and frozen or refrigerated for later use. It is a great way to serve shrimp in the summer. Yellow squash is tender and flavorful, and blending it with the shrimp makes for a distinctive dish. I like to stuff several squash, then wrap each set of two halves together, and freeze. I can use them as a side dish or as a main dish—whichever I prefer. You can also use this recipe to make **Zucchini Calhoun** by using 8 medium zucchini instead of the yellow squash.

Calories—268; Carb—33.5; Fat—15.5; Chol—149; Pro—22.6; Fib—1.3; Sod—661

HOLLANDAISE SAUCE

1 stick unsalted butter
4 large brown eggs, yolks
  only
2 tbsp. fresh lemon juice

1/4 tsp. Tabasco sauce
1/4 tsp. salt
ice shavings or cold water

Melt the butter over low heat (or in the microwave) and set it aside. In a small metal mixing bowl, combine the egg yolks, lemon juice, Tabasco Sauce, and salt. Use a small electric mixer—preferably one that has a wire whisk—to beat the mixture until it is blended.

In a saucepan that is small enough for the metal bowl to rest on top of, bring some water to boil. When the water is boiling, reduce heat to simmer so just a small amount of steam rises. Place the metal mixing bowl on top of the saucepan, and continue to beat the mixture as it cooks for about 2 minutes. The sauce should thicken to look somewhat like pudding.

Begin to add the melted butter, a little at a time, beating after each addition. Constantly scrape the sides of the bowl so the egg does not stick or scramble. Keep your hand on the bowl throughout the cooking process. If the bowl gets to hot for you, lift it from the heat—beating all the time—then lower it as soon as the sauce cools. The sauce is done when all of the butter is blended in and it is smooth. Serve over steamed vegetables, meats, seafoods, or anything else that needs some flavor. Makes about 1 cup.

Lagniappe: This is a sauce that should be made as you need it. If you have extra, store it in the refrigerator in a tightly covered bowl. When you are ready to use it, let it stand at room temperature for about 1 hour; then whip it with a fork. It will return to the consistency of the freshly made sauce.

Calories—77; Carb—.4; Fat—7.7; Chol—94; Pro—1.8; Fib—0; Sod—59

SWEET POTATO CHIPS

peanut oil
3 large sweet potatoes,
  peeled

1/4 tsp. cinnamon
1/2 cup powdered sugar

Preheat the peanut oil in a deep fryer to 375 degrees. Use enough oil for the chips to be able to be completely submerged. With a sharp knife, cut the potatoes into chips about the thickness of thick potato chips. Fry one potato's worth of chips at a time, until all the slices are a nice golden brown. Drain on paper towels. Mix the cinnamon and powdered sugar together until blended. Sprinkle the chips with the cinnamon sugar mixture, then serve hot. Serves 4.

Lagniappe: This recipe can be used as a vegetable, appetizer, or as a snack food. The chips can be made in advance and stored in a tight container after they have cooled, but they are really best if eaten right away. This is a good way to get the kids to eat sweet potatoes (and all that vitamin A).

Calories—453; Carb—68.6; Fat—18.7; Chol—0; Pro—3; Fib— 3.2; Sod—18

Desserts

ENCHANTING BAKED APPLE

4 medium baking apples
2 tbsp. light brown sugar
2 tbsp. dark brown sugar
3 tbsp. unsalted butter
1/8 tsp. salt

1/8 tsp. ginger
1/4 tsp. nutmeg
1/4 tsp. cinnamon
2 tsp. vanilla extract

Cut the top of the apple at an angle to remove the stem. Partially core the apple to remove the seeds, but do not go all the way through the apple to the bottom. Leave the bottom intact to form a hollow to hold the baking filling.

Place each apple in a round, lightly buttered individual ramekin. Combine the remaining ingredients until well blended. Spoon equal amounts of the mixture into each apple's center. Bake at 450 degrees for 5 minutes, then remove and let the apples stand for about 5 minutes. Serve hot as a dessert or as a side dish. Serves 4.

Lagniappe: You can prepare the apples early and set them aside until you are ready to bake. If you plan to use them at a later date, combine the juice of 1/2 lemon with 2 cups of water, then fill the center of the apple with the lemon water. Let them stand with the lemon water for about 2 minutes; then drain and fill them with the baking filling. Cover and refrigerate until you are ready to bake. This makes a splendid side dish with many meals. If you are going to serve it as a dessert, you might want to top each apple with a large spoonful of fresh whipped cream.

Calories—225; Carb—34.7; Fat—10.8; Chol—28; Pro—.4; Fib—2.8; Sod—9.9

FRESH BLUEBERRIES ON A CLOUD

8 extra large eggs, whites
  only
1 1/2 cups sugar
1 tsp. cream of tartar
2 tsp. vanilla extract

3 tbsp. powdered sugar
2 recipes Whipped Cream
  Topping (see index)
2 cups fresh blueberries,
  washed and drained

1/8 tsp. finely grated lemon rind	chocolate shavings
1 1/2 cups real chocolate chips	

Preheat the oven to 425 degrees. In a large mixing bowl, beat the egg whites until they are stiff. Gradually beat in the sugar; then whip in the cream of tartar, vanilla, and lemon rind. Lightly butter a 10 by 14-inch baking pan; then cover the bottom with the meringue. Bake for 3 minutes at 425 degrees; then remove from the oven and turn the oven off.

Let the meringue sit for 2 minutes, then return it to the oven for 5 minutes. Remove it again, and sprinkle the chocolate chips over the meringue. Sprinkle the powdered sugar on top, then return to the warm oven until it is completely cooled and the chips have melted somewhat.

When the dish is completely cool, spread one recipe of the fresh **Whipped Cream Topping** over the chocolate chips. Cover evenly with the two cups of blueberries, then top with the second recipe of **Whipped Cream Topping.** Garnish with a few blueberries and shavings of chocolate. Serve at once or refrigerate until you are ready to serve. Serves 8.

Lagniappe: What ecstasy! It's almost like paradise or biting into nothing. The fresh berries and chocolate blend together with the whipped cream to make this an absolutely elegant dessert. It can be made in advance and refrigerated for up to 12 hours but, after that, the whipped cream starts to decrease. It is great right after it is made, and equally delightful from the refrigerator.

Feel free to change the berries if you like. I use fresh blackberries when they are in season, and raspberries as well. Use 2 cups of fresh blackberries instead of the blueberries to make **Fresh Blackberries on a Cloud,** or use 2 cups of fresh raspberries to make **Fresh Raspberries on a Cloud.** Any berry you choose will produce a hit!

Calories—613; Carb—72; Fat—20.5; Chol—44; Pro—5.4; Fib—1.1; Sod—66

FRESH RASPBERRIES HEATHER

3 tbsp. sugar
1 tbsp. light brown sugar
3 tbsp. unsalted butter
2 cups fresh raspberries
2 tbsp. fresh orange juice

1/3 cup Grand Marnier
 liqueur
1/4 tsp. grated orange peel
2/3 cup cognac
vanilla ice cream

Heat a large skillet or flambé pan over medium heat. When it is hot, add the sugar and light brown sugar. Try to spread it out across the pan. As the sugars begin to melt, use a spoon to swirl the unmelted sugar into the melted sugar. When the sugar turns a golden brown, quickly blend in the butter. Do not wait too long, or the sugar will turn dark brown or even black.

Crush one cup of the raspberries with a spoon to make them give up some of their juice. Add the crushed cup of raspberries to the pan along with the orange juice. Stir in well. Add the Grand Marnier and the grated orange peel and let the sauce simmer for about 3 minutes, stirring a few times. Stir the remaining cup of raspberries into the sauce.

Add the cognac, let it heat up for a few seconds, then put a lit match near it to ignite the alcohol. Flambé until the flame burns itself out. Do not try anything fancy—just shake the pan a little. The sauce should be thickened when the flame goes out. Spoon generous amounts of the sauce over vanilla ice cream. Serves 8.

Lagniappe: Another flambé! Raspberries are so wonderful to work with. They are pungent and full of body. They utilize all of the taste-buds in your mouth. This is a dessert that can be made without much preparation and can finish off any meal. Try serving it over angel food cake or cheese cake. It is divine. You can refrigerate the surplus for later use. I like to use it cold as well.

Calories—214; Carb—25.5; Fat—11.9; Chol—42; Pro—2.7; Fib—1.5; Sod-60

CHERRY COBBLER

2 cups Bisquick mix
2 tbsp. dark brown sugar
3 tbsp. light brown sugar
1/2 tsp. ground nutmeg
1/8 tsp. orange peel spice
3 tbsp. unsalted butter,
   softened

2/3 cup evaporated milk
2 17-oz. cans pitted tart
   red cherries
1 tsp. fresh lemon juice
1 1/2 cups sugar
1 recipe Whipped Cream
   Topping (see index)

Preheat the oven to 425 degrees. Combine the first five ingredients in a large mixing bowl. Cut in the butter with a fork or pastry cutter. Blend in the milk to make a nice thick batter. Lightly butter a 10 by 14-inch baking pan; then pour in the batter and spread it evenly across the pan.

Drain the cherries and reserve their liquid. Spread the cherries out equally on top of the batter. Mix together the reserved cherry liquid, lemon juice, and sugar until the sugar is dissolved. Pour the liquid over the cherries. Bake at 425 degrees for about 30 minutes. Remove from the oven, allow the cobbler to cool slightly, then serve warm with a large spoonful of fresh whipped cream. Serves 8.

Lagniappe: This recipe uses mixes and canned fruit to make a great dessert with ease. I got this technique from a number of my cooking school students. I followed their directions and was quite pleased with the results. The more I travel, the more good—no make that great—ideas I get from students. Some of my best recipes have come from a student saying, "Couldn't you make that with . . . ?" I've learned to listen and take good notes. We all can learn from others if we remember to listen to their suggestions. If you have a good idea for a recipe, please write and let me know.

This recipe can be made in advance and either refrigerated or frozen for later use. It is a great last-minute dessert. I always have a few cans of fruit and a big box of biscuit mix handy in the pantry. You never know when someone will call to say they are on their way!

Calories—567; Carb—97.3; Fat—19.7; Chol—55; Pro—3.5; Fib—1.4; Sod—374

NO-FUSS PEACH COBBLER

2 1/4 cups sugar
1 1/2 cups all-purpose flour
2 1/2 tsp. baking powder
1/2 tsp. baking soda
1/2 tsp. salt
1/4 tsp. ground nutmeg
1 1/2 cup milk

1 tsp. vanilla extract
2/3 cup unsalted butter,
  melted
4 cups fresh peaches,
  peeled and sliced
1/8 tsp. finely minced fresh
  lemon rind

Preheat the oven to 350 degrees. In a large mixing bowl, combine 1 cup of the sugar with the flour, baking powder, baking soda, salt, and nutmeg until well blended. Stir in the milk and vanilla extract to form a batter.

Pour the melted butter into the bottom of a 3-quart shallow baking dish or a 10 by 14-inch cake pan; then tilt the pan to coat the entire bottom of the pan. Pour the batter on top of the butter. Do not stir.

In a separate bowl, mix together the fresh peaches, the remaining sugar, and the lemon rind until the peach slices are coated with sugar. Pour the peaches on top of the batter, but do not stir. Bake at 350 degrees for about 45 minutes. Serve warm. Serves 10.

Lagniappe: The hardest thing about this recipe is slicing the fresh peaches. You can drop them into boiling water for about 30 seconds, let them cool enough to handle, then easily remove the skin. Cut them in half, remove the seed, then cut them into slices. The batter will rise up to form the crust for this cobbler. The taste is delectable and, as you can see, the recipe is effortless.

You can make this dish in advance and keep it on the kitchen counter for up to 12 hours. For anything over twelve hours, I recommend refrigerating. You can also freeze this cobbler for later use. To serve, just defrost it in the refrigerator. If I want to serve it warm, I would then use the microwave to warm it. Top it with fresh **Whipped Cream Topping** or ice cream. My preferred topping for this recipe is the whipped cream—but the choice is yours.

Calories—305; Carb—52.9; Fat—18.1; Chol—5; Pro—5.3; Fib— 1.3; Sod—247

PEACH FLAMBE BOREL

5 fresh peaches	2 tbsp. fresh lemon juice
1/2 stick unsalted butter	1/2 cup peach brandy
1/4 cup light brown sugar	2/3 cup cognac
1/2 cup sugar	1 tbsp. cornstarch
1/4 tsp. minced fresh	1/4 cup cold water
lemon rind	vanilla ice cream
1/4 tsp. ground nutmeg	

Peel the peaches, remove the pits, and cut them into slices. In a large skillet or flambé pan over medium heat, melt the butter. Add the brown sugar, sugar, lemon rind, and nutmeg. Cook for 1 minute, stirring constantly; then add the peaches and cook for 4 more minutes, stirring. Stir in the lemon juice and peach brandy. Cook for 2 more minutes; then add the cognac carefully. Let it heat up for a few seconds, then put a lit match near the pan to ignite it. Flambé the peaches until the fire burns itself out. Do not do anything other than gently shake the pan.

Dissolve the cornstarch in the cold water, then pour it into the peach mixture. Blend it in as the mixture thickens. Spoon generous amounts of the peaches and sauce over vanilla ice cream. Serves 8.

Lagniappe: I really just love flambés. They are showy, tasty, and usually served over ice cream. What could be better? They are also quick and don't require a lot of preparation. The flambé is the ideal dessert. This dessert can be as little or as big as you and your guests would like.

This sauce is fine over cheesecake or pound cake. You can refrigerate the leftovers (if there are any) for later use. Just reheat either in the microwave or on the stove, and use it to top whatever you like. For frozen yogurt lovers, this is a marvelous yogurt topping.

Calories—312; Carb—47.8; Fat—13.3; Chol—46; Pro—3.3; Fib— .6; Sod—65

BLACKBERRY COBBLER

4 cups fresh blackberries
1 tsp. fresh lemon juice
1 cup sugar
1 cup self-rising flour
1 tsp. vanilla extract

1 large brown egg, slightly
   beaten
1 stick unsalted butter,
   melted

Preheat the oven to 375 degrees. Wash the blackberries and drain them well. Toss the berries in the lemon juice, then put them on the bottom of a 2 1/2-quart shallow casserole dish or baking pan. Combine the sugar, flour, vanilla, and egg to make a pasty crumb mixture. Crumble this mixture over the blackberries in the casserole. Pour the melted butter evenly over the dish; then bake at 375 degrees for about 35 minutes until golden brown.

Lagniappe: You can bake it, then refrigerate or freeze this cobbler for later use. It is elementary, yet the taste is scrumptious. I like to serve it with ice cream. You can substitute the fresh fruit of your choice if you don't have blackberries.

Calories—298; Carb—43.9; Fat—13.3; Chol—72; Pro—2.9; Fib—3.3; Sod—11

FRESH CHERRY PARFAIT PIE

4 cups fresh cherries,
    pitted
1/2 cup sugar
1/2 cup water
1 3-oz. pkg. cherry flavored
    gelatin

2 cups vanilla ice cream
1 recipe Graham Cracker-
    Ginger Snap Crust (see
    index)
1 recipe Whipped Cream
    Topping (see index)

In a medium mixing bowl, combine the cherries, sugar, and water and let the mixture stand for about 20 minutes. Drain the liquid from the cherries into a medium-sized saucepan. Bring to a boil over medium heat; then remove from the heat and stir in the gelatin until it has dissolved. Add the cherries and stir until they are all coated. Pour into a large mixing bowl, add the ice cream, and stir until the ice cream has completely melted. Cover and refrigerate until the mixture holds it shape when spooned.

Spoon the filling into the **Graham Cracker-Ginger Snap Crust** and refrigerate until firm. Cover with the **Whipped Cream Topping,** and serve. Serves 6.

Lagniappe: This is a gorgeous pie. You can refrigerate it for up to 2 days before using it. In fact, it really tastes better if you refrigerate it. Do not freeze it, and do not make the whipped cream until just before you are ready to serve.

This makes a great Sunday dessert or a special pie to bring to a gathering. You can use this recipe to make **Fresh Blackberry Parfait Pie** by substituting 4 cups of fresh blackberries for the cherries and using either blackberry or raspberry gelatin.

Calories—827; Carb—139; Fat—39.6; Chol—118; Pro—20.6; Fib—1.8; Sod—164

FRESH STRAWBERRY PIE

1 1/2 cup sugar
1/4 cup cornstarch
2 cups water
1 3-oz. pkg. strawberry
    gelatin

5 cups whole fresh
    strawberries
2 9-inch pie shells, baked

Mix together the sugar and cornstarch until well blended; then combine with the water in a saucepan and bring the mixture to a boil. Cook, stirring often, for about 4 minutes; then remove from the heat. Blend in the strawberry gelatin until it is dissolved, then allow the mixture to cool completely.

Remove the stems from the strawberries; then arrange them, pointed ends up, in the pie shells. Pour the liquid mixture over the berries, and chill until the jello mixture sets. Makes 2 pies.

Lagniappe: You can make these pies in advance and keep them refrigerated for up to 4 days. They are better if served within 24 hours, but they hold quite nicely in the refrigerator. Do not freeze these pies. Try to choose berries that are not too large. If the only berries you find are too big, then slice them before arranging them in the pie shells. You can top the pies with **Whipped Cream Topping** (see index); it is a nice touch.

Calories—298; Carb—50; Fat—10.3; Chol—0; Pro—2.7; Fib—1.3; Sod—23

SWEET POTATO PIE

4 medium-sized fresh sweet
  potatoes
1/4 tsp. salt
1 stick unsalted butter
1/2 tsp. nutmeg
1 tsp. vanilla extract
1/2 cup sugar

4 extra large eggs, well
  beaten
1/2 13-oz can evaporated
  milk
2 10-inch pastry pie shells
whipped cream (optional)

Preheat the oven to 350 deegrees. In a large pot over high heat, boil the potatoes in water with the salt. When a fork goes into the potatoes with ease, they are cooked (about 20 minutes). Remove the potatoes from the water and peel them. Mash the potatoes in a large bowl until smooth. Mix in the butter, nutmeg, and vanilla.

In a small bowl, dissolve the sugar in the milk; then add it to the potato mixture and blend until smooth. Pour the mixture into each pie shell, and bake for 70 to 75 minutes at 350 degrees. If a knife comes out clean when stuck into the center of the pie, the pie is cooked. Serve hot or cold. Top with fresh whipped cream just before serving. Serves 12.

Lagniappe: Although the cooking time for this pie is over an hour, the preparation time is quick. This pie is too good to leave out of this book. You can use canned sweet potatoes if you can't get fresh, but you can really tell the difference. If you really can't find fresh sweet potatoes, just use one 40-ounce can of sweet potato. Be sure to drain any water that may be in the can before proceeding with the recipe.

This is a great dessert for any time of the year, but it is especially nice during the holidays. Be sure to store this pie in the refrigerator, it is a custard pie that will spoil if not kept chilled.

Calories—503; Carb—73.2; Fat—21.4; Chol—119; Pro—6.4; Fib—1.5; Sod—100

RUM PIE

1/2 cup unsalted butter, softened
3/4 cup sugar
1/2 cup dark brown sugar
1/2 cup all-purpose flour
2 large brown eggs, slightly beaten
1 cup chopped walnuts

1 6-oz. pkg. semisweet chocolate chips
1 1/2 tsp. vanilla extract
1 tsp. rum
1 9-inch unbaked pie shell
1 recipe Whipped Cream Topping (see index)
1 tbsp. dark Jamaican rum

Preheat the oven to 350 degrees. In a large mixing bowl, cream the butter, sugar, and brown sugar until well mixed. Beat in the flour and eggs until smooth. Fold in the walnuts, chocolate chips, vanilla, and rum. Pour the batter into the unbaked pie shell; then bake at 350 degrees for about 45 minutes. Remove and allow the pie to cool.

Beat the dark rum into the **Whipped Cream Topping.** When the pie has completely cooled, cover it with the rum whipped cream. Serve at once. Serves 6.

Lagniappe: Although it does take a while to bake this pie, it doesn't take long to put it together. I recommend baking it in the morning and letting it cool; then refrigerating until you are ready to serve. Don't make the whipped cream until just before serving.

It is a wonderful dessert. With the small amount of rum that is in it, you will be surprised by the full rum flavor. If you are artistic, you can pipe the whipped cream with a pastry bag to make elegant designs. I like my whipped cream spread with a spatula about 3 inches deep.

Calories—734; Carb—70; Fat—48.7; Chol—193; Pro—7; Fib—.2; Sod—52

BAKED ALASKA LEBLANC

2 1-inch-thick slices pound
  cake
1 pint ice cream (in the
  round paper container),
  the flavor of your choice
4 egg whites

1/2 tsp. cream of tartar
1/2 cup sugar
1 tsp. vanilla
1 tsp. Grand Marnier
  liqueur

Place each slice of pound cake on a plate that can go from the freezer to the oven. Remove the round paper container from the ice cream. Cut the cylinder of ice cream in half, and place one round half on each slice of cake. Place the plates holding the cake and ice cream in the freezer.

Beat the egg whites and cream of tartar at high speed until they become foamy. Gradually beat in the sugar until stiff peaks form; then beat the vanilla and liqueur into the meringue. Remove the ice cream and cake from the freezer and cover them completely with the meringue. Use a spatula or knife to pull out nice points on the meringue peaks to create a light and airy appearance. Bake at 475 degrees for about 3 minutes, or until the meringue is a golden brown. Serve at once. Serves 2.

Lagniappe: This looks like a monster dessert, yet it is really quite reasonable to make. It will impress your guests because, for some reason, most people think Baked Alaska is extremely difficult to make. I guess the thought of putting ice cream in the oven is too much for some people to handle.

You will succeed with no trouble if you set the cake and ice cream in advance. You can use homemade pound cake or buy frozen or bakery cake from the supermarket. I recommend using a fancy blended ice cream such as Chocolate Sundae or Almond Amaretto. Do not make the meringue in advance. A friend of mine once prepared it and put it in the refrigerator. He wondered why the ice cream melted—he only left it in the refrigerator for 3 hours! If you follow the directions, you'll get perfect results every time.

Calories—806; Carb—137; Fat—13.9; Chol—120; Pro—18.8; Fib—1.2; Sod—990

FRESH PEACH CAKE

1 1/2 cups vegetable oil
3 large brown eggs, lightly
   beaten
2 cups sugar
3 cups all-purpose flour
1 1/2 tsp. baking powder
1/2 tsp. baking soda
1 tsp. salt

1/2 tsp. ground allspice
1 tsp. ground nutmeg
1/2 tsp. ground ginger
3 cups chopped and peeled
   fresh peaches
1 cup chopped pecans
2 tsp. vanilla extract
powdered sugar

Preheat the oven to 350 degrees. Cream the oil, eggs, and sugar until light and fluffy. Combine the flour, baking powder, baking soda, salt, allspice, nutmeg, and ginger until well blended. Add the flour mixture, peaches, and pecans, 1/4 at a time, to the creamed sugar mixture and beat with an electric mixer until smooth. Add the vanilla and blend in well. Pour into a lightly buttered and floured bundt cake pan, and bake for one hour at 350 degrees. Remove from the oven and allow it to cool, then sprinkle with powdered sugar. Serves 10.

Lagniappe: This is a moist cake that will keep for almost a week (if you can keep your family away from it). Keep it covered. You can also make wonderful **Peach Muffins** from this recipe by just pouring the batter into muffin tins and baking for 20 minutes at 350 degrees. This cake is great with a dab of **Whipped Cream Topping** (see index). I just had to include this recipe. With all the fresh peaches in the store, I've gone "peach crazy" (which is kin to "plum crazy," but it comes earlier in the year).

Calories—545; Carb—59.4; Fat—33.2; Chol—70; Pro—2.4; Fib—.5; Sod—18

MAPLE WALNUT POUND CAKE

3 sticks unsalted butter
3 cups dark brown sugar
1 cup light brown sugar
6 large brown eggs
3 1/2 cups cake flour (or
   all-purpose flour)
1/2 tsp. nutmeg

1 tsp. baking powder
1/2 tsp. salt
1 cup evaporated milk
1 1/2 tsp. vanilla
1 tsp. maple extract
1 cup chopped walnuts

Preheat the oven to 325 degrees. In a large mixing bowl, cream the butter until light and feathery. Add the brown sugars and blend together with the butter. Add the eggs, one at a time, whipping between each egg. Combine the flour, nutmeg, baking powder, and salt until well blended.

Beat the flour mixture and the milk, 1/4 at a time, into the creamed mixture with an electric mixer. Blend in the vanilla, maple extract, and walnuts. Pour the batter into a greased and lightly floured bundt pan, and bake at 325 degrees for about 75 to 90 minutes. When a toothpick inserted into the center of the cake comes out clean, the cake is done. Let the cake cool and serve. Serves 12.

Lagniappe: You can bake this cake in advance and freeze it, tightly wrapped, for later use. It is good right out of the oven or cooled. I like to serve it with a dab of **Whipped Cream Topping** (see index) or you can glaze it with **Chopped Walnut Glaze** (see index). Although this recipe takes longer than what I would normally consider for a quick cookbook, it is very easy to taste why I wanted to include it.

Calories—709; Carb—100; Fat—29.3; Chol—210; Pro—8.8; Fib— .1; Sod—190

DOUBLE CHOCOLATE CAKE

1 cup butter
6 1.55-oz. milk chocolate
  bars
4 large brown eggs
2 cups sugar
1 16-oz. can dark chocolate
  syrup
2 tsp. vanilla extract
2 1/2 cups all-purpose flour

1 tsp. baking soda
1/4 tsp. baking powder
1/2 tsp. salt
1 cup buttermilk
1 cup chopped walnuts or
  pecans
1 tsp. powdered cocoa
1/3 cup powdered sugar

In a small saucepan over low heat, melt the butter and chocolate bars. In a large mixing bowl, beat the eggs for 1 minute, then beat in the sugar until well mixed. Pour the melted chocolate mixture into the egg mixture, and beat until mixed. Blend in the chocolate syrup and vanilla. Combine the flour, salt, baking soda, and baking powder; then slowly blend it into the batter. Add the buttermilk and nuts, then blend until smooth.

Lightly grease and flour a bundt cake pan; then pour the cake batter into the pan. Bake at 350 degrees for about 1 hour, or until a toothpick inserted into the center of the cake comes out clean. Let the cake cool for a minute, then remove from the pan. Mix together the cocoa and powdered sugar. Dust the cake with the powdered mixture and serve. Serves 8.

Lagniappe: This cake is very moist and full of chocolate, and it needs to remain covered until you are ready to serve it. You can make it well in advance, and store it covered at room temperature for up to 2 days. I sometimes like to dab the cake with fresh whipped cream to contrast the white topping with the dark chocolate. Enjoy!

Calories—650; Carb—86.1; Fat—32.7; Chol—92; Pro—8.1; Fib—1; Sod—223

CAJUN SWAMP CAKE

1 cup unsalted butter
4 large brown eggs, beaten
1 1/2 cups sugar
3/4 cup light brown sugar
1 1/2 cups all-purpose flour
2/3 cup cocoa
1/4 tsp. salt
1/4 tsp. baking powder
2 tsp. vanilla extract

1 cup chopped pecans
2/3 cup coconut
3 1.55-oz. milk chocolate
   bars, chopped
1 10 1/2-oz. pkg. miniature
   marshmallows
1 recipe Cajun Swamp
   Icing (see index)

Preheat the oven to 350 degrees. Cream together the butter, eggs, sugar, and brown sugar until light and fluffy. Combine the flour, cocoa, salt, and baking powder; then blend it into the creamed mixture, a little at a time. Fold in the vanilla, pecans, coconut, and chopped chocolate bars.

Lightly grease a 9 by 13-inch baking pan; then pour the batter into the pan. Bake for 35 minutes at 350 degrees. Remove from the oven and cover with the miniature marshmallows. Return to the oven for about 3 minutes, or until the marshmallows are melted. Remove from the oven and spread with the **Cajun Swamp Icing.** Serves 8 to 10.

Lagniappe: This cake keeps well for up to one week. Make it; then hide it until you are ready to serve it because it will be all gone before you know it. The cake gets its name from the color it shares with the Louisiana swamps—but don't let that fool you, it is phenomenal!

Calories—813; Carb—115; Fat—38.8; Chol—161; Pro—6.3; Fib—.5; Sod—107

CHOCOLATE CHEESE CAKE

1 recipe Oreo Cookie Crust
  (see index)
2 lb. cream cheese,
  softened
4 1-oz. squares semisweet
  chocolate, melted

5 large brown eggs, lightly
  beaten
1/2 lemon, juice only
1 3/4 cups sugar
3 tbsp. vanilla
1/4 tsp. nutmeg

Preheat the oven to 400 degrees. Bake the **Oreo Cookie Crust** and let it cool for at least five minutes. Place all the remaining ingredients in a large mixing bowl and beat at medium-high speed until the mixture is very smooth. Pour the batter into the crust; then bake at 400 degrees for 20 minutes. Lower the temperature to 300 degrees and bake for another 20 minutes; then lower the temperature to 250 degrees and bake until the cake has set, about 1 hour and 15 minutes. Remove from the oven and cool completely before attempting to cut. Serves 10.

Lagniappe: This may not be a quick cheese cake, but it is too good to pass up. If you use a timer, it really isn't to hard to manage. Don't worry about the appearance of the cake when you remove it from the oven—it will look like the remains of a California earthquake. It will correct itself when it cools. I like to top the cake with whipped cream and chocolate shavings, but it is great plain.

Do not refrigerate it until the cake is cool, or it will form little drops of water and become mealy. The cake can be frozen as long as it has cooled beforehand. Cover it with plastic wrap and freeze it in the springform pan. After 48 hours, remove the cake from the pan, place it in a box or a plastic container, and put it back in the freezer. After it has been frozen, just let the cake thaw in the refrigerator, then serve. I always double the recipe to make two cakes, one to eat now and one to freeze and eat another day!

Calories—707; Carb—84.4; Fat—28.6; Chol—195; Pro—10.2; Fib—.1; Sod—517

CAJUN BROWNIE

2 1-oz. squares
  unsweetened chocolate
1/2 cup unsalted butter
1 tbsp. strong coffee
2 large brown eggs, slightly
  beaten
1 cup sugar
2 tbsp. light brown sugar
1 tsp. pure cane syrup

1 cup sifted all-purpose
  flour (or cake flour)
1 tsp. baking powder
1/4 tsp. salt
1/4 tsp. ground nutmeg
1 cup pecans, chopped or
  broken
2 tsp. vanilla

Preheat the oven to 350 degrees. In a small saucepan or double boiler over hot water, mix together the chocolate, butter, and coffee and heat until the chocolate is melted. In a large bowl, cream together the eggs, sugar, brown sugar, and cane syrup until light and fluffy. Beat the chocolate mixture into the egg mixture until it is thoroughly blended. Combine the flour, baking powder, salt, and nutmeg. Add the flour mixture and the pecans, 1/4 at a time, to the egg mixture and mix in well. Whip in the vanilla.

Lightly grease an 8 by 8-inch baking pan, and pour the batter into the pan. Bake at 350 degrees for about 35 to 40 minutes, or until a toothpick inserted into the center comes out clean. Allow the brownies to cool for a few minutes; then cut and serve. Makes about 20 brownies.

Lagniappe You can make these brownies in advance (secretly), and store them until you are ready to serve. They make a superb dessert or snack. Nicole, my oldest daughter, loves to make brownies. In fact, they may be tied with fudge as her favorite snack or dessert. This recipe is easy and quick and a lot cheaper than buying the boxed mix. You can freeze brownies for up to one month with excellent results. Just defrost and serve.

Calories—156; Carb—17.7; Fat—9; Chol—42; Pro—25; Fib—.3; Sod—60

FILTHY RICH CHOCOLATE CHIPS

1 cup unsalted butter
1 cup sugar
2/3 cup dark brown sugar
1/2 cup light brown sugar
2 large brown eggs
1 1/2 tsp. vanilla extract
2 1/2 cups uncooked oats
2 cups all-purpose flour

2/3 tsp. salt
1 tsp. baking powder
1 tsp. baking soda
1 12-oz. pkg. real chocolate
  chips
4 1.55-oz. chocolate bars,
  chopped
2 cups chopped pecans

Preheat the oven to 375 degrees. In a large mixing bowl, cream together the butter, sugar, dark brown sugar, and light brown sugar. When the mixture is light and creamy, add the eggs and beat until smooth.

Process the oats into a fine powder in a food processor or blender. Combine the powdered oats, flour, salt, baking powder, and baking soda. Add the oat mixture to the creamed mixture, a little at a time, alternating with the chocolate chips, chopped chocolate, and pecans. Continue mixing until all the oat mixture, chocolate, and pecans are blended into the creamed butter mixture. Roll the dough into balls about 1 inch in diameter. Place on an ungreased cookie sheet and bake at 375 degrees for about 9 minutes, or until they are nicely browned. Makes about 5 dozen cookies.

Lagniappe: This is a regal chocolate chip recipe! I think my daughter Nicole could eat a dozen or more in one sitting. Be very careful, they are highly addictive! You cannot eat just one.

You can make the dough and refrigerate it for later use, or you can bake the cookies and freeze them. They also keep well in a tightly covered cookie jar for about 1 week. If you make this cookie recipe once, I think you'll tolerate no other.

Calories—139; Carb—15.8; Fat—7.8; Chol—19; Pro—1.5; Fib—.3; Sod—65

DOUBLE NUT COOKIES

1 cup unsalted butter,
  softened
1/4 cup sugar
2 tbsp. light brown sugar
1/4 cup molasses
2 cups all-purpose flour

1/2 tsp. salt
1/2 tsp. baking powder
1 cup chopped walnuts
1 cup chopped pecans
1/2 cup powdered sugar

Preheat the oven to 350 degrees. In a mixing bowl, cream the butter, sugar, and brown sugar until fluffy and light. Add the molasses and beat until creamy. Combine the flour, salt, and baking powder; then slowly mix the flour mixture into the butter mixture. Fold the nuts into the dough, then roll the dough into balls the size of a walnut shell. Place the dough balls on an ungreased cookie sheet and bake at 350 degrees for about 15 minutes.

Put the powdered sugar in a large mixing bowl. When the cookies come out of the oven, dump them into the mixing bowl while they are hot. Roll them around to coat them with the powdered sugar, let them cool, then serve. Makes about 54 cookies.

Lagniappe: The cookie dough can be made in advance and refrigerated up to 4 or 5 days until you are ready to use it. This will allow you to have freshly baked cookies on the day you need them. You can just bake a portion of the dough to make a few cookies per day if you like cookies straight from the oven.

When I was a young boy, I had a paper route for years. One of my customers used to make a cookie similar to this, and she would give me some with a large glass of milk once or twice a month. It was definitely worth putting the paper inside her back screen door!

Calories—74; Carb—7; Fat—5; Chol—10; Pro—.7; Fib—.1; Sod—26

OLD FASHIONED SUGAR COOKIES

1/2 cup unsalted butter
1 large brown egg
1 cup sugar
1 tbsp. light brown sugar
1/2 tsp. ground nutmeg

2 tbsp. milk
1 tsp. fresh lemon juice
2 cups all-purpose flour
1 1/4 tsp. baking powder

Preheat the oven to 400 degrees. In a large mixing bowl, cream together the butter, egg, sugar, and brown sugar until smooth. Add the nutmeg, milk, and lemon juice and mix for 1 more minute. Combine the flour and baking powder, and slowly add it to the creamed mixture until all is blended in. Drop by large spoonfuls onto an ungreased baking sheet, then bake at 400 degrees for about 8 minutes until the cookies are a golden brown. Let them cool and serve. Makes about 3 dozen cookies.

Lagniappe: This is so quick that you don't need any shortcuts. Just bake the cookies and tightly cover them until you are ready to serve. This is the kind of cookie that used to be quite popular before we got elaborate. It is dated, modest, and uncomplicated yet still quite delectable. Have a few!

Calories—71; Carb—10.6; Fat—2.9; Chol—15; Pro—.9; Fib—Trace; Sod—18

FRESH COCONUT COOKIES

1 1/4 cups vegetable
   shortening
1 1/2 cups sugar
2 large brown eggs
3 1/2 cups all-purpose flour
2 1/2 tsp. baking powder

1 tsp. baking soda
1/2 tsp. salt
2 tsp. vanilla extract
3 cups fresh coconut,
   grated

Cream together the shortening and sugar with an electric mixer until smooth. Add the eggs, and continue to mix until blended. Combine the flour, baking powder, baking soda, and salt. Slowly beat the flour mixture into the creamed sugar mixture, then fold in the vanilla and fresh coconut.

Roll the dough into logs about 1 1/2 inches thick, then wrap them tightly with plastic wrap. Refrigerate for at least 12 hours or overnight. Cut the logs into slices 2/3 inch thick and place them on a lightly greased baking sheet. Bake at 375 degrees for about 10 minutes. Makes about 3 dozen cookies.

Lagniappe: You can store the cookie dough tightly wrapped for up to 1 week in the refrigerator. Slice and bake what you need. The flavor of the fresh coconut cannot be matched by packaged coconut, but you can use the packaged form if you don't have the time to use the fresh. Tightly covered, these cookies will keep well after they are baked as well.

Calories—161; Carb—17.6; Fat—9.7; Chol—16; Pro—1.6; Fib—.5; Sod—76

GRAHAM CRACKER-GINGER SNAP CRUST

1 1/2 cups ginger snaps, broken	1/4 cup unsalted butter, melted
1 1/2 cups graham crackers, broken	2 tbsp. sugar
	1 tsp. light brown sugar

Preheat the oven to 375 degrees. Put the ginger snaps and graham crackers in a food processor and chop at high speed until the cookies are turned into crumbs. Add the butter, sugar, and brown sugar and process for 1 minute. Pour the crumb mixture into a 9-inch pie pan. Press the mixture onto the bottom and sides of the pan to form an even crust. Bake at 375 degrees for about 4 minutes, then remove and cool. Use this crust as you would any graham cracker crust.

Lagniappe: If you don't have a food processor, place the cookies on waxed paper on a hard surface; then cover with waxed paper. Crush with a rolling pin until the cookies are turned into crumbs. Put the crumbs into a mixing bowl with the butter and sugars, then mash together with a fork or your fingers.

You can make this crust in advance and freeze it for later use. Leave it in the pie pan to prevent it from breaking in the freezer. The ginger snaps add zest to the graham crackers, making this a marvelous crust!

Calories—1981; Carb—303; Fat—91; Chol—132; Pro—24; Fib—2; Sod—1988

OREO COOKIE CRUST

1 20-oz. pkg. Oreo Cookies   1/2 stick butter, melted

Preheat the oven to 350 degrees. Place the Oreo cookies in a food processor or blender and process at full power until the cookies are fine crumbs. In a large mixing bowl, pour the melted butter over the oreo crumbs. Mix until completely blended. With your fingers, mold the crumbs evenly and equally onto the sides and bottom of a spring-form pan. Place the pan into the oven and bake for 5 minutes at 350 degrees. Remove from the oven and let the crust cool for at least 5 minutes before using. Use as a shell for pies and cakes. Makes one crust.

Lagniappe: This is a simple and a very tasty crust that is great for any chocolate pie or cake. If you don't have a food processor (you really need to get one), you can crush the cookies in the bag they come in by hitting them with a kitchen mallet. Don't hit them too hard, or you will have a chocolate cookie explosion and crumbs all over your kitchen. Be sure to leave the filling in the cookie, it helps to hold the crust together.

Calories—3232; Carb—400; Fat—61; Chol—132; Pro—20.4; Fib—1; Sod—3408

CAJUN SWAMP ICING

1 16-oz. box powdered sugar	1/3 cup evaporated milk
1 stick unsalted butter, melted	3 tbsp. cocoa
	1 tsp. vanilla extract
	1 cup chopped pecans

Beat together all the ingredients, except for the pecans, until smooth. Fold in the pecans, then spread this icing gently over the marshmallow cream on the top of the **Cajun Swamp Cake.** The recipe tops one cake.

Lagniappe: I like to use this icing on top of a plain yellow cake as well as the **Cajun Swamp Cake.** It is easy to make and it frosts well. It also makes a nice filling to put between two chocolate chip cookies. Make the cookies a little larger than normal, put about 2 tablespoons of icing on one cookie and put them together. I guess you can tell that I don't like sweets!

Calories—3063; Carb—458; Fat—145; Chol—290; Pro—13; Fib—2.4; Sod—92

CHOPPED WALNUT GLAZE

3/4 cup chopped walnuts	3 cups powdered sugar
1/2 cup light brown sugar	1 tsp. vanilla
3 tbsp. evaporated milk	5 tbsp. unsalted butter

Combine the walnuts, brown sugar, and evaporated milk in a saucepan over medium heat. Cook, stirring often, for about 3 minutes. Remove and allow the mixture to cool. Combine the powdered sugar, vanilla, and butter; then beat until smooth. Slowly beat in the walnut mixture until thoroughly mixed. Spread over the top and drizzle down the sides of a warm cake. Makes enough glaze for one pound cake.

Lagniappe: This is a quick glaze for almost any cake that would benefit from a nut glaze. Use this recipe on the **Maple Walnut Pound Cake,** or on the pound cake of your choice. For best results, make this recipe just after removing the cake from the oven. You want to put it on the cake when it is still warm (but not hot) to get the best effect.

Calories—3036; Carb—786; Fat—91; Chol—179; Pro—9.9; Fib— .3; Sod—65

WHIPPED CREAM TOPPING

1 cup heavy whipping **1 tsp. vanilla**
  cream **2 1/2 tbsp. sugar**

Put the beaters for the electric mixer into the freezer for about 10 minutes. In a cold mixing bowl (I put the bowl into the refrigerator before using it to make whipped cream), combine the heavy whipping cream and the vanilla. Remove the beaters from the freezer and beat the cream at high speed. While beating, add a little of the sugar at a time. Beat until the cream is heavy and stiff. Refrigerate until you are ready to serve. Makes about 2 to 2 1/2 cups.

Lagniappe: Yes, you can actually make whipped cream from heavy cream. I know this may surprise many people, but you will find heavy whipping cream in the dairy section of any store. You don't find it in plastic cartons in the frozen food section.

I was making this recipe one day when Nicole, my oldest daughter, asked me what I was making. When I told her, she looked very puzzled. She wanted to know what all that white liquid was. She told me that whipped cream comes in plastic containers or cans that spray. But once she tasted the real thing, she was hooked.

Whipped cream will store refrigerated for up to 24 hours with great results, just be sure it is whipped thoroughly and kept very cold. I freeze the beaters before using them because the cold metal pushes more air into the cream and keeps it coagulated, thereby helping it build faster and stay feathery.

Calories—23.7; Carb—.9; Fat—2.2; Chol—8.4; Pro—.1; Fib—0; Sod— 2.5

HOMEMADE LEMONADE

1 1/2 cups sugar
1 qt. water
1/4 tsp. vanilla

2/3 cup fresh lemon juice
ice cubes
fresh mint leaves

Combine the sugar and water until the sugar is completely dissolved. Stir in the vanilla and lemon juice. Fill six large glasses with ice cubes, and pour the lemonade over the ice. Garnish with fresh mint leaves. Serves 6.

Lagniappe: Why am I putting such an easy recipe into this book? I discovered that there are many people that actually think lemonade is made from a powder! I thought it was my duty to dispel this myth. Why is this recipe in the dessert section? Where else would you put something so sweet and delicious (especially if you do not have a drink section)?

Anyone can make fresh lemonade—even a child. It keeps well (if you can keep people from drinking it) in the refrigerator. Do not pour it over the ice until you are ready to serve.

Calories—191; Carb—48; Fat—0; Chol—0; Pro—.2; Fib—0; Sod—27

Index

derloin of Beef with Chanterelles Mushrooms, 184; Tenderloin of Pork Ella Marie, 202-3; Tenderloin of Pork Etouffée, 203-4; Tenderloin of Pork Faye, 200-201; Tenderloin of Pork Nicole Marie, 206-7; Tenderloin of Pork Thomas, 204-5

Toasting bread rounds, 34

Tomatoes: Beef Tenderloin Debbie, 185; Breast of Chicken Kebabs, 169; Casserole de Province, 189; Chicken Christine Noelie, 163; Chicken Sean, 161; Crabmeat Stuffed Tomatoes, 75; Fresh Tomato-Basil Soup, 65; Old Fashioned Shrimp Stew, 123; Pork Jambalaya, 198-99; Seafood Coubillion, 53-54; Shrimp Creole, 127; Stuffed Tomatoes Michelle, 27-28; Tenderloin of Pork Nicole Marie, 206-7; Tenderloin of Pork Thomas, 204-5

Topping: Whipped Cream Topping, 279

Trout Martiaze, 146

Turkey : Almond Turkey, 174; Pan Fried Turkey, 178; Turkey Au Sherry, 173; Turkey Hamic, 176-77; Turkey Skillet Fred Lawrence, 175

Turnips: Potato Soup Miller, 68; Stuffed Turnips Danielle, 192

Twice Baked Potatoes, 245-46

Unsalted butter: (why use it?), 231

Veal Scallopini Euphemie Borel, 215

Veal: Veal Marie Elena, 214; Veal Sanderford, 216-17; Veal Scallopini Euphemie Borel, 215

Vegetable Dips: Olive Spread, 28; Pineapple-Walnut Spread, 27; Roquefort Dip for Vegetables, 29

Vegetables: Artichokes Chad Thomas, 221; Asparagus Poydras, 223; Baked Cabbage Casserole, 226; Baked Eggplant Emile, 191; Bean Salad Acadie, 77; Black-eyed Pea Salad, 76; Black-Eyed Pea Soup, 56; Broccoli au Gratin, 224; Broccoli Salad

Jacques, 78; Butter Beans St. James, 233-34; Cajun Fried Onion Rings, 235; Cajun New Potato Salad, 82; Carrots Aunt Alice, 227; Cauliflower Salad Jacques, 78; Cheesy Potatoes, 242; Chilled Avocado Soup, 67; Chilled Cucumber Salad, 80-81; Corn and Crab Soup, 62; Crabmeat Stuffed Avocado,75; Crabmeat Stuffed Tomatoes, 75; Cream of Asparagus Soup, 60; Cream of Broccoli Soup I, 60; Cream of Carrot Soup, 60; Cream of Fresh Broccoli Soup II, 61; Cream of Mushroom Soup, 63; Cream of Summer Squash Soup, 60; Cream Peas, 236; Creamy Corn Soup, 62; Creamy Mushrooms Darrell, 229; Debbie's Red Beans, 197-98; Easy Corn on the Cob, 228; Eggplant Casserole la Lande, 190; Field Peas New Iberia, 238; French Fried Okra, 234; Fresh Brussels Sprouts Daniel, 222; Green Beans Louise, 231; Green Beans Rabalais, 230; Green Peas and Rice, 237; Just Great Peas, 239; Leeks Basil, 227-28; Lima Beans St. James, 233; Lovely Limas, 232; Navy Beans St. James, 233; Oyster and Corn Soup, 62; Potatoes Edna, 241; Quick Cauliflower au Gratin, 225; Quick Dirty Rice, 246-47; Quick Potato Pie, 186-87; Red Bean Salad, 76; Salad Luc, 79; Sautéed New Potatoes, 244-45; Sautéed Potatoes Terriot, 243; Spinach Spaulding, 247-48; Stuffed Bell Pepper Mire, 192; Stuffed Eggplant Crowley, 110; Stuffed Turnips Danielle, 192; Summer Squash Sauté, 249; Sweet Peas Bogalusa, 240; Sweet Potato Chips, 252; Sweet Potato Pie, 264; Twice Baked Potatoes, 245-46; Yellow Squash Calhoun, 249-50; Zucchini Calhoun, 250

Walnuts: Apple Walnut Muffins, 97; Chicken Christine Noelie, 163;